My Obsession

Haworth

IN MEMORY OF ROBBIE MILLAR AND ALAIN MOLS, BOTH OBSESSIVE,
TWO GREAT FRIENDS, TWO GREAT COOKS, TWO CHARACTERS,
WHO WERE TAKEN AWAY IN THEIR PRIME, WE WILL REMEMBER THEM FOR EVER.

NIGEL HAWORTH'S
OBSESSiON

DEFINITION:

"THE DOMINATION OF ONE'S THOUGHTS
OR FEELINGS BY A PERSISTENT IDEA,
IMAGE, DESIRE, ETC."

HOW A CHEF'S OBSESSION LED TO A DECADE OF FOOD FESTIVALS, ICONIC CHEFS AND CELEBRATED CUISINE AT NORTHCOTE

During his 25 years behind the stove at Northcote, Nigel Haworth has done many things. Among them are winning the hotel its Michelin star in 1996; putting Lancashire produce on the map with his appearances on The Great British Menu; and keeping customers coming through the dining room doors for a quarter of a century with his innovative, accomplished British cooking. As one of the country's best-loved chefs, we've come to expect these achievements from him, but few would have predicted the way that Northcote – which sits 30 minutes outside Preston in rural Lancashire – would, once a year, become an epicentre for nationally and internationally celebrated chefs and food personalities coming together to cook.

Throughout the Obsession food festival, which has been held every January at the hotel for the past ten years, this is exactly what it becomes. The festival has, over the past decade, positioned itself firmly as one of the gems of the foodie calendar – hosting the likes of Phil Howard, Raymond Blanc, Pierre Koffmann, Angela Hartnett and Dieter Koschina among many others in its kitchens, and serving up refined, and often forward-looking, food to diners over the years. But while Obsession has gained momentum and culinary clout each year since its inception, it started rather more modestly, as an idea on a flight home from California, as Nigel Haworth explains.

"I went over to the festival of Food and Wine at The Highlands Inn in Carmel, California, off the back of a recommendation from a friend, Ian Harkness (former Chairman of Shire Inns), and worked there for a week. I wasn't one of the billed chefs, but I was just going over there to work with the chefs to see what it was like. I stayed with Tony Baker, a former colleague of Ian's and now a great friend, who runs the Monterey Grill in Monterey. It was pretty inspirational – I ended up working with Charlie Trotter, Thomas Keller and Alice Waters, who was the doyenne of American food at that point.

"On my last day, after meeting Thomas Keller, we'd organised to go up to his three Michelin-starred restaurant, The French Laundry, and have lunch – which was, in retrospect, perhaps not the wisest thing to do before a flight home. Of course, we had an incredible lunch and I ended up missing my flight back to England. When I finally flew home, the week I'd had was fresh in my head. I started thinking about the possibility of doing something similar at Northcote. I knew we didn't have the same amazing wine culture as the Napa Valley but we did have great produce and stunning countryside in Lancashire. I was sure we could do something that would be interesting for the customers and be exciting and new. It also struck me that it would fill that quiet and gloomy time in January when there's nothing really going on. And so the festival was born."

When the idea was still very much in its embryonic stages, Nigel was down in London judging The Pierre Taittinger competition, when he got talking to Phil Howard (the two-Michelin starred chef of London's The Square restaurant). "I thought I'd be a bit cheeky and say, 'if I did a food festival would you be interested in coming up and cooking?' and he said 'without hesitation yes' and so, at Westminster College it started to take momentum." Soon after, Nigel won the 2000 Wedgwood Chef Potter competition, and the prize was a working holiday at The Saint Geran in Mauritius. It was here that during the filming of a food programme for Channel Four, he met and cooked with Rick Stein, Nick Nairn and Brian Turner, and convinced Nick Nairn to come on board.

An avid Blackburn Rovers supporter, every year Nigel goes to watch the team play away in Newcastle: the stomping ground of friend and fellow chef Terry Laybourne – and it was at one such match that he managed to entice Terry for the festival too. Together the four chefs started the first ever Northcote food festival in the January of 2001. Fast forward ten years and the Northcote festival has become a yearly routine for Nigel, who, over the years, has extended the bill to seven nights and seven chefs (with the exception of 2010's celebratory ten night event). But the first year was nerve-wracking and extremely tiring, as Nigel recalls. "I cooked on the Saturday night, and then a Jazz Brunch for 100 featuring Kenny Davern, a great character and jazz musician, on the Sunday. I slept all day Monday after doing that – I was absolutely knackered, it was a really big strain."

With top chefs appearing year after year (Phil Howard has accompanied Nigel on the bill every year since 2001), it's not difficult to see how Northcote manages to fill all of the nights comfortably each festival. Looking back on the first ever festival though, Nigel remembers his anxiety about getting bums on seats. "The reason we did it in January was because it's a quiet month and I also thought I'd be able to access the chefs better then. You've had Christmas and New Year, and so to have something exciting at the end of January is a real attraction for diners. We didn't know if it would work, and it wasn't easy to fill. We managed to fill it though, and we did 50-60 covers each night."

The formula for the festival is a simple one: chefs can cook what they want, it is really about them expressing themselves for one night on the plate. "It's also about them coming up, having fun and spending some time with their family," says Nigel. "There are no add-ons. I encourage them to use regional produce from Lancashire but don't insist. They can stay for the whole week if they want, which some do. We've had some very merry nights – and there are some nights you can't get to bed at all."

OBSESSION

ANDONI LUIS ADURIZ

ANDREW FAIRLIE

ANDREW PERN

ANGELA HARTNETT MBE

ANTHONY FLINN

ATUL KOCHHAR

BRETT GRAHAM

BRIAN TURNER CBE

BRUCE POOLE

CHARLES METCALFE

CHRIS GALVIN

CHRISTIAN OLSSON

CLAUDE BOSI

DANIEL CLIFFORD

DANYEL COUET

DARINA ALLEN

DAVID THOMPSON

DIETER KOSCHINA

ERIC CHAVOT

FERGUS HENDERSON MBE

GERMAIN SCHWAB

GIORGIO LOCATELLI

GLYNN PURNELL

HESTON BLUMENTHAL OBE

JACOB JAN BOERMA

JEFF GALVIN

JOHN CAMPBELL

KEN HOM OBE

LISA ALLEN

MARK EDWARDS

MARK HIX

MATTHEW FORT

MICHAEL CAINES MBE

MICHEL ROUX JR

NATHAN OUTLAW

NEIL WIGGLESWORTH

NICK NAIRN

NIGEL HAWORTH

PAUL CUNNINGHAM

PAUL HEATHCOTE MBE

PETER GORDON

PHIL HOWARD

PIERRE KOFFMANN

RAYMOND BLANC OBE

RICHARD CORRIGAN

ROBBIE MILLAR

ROWLEY LEIGH

ROY BRETT

SAT BAINS

SHANE OSBORN

SHAUN RANKIN

TERRY LAYBOURNE MBE

THEO RANDALL

TOM KITCHIN

TOM PARKER BOWLES

FOREWORD

OBSESSION – A PASSION FOR PERFECTION

I have been accused of being obsessed with food, but I've never quite seen it that way. It seems to me quite normal to wake up in the morning wanting to eat the best food my money can buy. It seems quite natural to talk about food when you're eating it, to start planning the next meal before you've finished the one you're eating. It seems no more than right and proper to consider the source of ingredients, their particular qualities, the best possible way of preparing them, to anticipate the pleasures that they will give you.

And what better way to whet your appetite for the pleasures of the plate than by musing through the recipes in this book. Even if you can't cook all of them, or even any of them, you will have filled your imagination with the creations that range from the carefully calculated complexities of Heston Blumenthal to the inspired Indian originality of Atul Kochhar, from the elegant French classicism of Eric Chavot to the earthy British honesty of Mark Hix, from Italian intensity of Giorgio Locatelli to the idiosyncrasy of Glyn Purnell, to name only a few. You will have chewed over the Obsessions of some of the finest and most original talents working in kitchens around the world (although there are a couple of chancers included; I'll leave it to you to work out who they are). The fact that they have all come and cooked and conquered at Northcote speaks volumes about the magic of the place, and of the respect with which Nigel Haworth and Craig Bancroft are held. They are two men with a passion for food, if ever there were.

But at what point does a passion become an Obsession? I've never quite known the answer to that. The great Carlo Petrini, founder and president of Slow Food, in answer to a question about why he was obsessed with food, replied, "If I wear a pair of Armani pants they do not become a part of Carlo Petrini. If I eat a slice of ham, it becomes a part of Carlo Petrini. That is why I am passionate about what I eat." Passion? Obsession? Does it matter? It's the food that counts. And the pleasure. And there's more than your fair share in these pages.

Matthew Fort.

Matthew Fort
2010

OBSESSiON

OBSESSiON

First published in 2010 by Network Publishing Ltd
Network House, 28 Ballmoor, Celtic Court, Buckingham MK18 1RQ

www.networkpublishingltd.com

Sponsored by Yes Chef! Magazine
www.yeschefmagazine.com

© Network Publishing Ltd, 2010

In association with:

Northcote, Northcote Road, Langho, Blackburn, Lancashire BB6 8BE
www.northcote.com

Printed by Buxton Press (Derbyshire)

ISBN 978-0-9562661-2-5

Printed in England

Publisher:	Peter Marshall
Managing Editor:	Shirley Marshall
Editor:	Sue Christelow
Assistant Editor:	Hilary Mayes
Assistant Editor:	Katy Morris
Design Director:	Philip Donnelly
Photography:	Myburgh du Plessis, with the assistance of Alice Warren, except:

Keith Pollard – Andrew Fairlie, Andrew Pern, Anthony Flinn, Atul Kochhar, Phil Howard, Roy Brett, Shaun Rankin, Terry Laybourne, Tom Kitchin

Hugh Adams – Andoni Luis Aduriz, Angela Hartnett, Christian Olsson, Danyel Couet, Darina Allen, Dieter Koschina, Nathan Outlaw.

Jacob Jan Boerma, Ken Hom and Raymond Blanc images supplied.

Contributor:	Rosie Birkett

PREFACE

Ten years of Northcote's Food and Wine Festival – our Obsession. I suppose on reflection we can't believe in many ways that a small idea has become a major part of our annual calendar, an obsession that really can never be let go. Ten years of great moments, brought to a 10th anniversary this year with ten incredible nights which we anticipated with true excitement. The evolution has been an incredible journey, the people we have met, the friends we have made, the respect that has been earned and the skills that have been shared. That's what the whole story is about, an obsession of food, flavour and friendship, like minds coming together in a week of brilliance in the wilds of Lancashire in the depths of a January winter.

In 2010 we added three nights to celebrate the milestone of ten years, a great gathering of superb chefs to help us pull ten years to a climax. Tom Kitchin, Theo Randall, Ken Hom, Angela Hartnett, Lisa Allen, Nathan Outlaw, Phil Howard, who we will allow to retire after this year, Jacob Jan Boerma and finally Andrew Fairlie – what a fabulous line-up full of anticipation and intrigue. We also added a twist by asking Matthew Fort and Tom Parker Bowles to cook alongside us as two men more obsessed about food and flavour would be hard to find.

This book, that we hope you will enjoy, is part of the ten years of our Obsession; a celebration and testament to everyone who has taken part over the years in whatever way. The journey could not have been possible without the commitment of all our teams of staff, both in the kitchen, front of house and behind the scenes over the years. Behind the scenes the administration and marketing have been huge and the organisation incredible, but each year we have made it unscathed so a big thanks must go to Kaye Mathew for the ten years' work behind this Obsession and its development. My head chefs over the years, Warwick Dodds in particular, have been fantastic but none have assisted more than the brilliant and dedicated Lisa Allen who, over the eight years she has worked for me and the five years she has been head chef, has maintained a drive and enthusiasm that has ensured we have delivered the festival on behalf of our guest chefs and our diners.

Sponsors deserve an enormous thank you – there are too many to mention all individually by name, but without them we could have never financed and driven this Obsession. I would, however, like to thank Nick Green and all the team at Villeroy and Boch for the brilliant support throughout the whole journey. EBLEX has supported us brilliantly over the years as has The Mall Group. Louis Roederer too for their constant and continued support, supplying us all with some of the finest Champagne available. A huge thanks must go to all our guests, family and friends who have stood by us and supported by filling the festival to join in our Obsession as without their willingness to attend there would be no festival. Lastly, a special thank you must go to our long-suffering wives, Kath and Helen, for their immense understanding throughout the ten years of Obsession and the development of The Northcote Group; without their support we wouldn't be able to have our Obsession!

This year the tenth anniversary is also about giving back and we have chosen to dedicate some of the proceeds each night to Hospitality Action, our industry's charity that does so much good for those in our profession who have been less fortunate than ourselves.

So it is here – ten glorious years of an incredible Obsession. We sincerely hope you enjoy the moment and continue to enjoy it for many years to come.

Nigel and Craig

2010...

The arrival of the 2010 festival after ten years was potentially daunting with our decision to run for ten nights to celebrate our tenth anniversary. Tom Kitchin, ably assisted by his team Dominic, Sebastian and David, arrived on Sunday night with his wife and business partner Michaela. It was great to see Tom and the team who enjoyed dining in the Northcote restaurant on the Sunday evening.

The following day Tom was up early, and on top form, he needed to be as there were record numbers for a first night – 98. I had talked to Tom briefly before about the adventurous nature of his menu with octopus, pig's head and razor clams, but he was confident that all would be well and he was right: the customers loved it. He also served his famous Great British Menu dish of beef wellington – a truly great dish that was just pipped to the post by that equally famous hot pot in the final. To finish he did chocolate and sea buckthorn – what a great ingredient – it's a berry that grows on the coast with a sort of earthy passion fruit flavour, harvested by Tom's personal forager – the must-have accessory of today's leading chefs.

Matthew Fort arrived the night before and in his own inimitable style he entertained the Northcote guest table on Tom Kitchin's night with his gastronomic stories. Tom Parker Bowles arrived at 4.30pm the following afternoon. Matthew was a little perturbed at the lateness of Tom's arrival as he had been toiling all afternoon preparing for their menu, but Tom hit the kitchen at full throttle. He swung on to his ceviche of bream and Morecambe Bay shrimps which proved to be a winner. Next up was John Dory with zabaglione, which I have to say would have got an eight or more on the Great British Menu. Duck on barley, then Eccles cake ice cream rounded

off the evening in a fittingly Lancashire style. It goes without saying that the bar was full until the early hours and legend has it that Tom nearly missed his train the next morning. A great night was had by all.

Theo Randall travelled up from London on Tuesday and arrived with his assistant, Sanjeewa Thommadura. Theo, a connoisseur of Italian cuisine, dined at Matthew and Tom's evening and thoroughly enjoyed it, in fact, he was incredibly complimentary. Simplicity with confidence was the start of Theo's menu, chicory shoots with red wine vinegar dressing, anchovies and capers. The scallops and veal pasta were outstanding but wonderfully rustic. To finish was the fantastic and memorable Amalfi lemon tart – a perfect conclusion especially with the Moscato d'Asti wine.

Ken Hom flew in from Rio with no jet lag, he was full-on from the start. Intense, articulate and, above all, very passionate about his food. Ken is a very naturally talented man who truly understands his food culture.

Ken was assisted by Lee Williams who had prepared the way for his arrival. Crispy Vietnamese spring rolls, wrapped in soft herbs and lettuce leaves. Hot and sour soup came next, then steamed turbot which, with a touch of Hom magic, was transformed into a bubbling, spicy Chinese dish. Roast belly pork (which we dried for 24 hours with electric fans) was sublime and to finish was warm mango, basil and vanilla ice cream – a refreshing end to a stunning night.

Angela Hartnett and our very own Lisa Allen made for the biggest night of the festival: 'girl power'. When Angela is at Northcote it's always a time for laughter with serious cooking. Angela arrived late the night before, just catching the main course of Ken's evening. She and Lisa joined forces in the bar after service with several drinks and decided to have an early

trip to Bury Market, perhaps, in hindsight, not the best Angela, who was assisted on the night by ex-head che Borthwick, started her menu with scallops, Pata Negra butternut squash, followed by one of her famous risott time with black truffles and artichoke, with roasted loca all brilliantly executed and cooked to perfection.

Home-grown Lisa Allen wowed us all with her duck consommé and crispy duck skins, then sent us into hea with two desserts, a lime and pineapple cream and the brilliant chocolate cylinder with a very silky sheep's mil ice cream.

Nathan Outlaw had just finished filming the Great E Menu and had travelled up from London on the late tra arriving in time to have drinks with Angela and Lisa. He be an 'Outlaw', but he is a true gentle giant and certain chef to watch. His night was packed to the rafters and fishy night was in store. Nathan kicked off with a beaut crab salad, followed by lemon sole on potato dumpling dish that was incredibly well received. Next was his sig dish wreck fish with mussels – a blend of the Cornish an Normandy shores. Venison was the main course with ch then to finish the night, a cosy rhubarb sponge with gir cream. Wow – what a great night. Those Cornish chaps drink – we limped to bed at 4.30am!

For the first time in ten years Phil Howard sent up assistant James Salkald who started his mise en place a Phil to arrive by train the next day. Having worked with over the past ten years, you notice the true style of the confident, comfortable and really accomplished. He kic off the night with beetroot and goat's cheese, to be fol by a sublime combination of Dover sole, oysters and sm eel. Ravioli of calves' tail with chanterelles was real com

food. Venison Wellington was a classic dish, followed by a beautiful taste of Roquefort, pear and port, and then a perfect ending of a memorable and warming rhubarb tart. Somehow life at the festival will never be the same – thank you, Phil.

Jacob Jan Boerma and I quickly became friends after cooking at the Vila Joya Food Festival together in 2009. Jacob's food was really outstanding and I was so pleased when he accepted my invite to cook at the 2010 festival. Jacob was accompanied by his partner, Kim, and Ewout, Marco and Arturo. We were not to be disappointed. Jacob is a chef that can really hit the high notes, with a delicacy of touch. We started with an amazing oyster Tokyo-style, unbelievably tasty, moved on to North Sea Crab and warm Dublin Bay prawns, followed by slow-cooked lobster – a real star of a dish, with great textures and flavours. Grilled turbot with pumpkin, scallops and black truffles came next, followed by French pigeon and than an Obsession of desserts. A real surprise as Jacob hadn't really explained what this Obsession of desserts entailed, but we were soon to find out. Three desserts, one after the other, were the climax to the evening. The first was a small selection of chocolate desserts – followed by red fruits and sorbet, then basil mousse with tropical fruits and basil oil. What an end to a truly hectic, frantic and all-absorbing evening.

It took me an awfully long time to get Andrew Fairlie down to the festival – nearly six years – but it was well worth the wait. He was assisted by Ian Scarramuzza, one of the chef de parties from Fairlies. Andrew launched the night with a stunning smoked eel and foie gras terrine, beetroot and apple. He had the balance of the terrine

just perfect – what a brilliant start. Baked king scallops were followed by a beautifully delicate cep tart with roasted sweetbreads and ceps, which Andrew tells me had been picked with his own fair hands. His assiette of pork consisted of confit of belly pork, a small croquette of brawn, pork filled with some smoky cabbage and apples, along with a beautiful bacon from Alsace. These were really great combinations and very well received by an adoring public. Andrew wrapped the night up with a carpaccio of pineapple and coconut parfait: a refreshing end to another great night. The bar afterwards was extremely full and Andrew and I relaxed and enjoyed a few beers, a great atmosphere and a brilliant night.

And so finally, the last night was here – after nine fantastic evenings, it was up to us to go out on a high, which was no mean feat after such a gastronomic journey. We started with the venison carpaccio, pickled damsons and hazelnuts, followed by goose consommé with faggots which Craig matched memorably with his infamous Madeira. My main course was Lakeland veal with trotters and sweetbreads which, although daring, was very well received. Finally, the menu was completed with a rhubarb and marshmallow dessert.

There was a special atmosphere on this final night, and the realisation of what had been achieved and how brilliantly the staff had pulled together in supporting our guest chefs through this marathon of ten days was incredible. To top things off, along the way we had managed to raise money for charity and I'd like to take this opportunity to thank you all for your support in raising over £10,000 for Hospitality Action.

2010...

Nigel Haworth and Phil Howard, the obsessive chef partnership

TOM KITCHIN

"I am completely obsessed with seasonality in my cooking. It is all about working with nature and understanding where produce comes from. My passion in cooking is all about appreciating and understanding beautiful fresh seasonal ingredients and creating new exciting taste sensations.

As a chef, it doesn't matter what level you're cooking at, if your heart doesn't start beating when you get the first asparagus of spring or the first woodcock in autumn, then you're not doing it for the right reasons."

Monday 25th January

TOM KITCHIN
The Kitchin, Edinburgh

CARPACCIO OF WEST COAST OCTOPUS
SERVED WITH PICKLED VEGETABLES,
LEMON & CAPER DRESSING
Encruzado, Dâo, Quinta dos Roques, 2008

BONED AND ROLLED PIG'S HEAD, SERVED
WITH ROASTED TAIL OF LANGOUSTINE
FROM ANSTRUTHER, CRISPY EAR SALAD
Blanc de Blancs, Clos Mireille,
Côtes de Provence, Domaines Ott, 2007

RAZOR CLAMS
La Val, Albariño, Rias Baixas, 2008

SCOTCH BEEF WELLINGTON,
À LA GREAT BRITISH MENU,
RED WINE SAUCE
Cheval des Andes, Vistalba, Mendoza, Cheval Blanc
and Terrazas de Los Andes, 2005

CHOCOLATE AND SEA BUCKTHORN
SPICED CHOCOLATE GATEAU SERVED WITH
EAST LOTHIAN SEA BUCKTHORN SORBET
AND CANDIED ORANGE
Vin de Constance, Klein Constantia, Constantia, 2004

INGREDIENTS

1	Carrot
1	Courgette
100ml	Vegetable oil
1	Lemon
8	Razor clams
2	Shallots, peeled and finely chopped
100ml	White wine
100ml	Whipping cream
50g	Chopped chives or parsley

Knob of unsalted butter

Salt & pepper

Garnish

Bunch of chives, chopped	
3	Sprigs of dill, chopped
Bunch of fresh amaranth leaves	
2	Sprigs of chervil, chopped

METHOD

Vegetables

Peel the carrot and cut into 5mm dice. Cut the green skin off the courgette and dice into 5mm pieces – you don't need the white part for this recipe. Gently sauté the diced carrot and courgette in 1 teaspoon of vegetable oil for 3-4 minutes and set them aside.

Zest the lemon and squeeze the juice. Set aside for later.

Razor clams

Wash the razor clams well in cold running water, making sure you rinse away any sand and grit. Take a pan large enough to hold all the razor clams and place it over a high heat. Add the clams, shallots and white wine and immediately cover the pan with a tight fitting lid so the clams steam. The razor clams should be cooked in 1 minute – don't be tempted to cook them any longer or they will become rubbery. Discard any clams that don't open.

Remove the clams from their shells – keep the shells for serving. Slice the razor clam meat thinly at an angle around the brown intestine. Set aside.

Reduce the white wine cooking liquor by half. Then add the cream and diced vegetables and chopped chives or parsley while the liquid is simmering, stirring constantly. Once the cream thickens slightly, add the sliced razor clams, lemon juice and zest, and finish with a knob of butter. Season to taste.

TO SERVE

Place some shells on each plate and pile in the razor clams, vegetables and creamy juices. Garnish with fresh herbs for decoration and added flavour.

MATTHEW FORT AND TOM PARKER BOWLES

"To adapt an observation of the great Liverpool manager, Bill Shankly, 'food isn't a matter of life and death. It's more important than that'."

Matthew Fort

"Greed is the root of all my passion for food, and the endless quest for great food, be it in the Michelin-starred glory of Northcote, or the most humble of Laotian noodle stores. I want good ingredients, cooked with love and skill."

Tom Parker Bowles

Tuesday 26th January
MATTHEW FORT
TOM PARKER BOWLES

TOM
TOM'S PORKY SCRATCHINGS
AND CIAUSCULO
(A SPREADABLE ITALIAN SAUSAGE)
Vinho Frisante Gaseficado, "Bomfinal" Vinhos Messias

TOM
TOM'S CEVICHE OF BREAM WITH
MORECAMBE BAY SHRIMPS
Gavi di Tassarolo, "Piedmont", La Zerba, 2008

SAN PIETRO CON ZABAGLIONE D'ACETO
(JOHN DORY WITH VINEGAR ZABAGLIONE)
Sauvignon Blanc, Marlborough, Isabel, 2008

MATTHEW
TAGLIATA WITH LANCASHIRE
PINEAPPLE SALAD
Hunter Semillon, VAT 1, Hunter Valley, Tyrrell's, 2002

MATTHEW
PETTO D'ANATRA CON ORZOTTO E ZUCCA
(DUCK BREAST WITH BARLEY RISOTTO
AND PUMPKIN)
Chianti Classico, Tuscany, Fattoria Ormanni, 2005

TOM
GINGER BRAISED PINEAPPLE WITH
ECCLES CAKE ICE CREAM
Muscat, Campbells, Victoria, Rutherglen NV

MATTHEW
CREMA DI LATTE CON MELE IN MIELE
Frangelico Liqueur, Barbero

PETTO D'ANATRA CON ORZOTTO E ZUCCA (DUCK BREAST WITH BARLEY RISOTTO AND PUMPKIN)

Serves 4

INGREDIENTS

1	Reg Johnson supreme duck

Fat (preferably duck fat)
Oil

1	Carrot
1	Onion
1	Leek
1	Celery stick
1	Bay leaf
1	Bottle full bodied red wine
1 tsp	Black peppercorns
1 tsp	Juniper berries
100g	Red onion marmalade

Handful deep-fried salsify

Barley risotto and pumpkin

140g	Barley (35g per person)
2l	Stock (vegetable if you're a vegetarian; chicken, quail or game if you're not)
600g	Pumpkin or butternut squash flesh
30g	Butter

Handful of kale
Salt & pepper

30g	Grated parmesan

METHOD

Preheat the oven to 230°C/450°F/ gas mark 8. Brown the duck crown in hot fat by slipping it into the oven skin side down for 15-18 minutes. Remove from the oven and allow to cool.

Cut the legs off the duck. Cut the undercarriage of the duck away, leaving the crown. Chop up the undercarriage and brown in hot oil. Add the vegetables. Turn in the hot fat for a few minutes. Pour over the red wine and bring to the boil. Skim off the disagreeable foam. Turn down to a gentle simmer. Add the spices and bay leaf and the duck legs. Simmer for 1½ hours. The duck legs may possibly fall apart before this, in which case take them out, take off the skin and shred the flesh. Strain the duck stock into a clean pan and reduce to the desired intensity.

Barley risotto and pumpkin

Put the barley and stock in a saucepan. Bring to the boil. Simmer gently until the barley is cooked – about 40 minutes. Peel, de-seed and chop up the pumpkin flesh into chunks. Put inside a roasting bag or bowl and microwave for 8 minutes at full power until soft (or cook in a saucepan with a little water and the butter, remembering to boil off the water; or roast until soft). Liquidise in a food processor along with the butter. Season to taste. Stir the liquidised pumpkin into the barley.

Blanch the kale until well cooked and cut up finely. Stir into the orzotto con zucca (pumpkin risotto) along with the shredded duck's legs. Season again. Beat in the parmesan.

TO SERVE

Remove the duck breast from the crown and keep warm. Place the orzotto con zucca in the centre of a plate. Slice the duck breasts and place on top, dividing them equally between the plates. Place the duck liver at the side, garnish with the onion marmalade and deep-fried salsify. Sauce around.

THEO RANDALL

"I'm obsessed with food and cooking because when I was very little my family instilled in me a love of food. It's always been a part of me and it's the tasting I love – remembering a flavour or smell. I knew it's something I really liked so I started working in kitchens and I cooked at home a lot, and used to help my mother bake and cook. We used to grow lots of produce in the garden and it was very common for me to go out into the garden and pick fresh vegetables to cook. Then I really got into it and loved the idea of being a chef, because it's not regular hours and there's this amazing pressure and the fulfilment at the end of the day when you make people happy – then start over the next day. It's the simplicity of food I love."

Wednesday 27th January

THEO RANDALL
Theo Randall at the Intercontinental

PUNTARELLE ALLA ROMANA, THINLY
SLICED CHICORY SHOOTS WITH RED WINE
VINEGAR, ANCHOVY AND CAPERS
Pinot Gris, Le Fromenteau, Alsace, Josmeyer, 2006

PAN FRIED SCALLOPS WITH CHILLI, SAGE,
CAPERS AND ANCHOVIES
Vouvray, Le Mont Sec, Domaine Huet, 2007

CAPPELLETTI DI VITELLO, FRESH PASTA
STUFFED WITH SLOW COOKED VEAL
AND PANCETTA WITH PORCINI
MUSHROOMS SAUCE
Dolcetto di Dogliani, San Luigi, Piedmont,
Pecchenino, 2008

COSTATA DI AGNELLO – ROAST RACK
OF SOMERSET LAMB (PINK) WITH
WOOD ROASTED CARROTS, JERUSALEM
ARTICHOKES, ONION SQUASH, FENNEL
AND SALSA D'ERBE
Reserva, Alión, Ribera del Duero,
Bodegas y Viñedos, 2005

AMALFI LEMON TART
Moscato d'Asti, Piedmont, Pio Cesare, 2008

PAN FRIED SCALLOPS WITH CHILLI, SAGE, CAPERS AND ANCHOVIES

Serves 4

INGREDIENTS

250g	Cima di rapa or purple sprouting broccoli, tough stems removed
600ml	Water
	Salt & pepper
1	Garlic clove, sliced finely
	Olive oil
12	Cleaned large scallops
1	Red chilli – sliced and seeds removed
1 tsp	Capers
8	Sage leaves
4	Anchovy fillets, salted in oil
250g	White polenta flour
½ tsp	Red wine vinegar

METHOD

Blanch the cima di rapa in salted boiling water. Remove when tender and cool down in a colander.

Fry the garlic in a saucepan and add the cima di rapa and cook for 3 minutes. Season and put to one side.

In a deep saucepan boil the water and add a pinch of salt then whisk the polenta into the boiling water and cook for 30 minutes. Season and add 2 tablespoons of olive oil.

Heat a frying pan until it smokes. Toss the scallops with salt and pepper and a little olive oil. Place in a hot pan carefully and colour on one side. Turn over, add the chilli, capers, sage and anchovy and a dash of olive oil then take off the heat and add half a teaspoon of red wine vinegar.

TO SERVE

Plate up by putting the polenta in the middle of the plate. Place the cima di rapa on top followed by the scallops, sage, anchovy and capers.

25

KEN HOM

"I am often asked what is it that motivates me to cook and without hesitation I always say it's an Obsession which is defined as a strong and barely controllable emotion. This strong feeling is hard to quantify but it has guided me throughout my life and career whether it be cooking, learning, writing or broadcasting.

Without a doubt, there have been many trying times when I questioned my Obsession with food and cooking and was unsure if I should continue to follow it. Even my mother had her doubts. She kept asking me for years when I was going to give up my passion for cooking and get a normal job. Finally, after 23 years, I got the chance to cook for the Chinese president at No 10 on his first ever state visit to this country which resulted in global headlines that reached even Chinese newspapers. My mother called and said perhaps I should keep my day job. That is when Obsession pays off!"

Thursday 28th January

KEN HOM
Maison Chin, Bangkok

CHA GIO NUOC CHAM
(CRISPY VIETNAMESE SPRING ROLLS WITH
DIPPING SAUCE)
Grüner Veltliner, Kamptal, Fred Loimer, 2008

SPICY HOT AND SOUR SOUP
Saké, Daiginjo, Akashi-Tai Brewery, Akashi

STEAMED CANTONESE STYLE FISH
Riesling Saering, Grand Cru, Alsace,
Schlumberger, 2007

CRACKLING CHINESE ROAST PORK WITH
STIR-FRIED CHINESE GREENS
Robert Arnoux, Bourgogne 'Pinot Fin', 2007

WARM MANGO COMPOTE WITH BASIL
AND VANILLA ICE CREAM
Goldackerl, Beerenauslese, Willi Opitz, 2007

SPICY HOT AND SOUR SOUP

Serves 4

INGREDIENTS

1.2 litre	Homemade chicken stock
2 tsp	Salt
125g	Lean boneless pork, finely shredded
1 tsp	Light soy sauce
1 tsp	Shaoxing rice wine or dry sherry
½ tsp	Sesame oil
½ tsp	Cornflour
Pinch of salt	
Pinch of sugar	
2	Eggs, beaten with a pinch of salt
2 tsp	Sesame oil
25g	Dried Chinese mushrooms, soaked, stems removed and finely shredded
15g	Dried 'tree ear' mushrooms, soaked, stems removed and finely shredded
250g	Fresh firm beancurd, drained and shredded
1½ tbsp	Light soy sauce
1 tbsp	Dark soy sauce
1 tsp	Freshly ground white pepper
6 tbsp	Chinese white rice vinegar or cider vinegar
2 tsp	Sesame oil
2 tsp	Chilli oil
2 tbsp	Fresh coriander, finely chopped

METHOD

Bring the stock to a simmer in a large pot and add the salt.

Combine the pork with the soy sauce, rice wine, sesame oil, cornflour, salt and sugar. Mix well and set aside.

In a small bowl, combine the eggs with the sesame oil and set aside.

Stir the pork into the stock mixture and simmer for 1 minute. Then add the two types of mushrooms with the beancurd and continue to simmer for 2 minutes. Add the egg mixture in a very slow, thin and steady stream. Using a chopstick or fork, pull the egg slowly into strands. Remove the soup from the heat, and stir in the soy sauces, pepper and vinegar. Give the soup a good stir, then finally add the sesame oil, chilli oil, fresh coriander and stir.

TO SERVE

Ladle into individual bowls or in a large soup tureen and serve at once.

ANGELA HARTNETT AND LISA ALLEN

"I'm passionate about food because you get the chance to express your character, ability and flair in a plate of food. For me cooking is very emotional – there are so many emotions you go through: frustration, joy, passion and love, and that all comes through in cooking. You have to be obsessed to be a chef."

Lisa Allen

"I'm obsessed with food because I like to eat – simple as that. I was fortunate as a kid to grow up in a household that cared a lot about what we ate, and when you have that as a child it spoils you and becomes a part of what you want to do. I love my job, and I love cooking, end of story."

Angela Hartnett

Friday 29th January

ANGELA HARTNETT
LISA ALLEN

Angela Hartnett, Murano, Mayfair, London and
Lisa Allen, Northcote, Lancashire

ANGELA
SEARED WEST COAST SCALLOPS, PATA
NEGRA AND BUTTERNUT SQUASH
Vinhas Velhas Branco, Bairrada, Luis Pato, 2008

ANGELA
RISOTTO OF JERUSALEM ARTICHOKES,
ITALIAN BLACK TRUFFLE VINAIGRETTE
Roero Arneis, Piedmont, Giacosa, 2008

LISA
ESSENCE OF GOOSGNARGH DUCKLING,
CRISPY SKIN AND BITS
Amontillado (c18th Solera) Bodegas Tradicion

ANGELA
ROAST RACK OF LONK LAMB, AUBERGINE
PARMIGANO, ROASTING JUICES
Leione, Dominio Dostares, Castile y Leon, 2005

LISA
PINEAPPLE CREAM, LIME CARAMEL
AND ICE
Riesling Late Harvest, Niagara-on-the-Lake,
Château des Charmes

LISA
VALRHONA CHOCOLATE CYLINDER,
SMOKED NUTS, SALTED ORGANIC SHEEP'S
MILK ICE CREAM
Ramos Pinto LBV, 2004

SEARED WEST COAST SCALLOPS, PATA NEGRA AND BUTTERNUT SQUASH

Serves 4

INGREDIENTS

Apple vinaigrette
(makes more than enough for 4)

1 litre	Apple juice
500ml	Olive oil
70ml	Cider vinegar
Salt	

Butternut squash purée
(makes more than enough for 4)

1kg	Ripe pumpkin diced
50g	Butter

Candied walnuts

100g	Shelled walnuts
200g	Sugar
	Butter

Shallot chutney

3	Shallots
100ml	Chardonnay vinegar
Salt	
Thyme	
Bay leaf	

Scallops

8	Large scallops
	Olive oil
	Curry seasoning (1:1 mild curry powder to salt)
1	Granny Smith apple
½	Cucumber, peeled
Chopped chervil	
Pata negra ham sliced	
Mixed cresses	

METHOD

Apple vinaigrette

Bring the apple juice to the boil and reduce to 100ml.

Mix the olive oil, cider vinegar and salt together with the reduced apple juice.

Butternut squash purée

Sweat the butternut squash dice in butter and season with salt.

Cover with a lid and let it steam for 15 minutes, or until the butternut squash has released its juices.

Take the lid off and cook on a medium heat until the butternut squash has gone soft and the liquid has evaporated.

Blend in a Vitamix (liquidiser) adding some of the diced cold butter.

Season and pass through a chinoise (conical sieve).

Candied walnuts

Toast the walnuts in the oven at 180°C/ 350°F/gas mark 4 for 2 minutes so that the walnuts are hot.

Heat the sugar to make a caramel.

When golden, add the walnuts, a pinch of salt and enough butter to cover the walnuts.

Mix for a few seconds and then pour onto parchment paper.

Leave to cool then roughly chop.

Shallot chutney

Dice the shallots into 2cm cubes. Cover with the vinegar, add the aromats, season and cook at a very low heat, until the liquid has evaporated and the shallots are cooked.

Scallops

Cut the scallops in half, sprinkle with curry seasoning and pan fry in a hot pan with the olive oil.

Dice the apple and cucumber into equal cubes (roughly 0.5cm³).

Mix the diced apple and cucumber with a spoonful of shallot chutney, walnut crunch, chopped chervil and the apple vinaigrette.

Arrange the purée on the plate, scallops on top, spoon the apple garnish on and around.

Finish with a slice of pata negra on top and then the cresses.

VALRHONA CHOCOLATE CYLINDER, SMOKED NUTS, SALTED ORGANIC SHEEP'S MILK ICE CREAM

Serves 4

INGREDIENTS

4   Chocolate cylinders (see below)
Chocolate mousse (see below)
Condensed milk caramel (see below)
Salted sheep's milk ice cream (see below)
Sugar pull (see below)
Vanilla soaked sultanas (see below)
Smoked nuts (see below)
Chocolate paint (see below)

Chocolate cylinders

600g   Valrhona 55% Equatorial Chocolate Pistols

Chocolate mousse

140g   Valrhona chocolate
30g   Butter
60g   Egg yolks
15g   Caster sugar
50ml   Cream
100g   Egg whites
60g   Icing sugar

Salted sheep's milk ice cream

½l   Sheep's milk
¼l   Cows' milk
75g   Glucose
75g   Milk powder
2.5g   Stabiliser – stab 2000
75g   Sugar
5g   Maldon sea salt

Condensed milk caramel

400g   Carnation condensed milk or a can of ready caramelised condensed milk

Sugar pull

200g   Fondant sugar
40g   Glucose syrup
10g   Smoked nut dust

Vanilla soaked sultanas

100g   Water
50g   Sugar
½   Vanilla pod
5g   Minus 8 vinegar
60g   Yellow sultanas

Smoked nuts

30g   Roasted pecan nuts
30g   Roasted hazelnuts
30g   Roasted walnuts

Chocolate paint

62g   Sugar
62g   Water
20g   Cocoa powder
62g   Double cream

To serve

1   Cylinder
1   Sugar pull
Smoked nut dust
Melted chocolate
Salted sheep's milk ice cream
Condensed milk caramel
Chocolate paint

METHOD

Chocolate cylinders

Melt 200g of the chocolate to 55°C. Stir in the remaining 400g of pistols, work briskly to melt the beans but be careful not to incorporate any air. The chocolate should end up at around 33°C. Leave the chocolate in a cool dry place to cool to 28°C. The chocolate will begin to set around the outside. Gently heat the chocolate back up to 31°C, stirring in the solidified chocolate as you go. IF YOU EXCEED 32°C THE PROCESS WILL HAVE TO BE REPEATED.

To make the cylinder, cut pieces of acetate to 18x15cm and attach parcel tape to one of the longer sides. Spread the chocolate across half of the acetate away from the tape and roll, securing with the tape at the other side. If necessary, drizzle a little more chocolate down the tube to seal the edge of the cylinder. Allow to set in a cool dry place, preferably for 24 hours. To assemble the cylinder pipe a little condensed milk caramel into the tube, try to get some running the full length. Pipe chocolate mousse into the tube. Follow by adding some of the nuts and sultanas. Repeat the process until the tube is filled. Cap each end with condensed caramel and refrigerate.

Chocolate mousse

Melt the chocolate and butter, mix until fully incorporated. Whisk egg yolk and sugar until light and double in size. Boil the cream and pour over the chocolate and butter. Fold the yolk mixture into the chocolate. Whisk egg whites until soft peaks, slowly adding icing sugar. Fold into the above. Lastly, refrigerate until cold and ready to use.

Salted sheep's milk ice cream

Bring both milks to the boil. Add the glucose, milk powder, stabiliser and sugar and simmer for a further 2 minutes then blitz with a hand blender, pass through a fine sieve and mix in the Maldon sea salt. When cool, place into the Pacojet and freeze to –20°C. Once frozen, paco once then paco again before serving. An ice cream maker could be used for this.

Condensed milk caramel

Place an unopened tin of condensed milk in a pan of boiling water and simmer for 4 hours.

Check the pan occasionally to ensure it doesn't boil dry. When cooked, leave the tin to cool completely before opening. Open the tin, empty the contents into a bowl and stir to ensure an even colour. Put into a piping bag ready for use.

Sugar pull

Bring both sugar and glucose syrup to the boil and cook to 121°C. Stop the cooking by dipping the base of

the pan into cold water, add the nut dust, pour out onto a silpat mat. When cooled a little, pull thin sheets of sugar and form over a rolling pin or other cylindrical object. Dip your thumb into one end of the sugar pull to provide space to place the ice cream.

Vanilla soaked sultanas

In a small pan bring to the boil the water, sugar and vanilla pod and boil for 3-4 minutes.

Remove from the heat, add the minus 8 vinegar and the yellow sultanas. Leave to cool and marinate for at least 1 day.

Smoked nuts

Place the nuts onto a tray and into a smoker with hickory smoking tablets for 45 minutes.

Once smoked cut the nuts into bite-size pieces. Reserve for the cylinder and the small nuts for the nut dust.

Chocolate paint

Bring the sugar and water to the boil. Add the cocoa and whisk in well, pour into a small bowl and place on ice water. Once cool, whisk in the double cream, pour into a squeezy bottle and refrigerate.

TO SERVE

Brush the plate with the chocolate paint. Pipe a little condensed milk caramel to secure the cylinder. Unwrap the cylinder, be careful not to mark or get fingerprints on the surface of the chocolate. Dip the ends in the smoked nut dust, secure on the plate with the condensed milk caramel. Place the sugar pull over the cylinder. Finally position a quenelle of ice cream in the end of the sugar pull and serve.

NATHAN OUTLAW

"Food and cooking have always been an Obsession for me, since I was a small boy. Watching my dad prepare and cook in his kitchen always got me excited and from his point of view I probably got in his way! The most exciting thing about cooking is the eating and I definitely have an Obsession for that – as you will have noticed if you have met me. There aren't many people in this world who can say they are obsessed with their work, but I am one of those lucky people who can say they are. Being obsessed with something cannot be taught, it comes from within. A hunger to learn more and get better and better produce from my area is what drives my passion to cook every day. The day that passion isn't there is the day I hang up my whites."

Saturday 30th January

NATHAN OUTLAW
*Restaurant Nathan Outlaw,
St Enodoc Hotel, Cornwall*

CRAB SALAD WITH APPLE AND CURRY
Sauvignon Blanc, Single Vineyard, Marlborough,
Fairhall Downs, 2007

LEMON SOLE, WILD GARLIC AND POTATO
DUMPLINGS, OLIVE OIL AND LEMON
Redoma, Douro, Dirk Niepoort, 2008

WRECK FISH, MUSSELS AND SAFFRON WITH
RED PEPPER AND BLACK OLIVES
Gran Reserva, Blanco "Capellania",
Marqués de Murrieta, 2004

VENISON, CHICORY AND PARSNIPS WITH
ORANGE AND ESPRESSO
Zinfandel, Geyserville, Santa Cruz,
California, Ridge Vineyards, 2006

RHUBARB SPONGE
WITH GINGER ICE CREAM AND
ALMOND CREAM
Vino Dolce, Vulcaia Après, Veneto, Inama, 2004

WRECKFISH, MUSSELS AND SAFFRON WITH RED PEPPER AND BLACK OLIVES

Serves 4

INGREDIENTS

Mussels

500g	Live mussels
Water to cook	

Saffron sauce

750ml	Fish stock
250ml	Shellfish stock
2	Chopped ripe tomatoes
1	Sprig tarragon
Pinch of saffron	
50ml	Unsalted butter

Shellfish stock

1	Onion, chopped
2	Carrots, peeled and chopped
4	Ripe tomatoes, chopped
6	Garlic cloves, halved
1kg	Frozen shell-on prawns
1	Orange, zest and juice
Few knobs unsalted butter	

Potatoes

16	Medium Roseval (salad) potatoes
100ml	Olive oil
Pinch of salt	

Red pepper

1	Large red pepper

Wreckfish

4 x 200g Fillet portions of wreckfish
Oil for cooking
Salt for seasoning

Garnish

600g	Washed baby spinach
40g	Pitted black olives, roughly chopped
Extra virgin olive oil	

METHOD

Mussels

Heat a pan with a tight fitting lid until it is very hot. Add the mussels and carefully add the water. Place the lid on and steam open the mussels for 2 minutes. Drain the mussels, reserving the juices. Pick the mussel meat out of the shells and wash off the sand and grit, if any. Chill down the mussels and place in the fridge.

Saffron sauce

Place all the ingredients into a pan and reduce to a sauce. Pass through a sieve and keep warm.

Shellfish stock

Place the prawns onto a tray and roast for 45 minutes. Sweat off the vegetables and orange zest in a pan until coloured and add the prawns. Cover with water and juice and simmer for 1 hour. Pass the stock through a sieve and reduce by half in a fresh pan. Chill and refrigerate.

Potatoes

Peel the potatoes and place them in a vacuum pack bag with the oil and salt. Seal the bag and place it into a water bath at 95°C. They will take 30-40 minutes to cook. To serve add a little of the oil to a pan, add the potatoes and colour them all over. Season and serve.

Red pepper

Place a wire rack or trellis over a naked flame. Place the pepper over the flame and blacken all over. Transfer the pepper to a tub and cover with cling film. Leave for 20 minutes then peel the black skin away and de-seed the pepper. Cut the pepper into 1cm squares. Reserve.

Wreckfish

Preheat the oven to 180°C/350°F/gas mark 4. Heat a non-stick pan on the stove and add some oil. Place the fish skin side down into the pan and season with salt. Cook the fish on the skin until it starts to turn golden, then place it in the oven and cook for 4-5 minutes. Remove from the oven and flip the fish over on to the flesh side and remove from the heat. This should be cooked at the very last moment and served immediately.

TO SERVE

Bring the shellfish stock to the boil and whisk in the unsalted butter. Warm 4 bowls. Place the potatoes in the centre of the plates. Add a little shellfish stock. Mix together the spinach, olives and red pepper and wilt in a pan, add the mussels and warm through. Season and plate up around the potato. Warm the sauce and spoon over the garnish and finish with the extra virgin olive oil. Finally, top with the fish.

PHIL HOWARD

"My life has seen many interesting moments, but none more significant and random than the all-consuming Obsession with food and its production while I was at university. Furthermore, many interests, some fanatical, have come and gone but my interest and love of food is as intense now as it ever was. For me it is all an internal and intuitive thing – there is simply no desire to innovate or impress – my fulfilment has always been derived from the simple pleasure of cooking delicious food and the satisfaction that it has the capacity to give to its consumers."

Well, here it is, the 10th year. It is testament to Nigel's status in the industry, to the fact that he has managed to keep a full house of impressive chefs for a decade. It is easy to pull it off for a year or two but 10 is another story.

I have had many, many fantastic times cooking at Northcote and have to confess to having my professional life enriched by the relentless displays of welcoming northern hospitality and the variety of cooking going on in that kitchen. Nigel and Craig have become great mates and people for whom I have the utmost respect.

Sunday 31st January

PHIL HOWARD
The Square, London

THINLY SLICED BEETROOT WITH GOAT'S
CURD, VINTAGE BALSAMIC
VINEGAR AND TUSCAN OLIVE OIL
Sancerre Rosé, Pascal Jolivet, 2008

TERRINE OF DOVER SOLE WITH SMOKED
EEL AND OYSTERS
Sauvignon Blanc, Te Koko, Marlborough,
Cloudy Bay, 2006

RAVIOLI OF CALF'S TAIL WITH
CHANTERELLES AND TRUFFLE
Sito Moresco, Langhe, Piedmont, Gaja, 2006

VENISON WELLINGTON WITH BAKED
CELERIAC AND GREEN PEPPERCORNS
Réserve de La Comtesse, Pauillac, Bordeaux, 2001

ROQUEFORT, PEAR AND PORT
Quinta da Ervamoira, 10 Year Old Tawny, Ramos Pinto

RHUBARB AND ALMOND TART WITH
SAUTERNES ICE CREAM
Château Bastor-Lamontagne 2005

TERRINE OF DOVER SOLE WITH SMOKED EEL AND OYSTERS

Makes one terrine (12-14 portions)

INGREDIENTS

3	Large Dover soles (1.2kg skin removed both sides)
	Salt & pepper
	Juice of a lemon
150ml	Crème fraîche
3	Leaves of gelatine

Garnish (for 8)

20	Large rock oysters, carefully shucked, juice retained
2	Egg yolks
200ml	Grapeseed oil
	Juice of ½ lemon
75g	Sugar
1 tbsp	Lemon olive oil
	½ bunch of chives, finally chopped
¼ tsp	Sosa Gelespressa or xanthan gum
1 x 330ml	Bottle of beer
12g	Fresh yeast
1 tsp	Sugar
280g	Flour
1	Smoked eel, skinned
1	Cucumber, peeled and cut into 3x5cm lengths
100ml	White wine vinegar
24	Sprigs of chervil, to garnish

METHOD

Season the Dover soles, vacuum pack them individually and cook for 15 minutes at 65°C in a water bath. Remove from the bath and leave to rest for 10 minutes. Remove the soles from the bags, reserving the juices, and carefully lift the fillets from the bone. Lay them all out on a tray and lightly season with salt and pepper and give them a squeeze of lemon juice. Measure out 150ml of the sole juices, add the crème fraîche and warm, whisking to combine.

Soften the gelatine in cold water and dissolve in the crème fraîche mix to make a jelly. Set aside and keep warm.

Line a standard terrine mould with cling film. Place two sole fillets in the base, trimming as required, and spoon over ½ tablespoon of crème fraîche jelly. Continue filling the terrine with sole fillets making sure you add a small quantity of crème fraîche mix between each layer. Once all the fillets are in, wrap the terrine in cling film and chill overnight.

Place 4 oysters and the egg yolks in a blender and blend until smooth. Add 50ml oyster juice and re-blend. Now gradually add the grapeseed oil. This will give a creamy oyster mayonnaise. Check and adjust the seasoning with salt, pepper and lemon juice. Set aside in the fridge.

Make the beer batter by gradually whisking the beer into the yeast, sugar and flour. Whisk until homogeneous and leave to prove in a warm place.

Cut the eel in 3, blast chill until firm and, with the use of a slicer, slice wafer thin slices of eel from each side of the central spine. You will need 16 slices. Lay on parchment paper and set aside in the fridge.

Cut a total of 16 thin slices off the cucumber blocks. Dissolve the sugar in the vinegar, add the cucumber and leave for 1 hour.

Chop 8 of the oysters into quarters. Thicken the remaining oyster juice (about 100ml) by blending with the Sosa Gelespressa. Add the chopped oysters, the lemon olive oil and chives and stir gently to combine. Dip the remaining 8 oysters in the beer batter and deep fry at 180°C until crisp and pale golden. Drain on absorbent paper.

TO SERVE

Remove the terrine carefully from the moulds and, using a sharp carving knife, take 8x1cm slices from the terrine. Place one on each of 8 plates and drape over 2 slices of cucumber. Place small dots of oyster mayonnaise onto the plates and spoon some of the oyster vinaigrette over the terrine. Garnish with a deep fried oyster and sprigs of chervil.

JACOB JAN BOERMA

"Food is a human interest and to cook serves man's survival. Professional cooking came in my life by chance. From the beginning the work in the kitchen obsessed me. I loved the richness of smells, tastes, textures and colours of the ingredients and the dishes that came from them. I perceived my capacity to make things with my own hands and to be original and imaginative. Cooking proved to be a way of pleasing others and get appreciation, eating together is a social activity. Every year my ambition is to be better than the year before; you may call it an Obsession, for me it is a lifetime vocation."

Monday 1st February

JACOB JAN BOERMA
Restaurant De Leest, te Vaassen,
The Netherlands

OYSTER "TOKYO STYLE"
CHLOROPHYLL, SOJA, PONZU
AND SEAWEED
Louis Roederer, Blanc de Blancs , Reims 2003

FRESH NORTH SEA CRAB, APPLE AND
CURRY WITH ROASTED DUBLIN BAY
PRAWNS AND LEMON-BELOTTA VARIETIES
Chablis, I'er Cru 'Beauroy', Domaine Hamelin, 2007

SLOW PREPARED LOBSTER AND TARTAR OF
LOBSTER WITH TEXTURES OF GREEN PEAS,
SLICED GREEN BEAN AND MINT ESSENCE,
JUS OF SPICES, COCONUT
AND LEMONGRASS
Condrieu, Les Chaillets, Yves Cuilleron, 2008

LIGHTLY GRILLED TURBOT WITH PUMPKIN,
TWO PREPARATIONS OF SCALLOPS,
WINTER TRUFFLE, PURSLANE AND JUS OF
TRUFFLE AND OLIVE OIL
Chardonnay Reserve, Franschhoek, Chamonix, 2008

FRENCH PIGEON PREPARED ON CARCASS
WITH JELLY OF PARMESAN CHEESE,
ROASTED ONIONS, MOUSSELINE OF
POTATOES AND CHAVROUX CHEESE AND
ITS OWN GRAVY
Châteauneuf-du-Pape, Les Vieilles Vignes Domaine de
Villeneuve, 2005

PETIT GRAND DESSERT
A SMALL COLLECTION OF OUR DESSERTS
Tokaji Aszú, 5 Puttonyos, Oremus, 2000

LIGHTLY GRILLED TURBOT WITH BUTTERNUT SQUASH, TWO PREPARATIONS OF SCALLOPS, WINTER TRUFFLE, PURSLANE AND JUS OF TRUFFLE AND OLIVE OIL

Serves 4

INGREDIENTS

1	White onion
6	Pieces of lemongrass, chopped
1	Piece ginger
Olive oil	
Salt & pepper	
2	Laurel leaves
2	Pieces of lemon peel
1 tsp	Curry powder
Small amount of curry paste	
150ml	White wine
400ml	Chicken fond (bouillon made from chicken meat and carcasses)
8	Scotch scallops
Mayonnaise	
1	Winter truffle, chopped
1	Piece of parsley
500g	Butternut squash, half diced and half sliced
4 x 100g	Pieces of turbot
Japanese vinegar	
Natural fish sauce, to serve	
Truffle vinegar, to serve	
Purslane or lettuce leaves, to serve	

METHOD

Cook the onion with chopped lemongrass and the ginger in olive oil with some pepper and salt, then add the laurel leaves, lemon peel, curry powder, curry paste and white wine and wait until it is reduced. Put in the chicken fond and cook until boiled. Remove the ginger and the laurel leaves. Blend the juice in a thermo blender.

Make a scallop tartare sauce by taking 4 scallops and mixing them with some mayonnaise, chopped truffle and parsley.

Boil the butternut squash squares and slices in salted water until almost well done and then marinate them in Japanese vinegar and olive oil.

Put some salt, pepper and olive oil on the turbot, grill them then put into the oven to steam at 120°C/250°F/gas mark ½ for between 2½ and 4 minutes.

Cut the other 4 scallops in half, season and sauté on one side.

TO SERVE

Place 2 sautéed scallops on a plate, sautéed side up, then put some scallop tartare on top followed by a slice of marinated butternut squash. Put some stripes of butternut squash purée around the plate with some squares of butternut squash. Place the turbot in the middle, then put some natural fish sauce on top of it. Dot truffle vinegar around and garnish with purslane or salad leaves.

JACOB JAN BOERMA

A N D R E W
F A I R L I E

"I was very fortunate at a young age to find something that I had a natural talent for and that's continued to grow – the more I discovered, travelled and the harder I worked, the more passionate I became about it. At this level it's become a lifestyle. If you're a chef restaurateur you're in a fortunate position to be enjoying it 25 to 30 years later. If the food is right then everything else falls into place. The noise and the buzz got me into the job in the first place – now it's double the pleasure."

Tuesday 2nd February

ANDREW FAIRLIE
Restaurant Andrew Fairlie,
The Gleneagles Hotel, Perthshire

SMOKED EEL AND FOIE GRAS, BEETROOT
AND APPLE SALAD
Pinot Gris, Marlborough, Fairhall Downs, 2006

BAKED KING SCALLOP, YUZU AND
GINGER BUTTER
Chardonnay, Hermanus, Walker Bay,
Hamilton Russell, 2007

CEP TART, ROASTED CALF'S SWEETBREAD
Crozes Hermitage, Domaine Mule Blanche, Paul
Jaboulet Aîné, 2007

ASSIETTE OF PORK GASCONY
Garrafeira, Casa de Saima,
Bairrada, Graça Miranda, 2001

CARPACCIO OF PINEAPPLE, COCONUT
PARFAIT, LYCHEE SORBET
Jurançon Moëlleux, Séléction des Terrasses,
A Capcéu, Domaine Larreyda, 2006

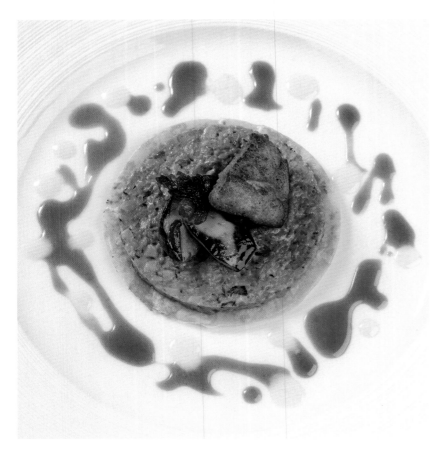

INGREDIENTS

2	Sheets of filo pastry
50g	Melted butter
1	Sprig of thyme
70g	Grated parmesan
250g	Firm ceps
150g	White button mushrooms
150g	Butter
Salt	
2 tbsp	Lemon juice
2	Shallots, finely chopped
1	Small garlic clove, crushed
75ml	Chicken stock
1 tbsp	Double cream
Vegetable oil	
1	Large nugget of soaked and trimmed calf's sweetbread
1 tsp	Chopped tarragon
Flat parsley	
2 tbsp	Madeira sauce

METHOD

Preheat the oven to 180°C/350°F/gas mark 4.

Brush one sheet of filo pastry with melted butter, remove the thyme leaves from the sprig and sprinkle over the filo with 20g of the grated parmesan. Place the other sheet of filo on top and run your hand over the top to dispel any air that may be trapped. Brush this top sheet with the remaining butter. Cut out a large round using a pastry cutter or cut round a saucer. Place the round in between two silpat mats (silicon paper can be used) and bake for exactly 8 minutes. Remove the crispy rounds and place on a wire rack to cool.

Pick out one perfectly shaped cep for roasting and presentation. Cut the remaining ceps into 3mm dice, keeping all the trimmings to one side.

Finely slice the button mushrooms.

Melt 50g of the butter in a small saucepan, add the cep trimmings and the button mushrooms, season with a little salt and the lemon juice, cover with a lid. Cook gently over a medium heat until the mushrooms are completely soft. Blend to make a very smooth purée. Keep until needed.

Melt another 50g of butter in a saucepan, add the chopped shallots and crushed garlic, sprinkle with a little salt and cook gently for 4 minutes. Add the diced ceps, turn the heat up a little and cook until the ceps just begin to take colour. Add the stock and cream and boil until almost evaporated. Remove from the heat until needed.

Heat a small frying pan with a little vegetable oil. Season the sweetbread and fry over a medium heat until golden brown, add the whole cep and continue to cook until both are nicely caramelised. Add the remaining butter and baste continuously until both the sweetbread and cep are cooked. Remove from the pan and drain on a cloth.

TO SERVE

Put the filo disc into the oven to reheat.

Heat the diced cep mixture; when hot fold in the mushroom purée and the grated parmesan. Check the seasoning and add the chopped tarragon.

Place the warmed disc onto a tray, place a cutter slightly smaller than the disc onto the disc and press the mushroom mixture into the cutter and smooth with the back of a spoon.

Place this mushroom tart onto the centre of a warmed plate, place the caramelised cep and sweetbread on top and garnish with a piece of flat parsley.

Drizzle a little Madeira sauce around and serve immediately.

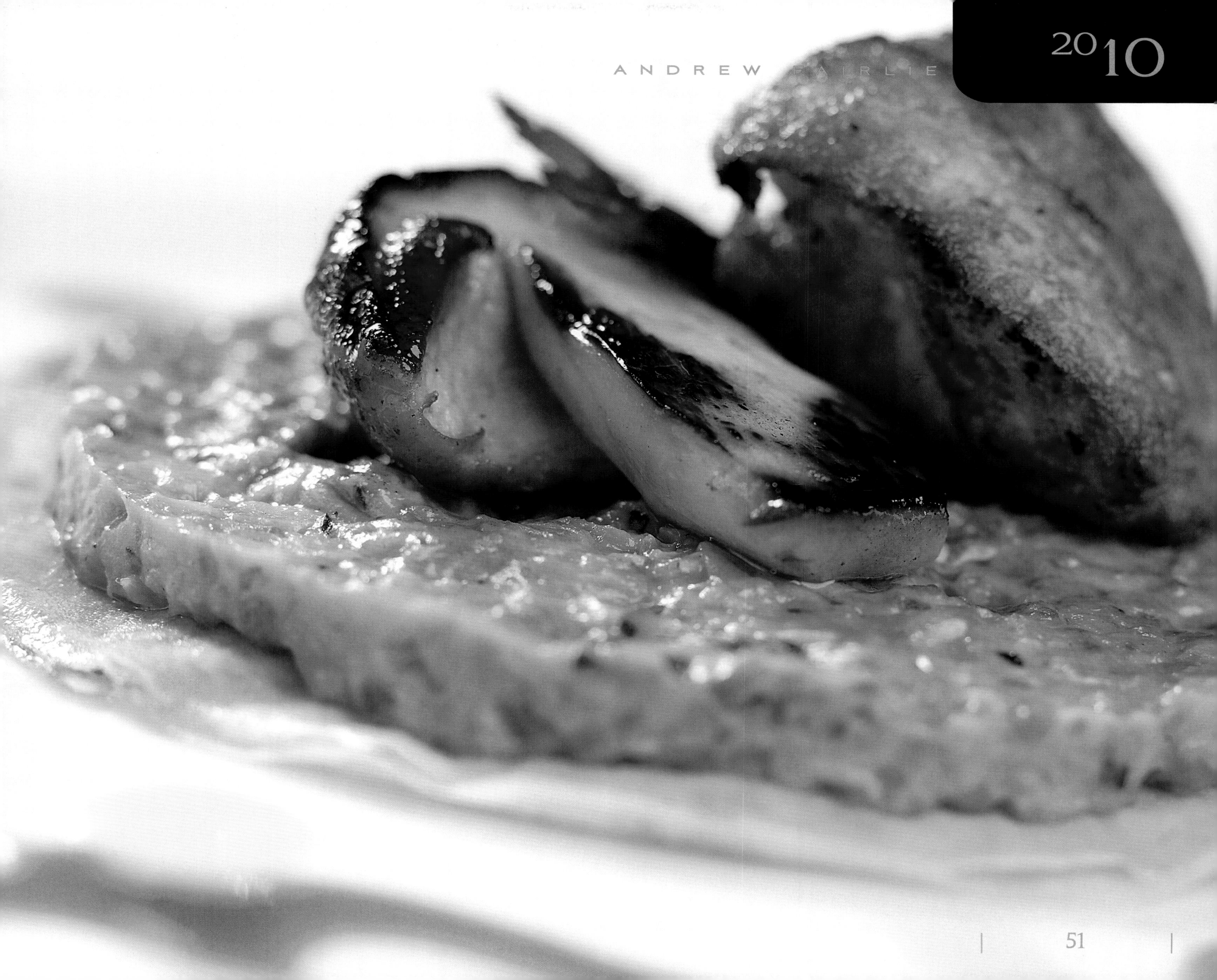

NIGEL HAWORTH

"To be obsessed by something you love is wonderful, some people work just for money."

Wednesday 3rd February

NIGEL HAWORTH
Northcote, Lancashire

VENISON CARPACCIO, MUSHROOM PÂTÉ,
PICKLED DAMSONS, HAZELNUTS
Rose of Virginia, Rosé, Barossa Valley,
Charles Melton, 2008

SOFT HERB DUMPLINGS, CUMBRIAN
LANGOUSTINES, CHICKEN SKINS
Sancerre Blanc, Harmonie, Vincent Pinard, 2006

GOOSE CONSOMMÉ, FAGGOTS,
DRIED MULLED PEARS
Vinhos Barbeito, Single Harvest Madiera, 1997

LOIN OF WELFARE FRIENDLY VEAL,
TROTTERS, SKIN AND SWEETBREADS,
FOREST MUSHROOM RAVIOLIS, MARJORAM
Vosne Romane, Burgundy, Vosne Romanée René
Engel, 2002

YORKSHIRE RHUBARB, MARSHMALLOW,
BLOOD ORANGE JELLY AND CUSTARD
Red Muscadel, Nuy Winery, Worcester, 2007

VENISON CARPACCIO, MUSHROOM PÂTÉ, PICKLED DAMSONS, HAZELNUTS

Serves 4

INGREDIENTS

1 x 300g Piece of venison cushion (silverskin removed and trimmed)
Tarragon pesto (see below)
8 Pickled damsons, deseeded and cut in half (see below)
Mushroom pâté (see below)
Crème fraîche and horseradish cream (see below)
4 Bread wafers (see below)
Few drops lemon olive oil
Maldon salt
20g Red onions, finely diced
8 Whole smoked hazelnuts, roasted and halved
4 Caper berries
Salad leaves

Mushroom pâté

100g Sliced white button mushrooms
25g Shallots, finely sliced
1 tbsp Olive oil
½ Garlic clove, crushed
Salt & pepper

Pickled damsons

225g Damsons
110g Sugar
1 Cinnamon stick
3 Cloves
10g Fresh root ginger, peeled and sliced
150ml White wine vinegar

Tarragon pesto

50g Tarragon (picked and cut with scissors)
10g Roast pine nuts
1 Garlic clove, finely chopped
150ml Olive oil
60g Parmesan
Pinch of salt

Crème fraîche and horseradish cream

50g Crème fraîche
20g Horseradish sauce
25g Whipping cream, semi-whipped
Salt
Pinch of cayenne pepper

Bread wafers

100g White bread dough
Salt & black pepper

METHOD

Roll the venison cushion tight in cling film, place in a blast chiller to semi freeze. Remove from the chiller and cut ½cm off each end to form a rectangle 11cm long and 6cm wide. Slice at number 1 (approx 1cm thick) on the meat slicer, then place directly on to the plate, overlapping slightly, three slices per plate.

Mushroom pâté

Sweat the mushrooms and shallots in the olive oil in a pan for 2-3 minutes until soft, add the garlic and season with salt and pepper. Cook for a further 8-10 minutes until all the liquid has evaporated. Place into a food processor and blitz to a rustic pâté, check the seasoning and remove from the food processor.

Pickled damsons

Preheat the oven to 140°C/275°F/ gas mark 1.

Prick the damson skins with a needle to prevent them splitting, then put into an earthenware dish and sprinkle with sugar. Scatter the cinnamon, cloves and ginger over the fruit and cover with the vinegar. Put the dish at the bottom of a warm oven and leave to cook very slowly for about 20 minutes. Remove when the damsons begin to feel soft and the juice is running and set aside to cool.

When cold, strain the juice, boil it for 5 minutes and pour over the damsons. Put them into a jar. They are best kept for two weeks before use.

Tarragon pesto

Place all the ingredients into a liquidiser, blend well to make the pesto. Remove from the liquidiser and check the seasoning. Reserve.

Crème fraîche and horseradish cream

Mix together the crème fraîche and horseradish sauce. Pass the mix through a fine sieve. Place into a bowl, fold in the semi-whipped cream, season with salt and cayenne pepper. Put into a piping bag ready for use.

Bread wafers

Roll the dough through a pasta machine, working down the numbers to number one. Dust the dough lightly with flour to prevent it from sticking. Once the dough is thin (you should be able to see your hand through it) lay it flat on to a dusted tabletop. Cut into long rectangles 16cm long by 2½cm wide. Season with salt and black pepper. Place the cut bread dough on to a metal wavy rack, bake in the oven at 190°C/375°F/gas mark 4 for 8-10 minutes until golden. Remove from the oven, leave to cool then remove from the wavy rack.

TO SERVE

Lightly brush the venison with the lemon olive oil and season with Maldon salt.

Take the bread wafers and put on two small spoons of mushroom pâté and a little horseradish cream, reserve.

Put 2 small teaspoons of mushroom pâté on to the venison, pipe 6 tiny cones of horseradish cream and sprinkle around the diced onion. Also place on the plate some hazelnuts, a caper berry and pickled damsons. Add a bread wafer and finish with the tarragon pesto and salad leaves.

NIGEL HAWORTH

2009

Daniel opened the 2009 Festival. I had met Daniel Clifford at Midsummer House while visiting St John's College, Cambridge where I was doing a talk on provenance. His first dish was cep, pumpkin and parmesan with fantastic flavours. This dish was followed by scallops and bay leaves, venison was the main course with a stunning chestnut ravioli and to finish a top dessert of roasted pineapple on a coconut and lime gateau.

Shaun Rankin was our next guest, probably a chef whose food we have eaten more of than many with our trips to Jersey. Shaun cooked his signature dish of a lightly poached royal bay oysters with sevruga caviar and they went down a treat. Jersey has some incredible seafood. Shaun's main course was a combination of raw and cooked beef with woodland mushrooms and winter truffles which took a few people by surprise but the result was a winner.

Where was Glynn Purnell? Glynn was due to arrive the night before, rooms were booked, Hot Pot prepared, staff on stand by, but there was no sign of Glynn. Alas, we went to bed at 2am, thinking that it could be a worrying day, but he arrived the next day with a full brigade, having closed his restaurant and it was an absolute joy. Of course he cooked a version of his fish curry that won the Great British Menu in 2008. Glynn's flavours really shone

through, everyone loved it, a really star dish. His famous egg dish with blackberries and crystallised tarragon was a beauty of a dessert.

It was great to have Phil Howard and Brett Graham – Brett opened the night with the warm game canapés and pigeon tea that was garnished with smouldering bay leaves which wafted throughout the room in an ecclesiastical way. He followed with Pyrenean lamb and truffled potato which was a delight. Phil reworked kedgree and I had to remind him it was a dinner, not a breakfast; joking aside it was a fabulous interpretation. Foie gras is always a feature and it made its way back on the menu to great acclaim; salted caramel nougatine was a modern twist on a great dessert.

Atul Kochhar arrived with his wife and children and his two trusted assistants from Benares. Atul cooked a fantastic carpaccio of venison with subtle spicing and great flavour. The Goan spiced lobster was an incredible dish with fresh flavours and soft spices. Then he finished with an interesting interpretation of a classic bread and butter pudding, introducing the flavours of fennel and ginger.

Jason and his team delivered his formidable repertoire in a precise and focused way. Tongue in cheek, a classic Atherton dish, was particularly well-received. Sweetcorn panna cotta followed, with salted caramel and

popcorn sherbet – an unusual dish that was brilliantly delivered with real theatre. Jason finished with bitter chocolate and hazelnut parfait with a milk mousse, a wonderful way to close a great menu.

To wrap it up in 2009, I cooked with my old friend Paul Heathcote. I had always wanted Paul to take part in the festival but had never managed to squeeze in the invitation in-between his many skiing holidays. This year we were in luck and finally we were cooking together. Preparation done and all in place we joined a fellow chef and great friend, Michael Golowitz, who was staying at Northcote, for a few minutes relaxing and watching football before service. Paul cooked braised turbot and scallops with leeks and wild mushrooms, a classic Heathcote dish from his former two Michelin star repertoire. He closed with Heathcote's bread and butter pudding, one of Paul's signature dishes and renowed for its depth of flavour and lightness. I cooked a beef tea then Herdwick mutton and smoked mash potato. Finally, tiny melting Valrhona chocolate desserts which were inspired by Lisa Allen. A final night at the bar saw us sipping a stunning red Vinha Pan from Luis Pato in front of the fire.

obsession
northcote
FESTIVAL OF FOOD & WINE, TWO THOUSAND & NINE

DANIEL CLIFFORD

"When I fall in love with something I give it 100 per cent. Food has always been my first love and it was the first thing that I found in life that I truly enjoyed. Every day I am learning. It's not a job, it's a lifestyle."

Monday 26th January

DANIEL CLIFFORD
Midsummer House, Cambridge

AMUSE BOUCHE
CEP, PUMPKIN AND MUSHROOM
Châteauneuf-du-Pape Blanc, La Bernardine,
M.Chapoutier, 2006

SAUTÉ SCALLOP, BAY LEAF, PIG'S TROTTER
Rully l'er Cru "Les Clous", Olivier Leflaive, 2006

ROAST SADDLE OF VENISON,
PARSNIP PURÉE, BLUE CHEESE,
CABBAGE, CHESTNUT CANNELLONI,
ROASTING JUICES
Sito Moresco, Langhe, Piedmont,
Gaja, 2006

VANILLA, RHUBARB AND APPLE PINEAPPLE
VANILLA ROASTED PINEAPPLE,
COCONUT GATEAUX, PINEAPPLE SORBET,
FRESH LIME
Jurançon Moëlleux, Séléction des Terrasses,
A Capcéu, Domaine Larredya, 2006

AMUSE BOUCHE CEP, PUMPKIN AND MUSHROOM

Serves 8

INGREDIENTS

Mushroom purée

1kg	Mushrooms, roughly chopped
	Oil or clarified butter
2	Shallots, sliced
2	Garlic cloves
	Thyme and bay leaves
170ml	Vegetable stock
50ml	Madeira
	Salt & pepper
1 tbsp	Whipping cream per serving
1 tsp	White truffle oil per serving

Cep jelly

300ml	Cep essence, seasoned (see below)
15g	Vegi Jell (Sosa)

Cep essence

1	Onion
½	Shallot
1	Garlic clove
1	Stick of celery
600g	Button mushrooms
50g	Dried ceps
150ml	Madeira
500g	Fresh chicken stock

Gnocchi

140g	Potatoes
	Salt
55g	Pasta flour
5g	Cep powder
	Salt & pepper
½	Egg
	Olive oil
	Butter

Pumpkin soup

2	Onions, chopped
4	Garlic cloves
140g	Pumpkin, chopped
190g	White chicken stock
	Small pinch of saffron
100ml	Double cream
50g	Beurre noisette
	Sherry vinegar
50g	Pumpkin seeds

METHOD

Mushroom purée

Sauté the mushrooms in very hot oil, so they colour quickly. Continue cooking until they start to render their juices. Strain off the liquid, but reserve it. Add the shallots and garlic to the pan and cook with the mushrooms. Add the stock, thyme and bay leaves and simmer until well reduced. Flavour the mushrooms with Madeira. Season.

Add back the reserved juice. Remove the bay leaves and liquidise the mushrooms, add the whipping cream and truffle oil, and pass through a tammy cloth.

Cep jelly

Whisk the cep essence and vegi jell/Sosa together. Boil, pass through a sieve and onto a small shallow tray and allow to set. Dice.

Cep essence

Sweat the onion, shallot, garlic and celery until soft, add the mushrooms and ceps and sweat again. Add the Madeira and reduce by half. Add chicken stock and boil.

Simmer for 2 hours then pass through muslin.

Gnocchi

Bake the potatoes on salt. Once cooked pass through a drum sieve. Add the flour and cep powder and season. Bind with the half egg. Pipe into shapes of ½ cm diameter. Blanch in salted boiling water until the gnocchi float. Lightly coat in olive oil and pan fry in foaming butter.

Pumpkin soup

Sweat the onions with the garlic. Add the pumpkin and cook for a couple of minutes. Add the white chicken stock and boil for 7 minutes with the saffron, then add the cream and cook for a further 2 minutes. Add the beurre noisette and blend, pass twice through a sieve.

Boil the sherry vinegar and add to taste. Pour 500g into a foam machine, gas with one cartridge, shake and keep at 57°C until needed.

TO SERVE

Take a glass and add pumpkin seeds, diced jelly, gnocchi then the soup. Put foam on the soup and serve.

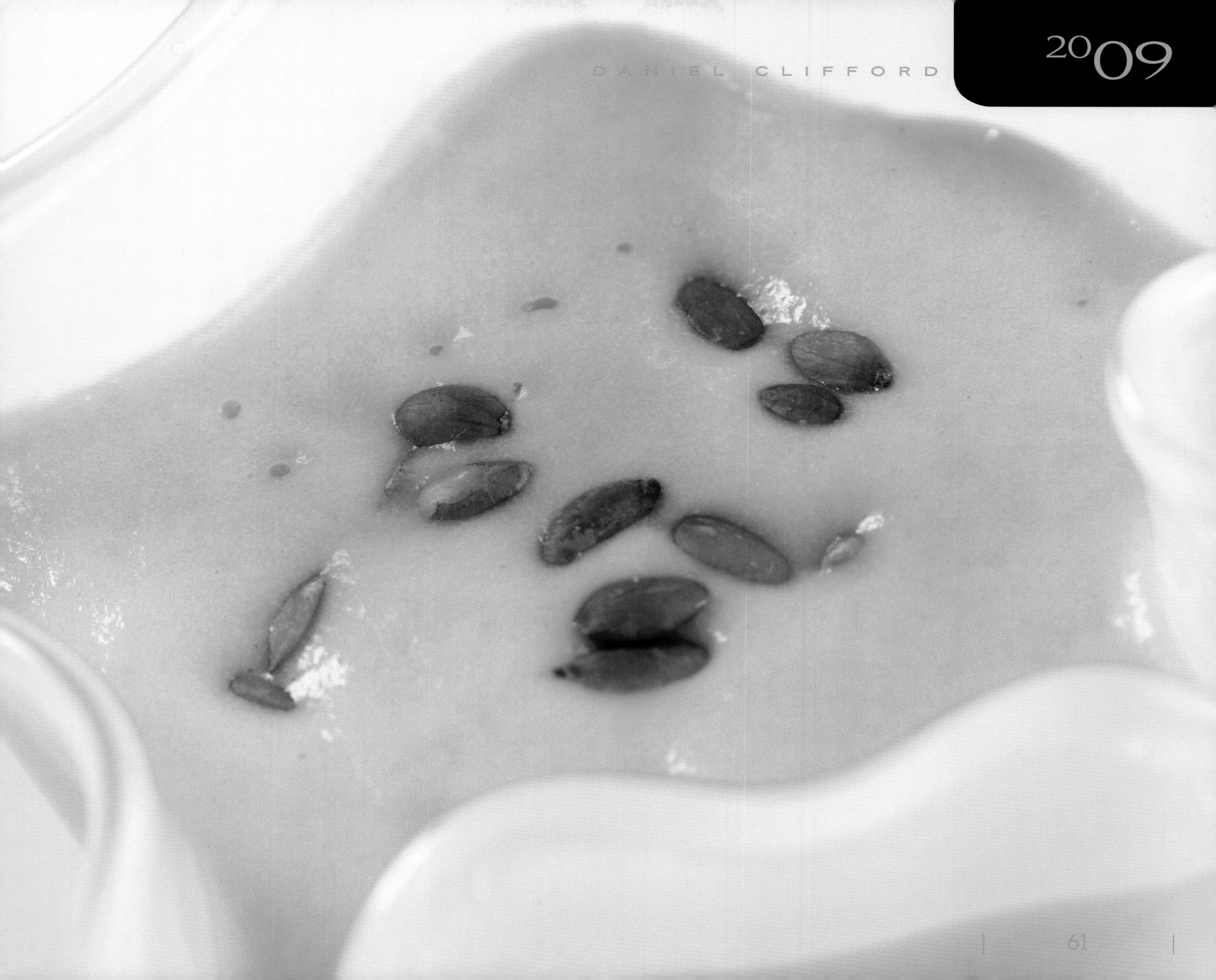

SHAUN RANKIN

"My Obsession is really with ingredients because it all starts with them. Ingredients define what I do. I call Jersey my nine-mile kitchen garden and for me it's all about sourcing local produce and ingredients. I started cooking because I loved the whole thing — I used to love cooking with my mum and that took me into catering, but from the age of 16 it's a job and you're cutting your teeth, I think a deeper understanding of ingredients doesn't come until a later age. My passion is growing more and more and I source better produce the older I get — it's a life work."

Tuesday 27th January

SHAUN RANKIN
Bohemia Bar and Restaurant, Jersey

TERRINE OF FOIE GRAS
WITH CARAMELISED PINEAPPLE CHOP,
PASSIONFRUIT JAM,
MANGO SORBET AND GINGER CRUMB
Mönchhof Erdener Treppchen, Riesling Kabinett, 2002

LIGHTLY POACHED ROYAL BAY OYSTERS
WITH SEVRUGA CAVIAR,
SAFFRON NOODLES AND LEMON BUTTER
Chablis I'er Cru, Fourchaume,
Domaine Séguinot-Bordet, 2007

ROAST ANJOU PIGEON,
ROQUEFORT RISOTTO, PICKLED WALNUTS
AND PRESSED ASIAN PEAR
Fugue de Nenin, Pomerol, 2002

SLOW COOKED SHIN AND CARPACCIO
OF RIBBLE VALLEY BEEF FILLET,
SAUTÉ OF WOODLAND MUSHROOMS,
WINTER TRUFFLE SALAD
Shiraz, T & C Soderstrom, Barossa Valley, Viking, 1999

LEMON CRUMBLE SOUFFLÉ,
CANNELLONI OF ESPRESSO SEMI-FREDO,
MACADAMIA NUT BISCOTTI
Sauvignon, Late Harvest Maule Valley,
Concha y Toro, 2004

LIGHTLY POACHED ROYAL BAY OYSTERS WITH SEVRUGA CAVIAR, SAFFRON NOODLES AND LEMON BUTTER SAUCE

Serves 4

INGREDIENTS

Oysters and caviar

12	Fresh oysters
1	Cucumber
	Sevruga caviar
	Chives
	Micro celery

Butter sauce

300ml	White wine
6	Black peppercorns
1	Sprig of thyme
1	Bay leaf
1	Shallot, finely chopped
2 tbsp	Double cream
250g	Diced unsalted butter
	Lemon juice

Pasta

600g	Pasta flour
	Pinch of salt
3	Eggs
6	Egg yolks
3 tbsp	Saffron reduction
1tsp	Olive oil

METHOD

Pasta

Sieve the flour and salt together and place in a food processor along with the eggs, egg yolks, saffron reduction and olive oil.

Process until the mixture comes together. Stop the machine, tip the ingredients onto a board and knead well until you have a firm smooth ball of dough.

Wrap in cling film and leave to rest for a minimum of 30 minutes.

On a lightly floured surface divide the dough into 4 equal pieces.

Take one part of the dough and roll out with a rolling pin to a rectangle approximately 5mm thick.

Feed the dough through the pasta machine several times on the thickest setting, adjusting the setting by one notch each time.

Finish with the thinnest setting, then using the linguine attachment run the dough through the machine.

Let the linguine hang over a wooden pole to dry before cooking in boiling salted water.

Drain and refresh in iced water then drain and toss with a little olive oil and set aside until needed.

Butter sauce

Take a small sauce pan, add the white wine, peppercorns, thyme, bay leaf and chopped shallot.

Bring to the boil and reduce the liquid by half its volume.

Pass through a fine sieve into a clean saucepan.

Add the cream, bring back to the boil then pull the pan to the edge of the stove.

Keeping warm, slowly add the diced butter a little at a time making sure the sauce does not boil.

Add the lemon juice, season with pepper and keep warm until needed.

Oysters

Carefully open and cut out the oysters, place in a bowl with their juices. Peel and cut the cucumber into small batons for the top of the oyster.

TO SERVE

When ready, reheat the noodles in boiling salted water.

Drain and, with a carving fork, make three little bobbins for each plate.

Warm the oyster juice in a saucepan and drop the oysters in for approximately 8 seconds.

Spoon them out onto a clean cloth and drain well.

Place on top of each pasta bobbin.

Top with the cucumber batons and caviar.

Chop the chives and place in the warm lemon butter sauce.

Spoon over the oysters and noodles, garnish with the micro celery and caviar, and serve straight away.

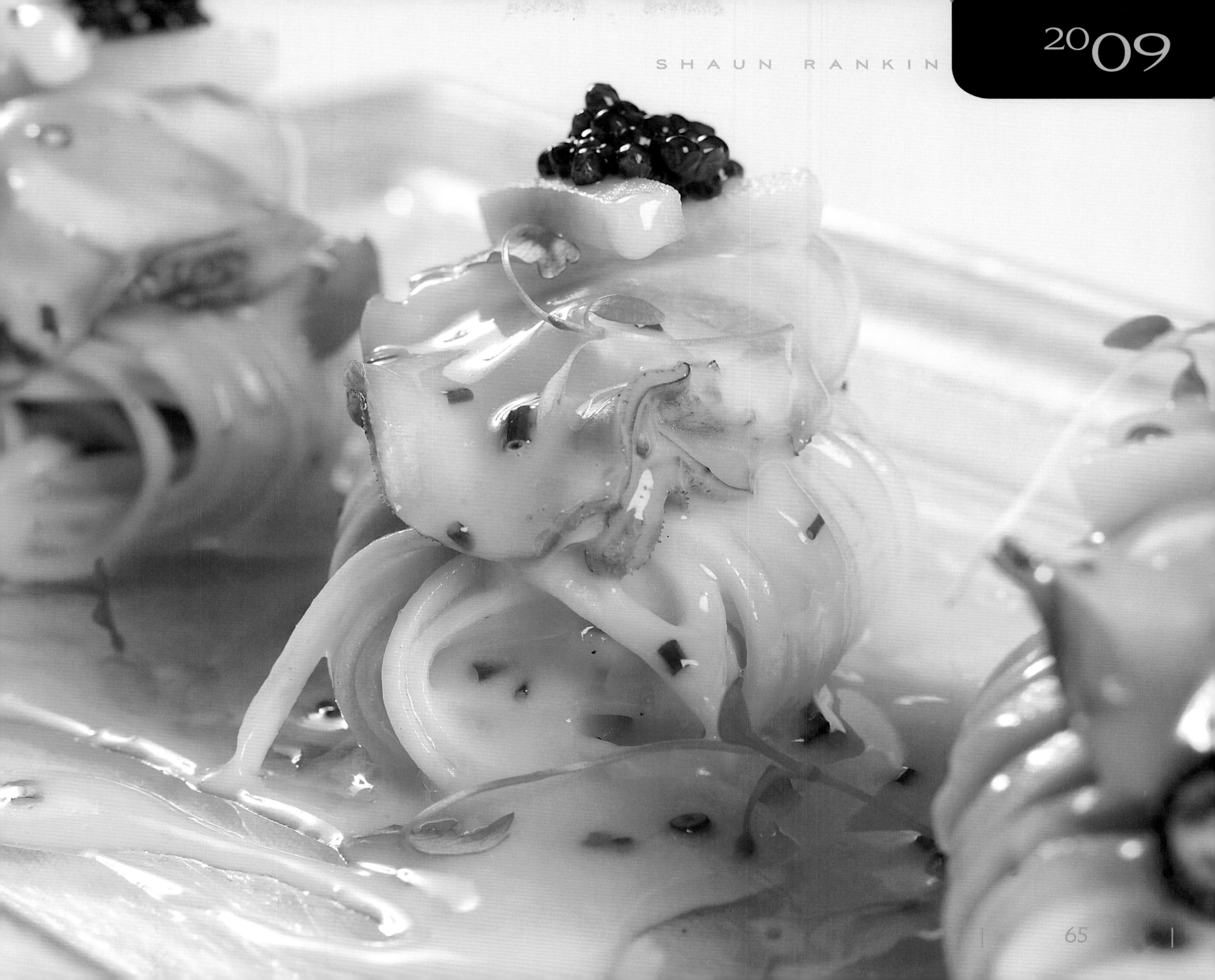

G L Y N N
P U R N E L L

"I got into cooking when I was about 10 and the Obsession
started when I went to the market with mum. It was wild: food
had faces and from then I was obsessed with the way food changes
when it's cooked - like when you fry an egg and how cheese goes
stringy when it's hot. Then it really kicked in when I walked
into my first kitchen at 14 and I realised it's not a job;
it's a way of life. First I thought, why are all these people
shouting? But it was instant - the hair on the back of my neck
was standing up and it was a total buzz. You can't describe the
feeling, but I knew that's what I'd do for the rest of my life
and that Obsession has never been dampened - if anything it's
grown. Even when I'm away from the restaurant I think about
food. It's food, food, food! You can't be any more intimate with
someone (other than sex) than when you're cooking for them."

Wednesday 28th January

GLYNN PURNELL
Purnell's, Birmingham

CUCUMBER SORBET,
RAS AL-HANOUT CREAM,
CRISPY BLACK JAPANESE RICE, MINT OIL
Verdejo, Conclass, Sitios de Bodega, 2007

POACHED EGG YOLK,
SMOKED HADDOCK MILK FOAM,
CORNFLAKES,CURRY OIL
Pouilly-Fuissé, Métertière, Thierry Drouin, 2006

ROYALE OF GOAT'S CHEESE,
CONFIT PINEAPPLE AND
WATERCRESS PURÉE

BRILL POACHED IN COCONUT MILK,
INDIAN LENTILS,
TOFFEE CUMIN CARROT,
RED PEPPER PURÉE
Riesling, Les Princes Abbés, Organic, Domaines
Schlumberger, 2005

OX CHEEK, BUTTERNUT SQUASH PURÉE,
BUTTERED CABBAGE, LEMON
Cabernet Sauvignon, Don Melchor, Puento Alto
Vineyard, Concha Y Toro, 1998

ENGLISH BURNT CREAM EGG CUSTARD
SURPRISE, WITH FRESH BLACKBERRIES,
CRYSTALLISED TARRAGON,
BLACK PEPPER HONEYCOMB,
MULLED JELLY
Muscat de Beaumes de Venise, Le Chant des Griolles,
Paul Jaboulet Aîné, 2006

Curry oil

300ml	Sunflower oil
2 tbsp	Medium curry powder

Haddock

400ml	Whole milk
250g	Undyed smoked haddock, skin on
½ tbsp	Xanthan gum (available from health food shops and online)
4	Free-range egg yolks
20	Cornflakes

METHOD

Curry oil

Place the oil and curry powder into a small pan over a very low heat and heat gently for one hour. Allow to cool, then strain.

Haddock

Place the milk into a wide deep pan over a low heat and bring to a gentle simmer. Add the smoked haddock and poach until the fish begins to flake and the milk has taken on the flavour of the fish.

Strain the haddock through a fine sieve into a bowl, squeezing as much moisture from the haddock as possible. Transfer the milk to a clean pan over a low heat. Discard the haddock (or use in other dishes, such as kedgeree).

Add the xanthan gum to the milk and whisk to dissolve and thicken it. Pour into a siphon, then place the siphon into a jug or bowl of hot water to keep the milk mixture warm.

Poach the egg yolks in gently simmering water for 1-2 minutes, then remove with a slotted spoon.

TO SERVE

Pipe out the thickened milk from the siphon into each serving bowl into a round shape. Place an egg yolk into the centre of the milk (so the milk and yolk resemble a fried egg).

Place or sprinkle the cornflakes over the milk, then drizzle the curry oil over the egg in a zig-zag pattern.

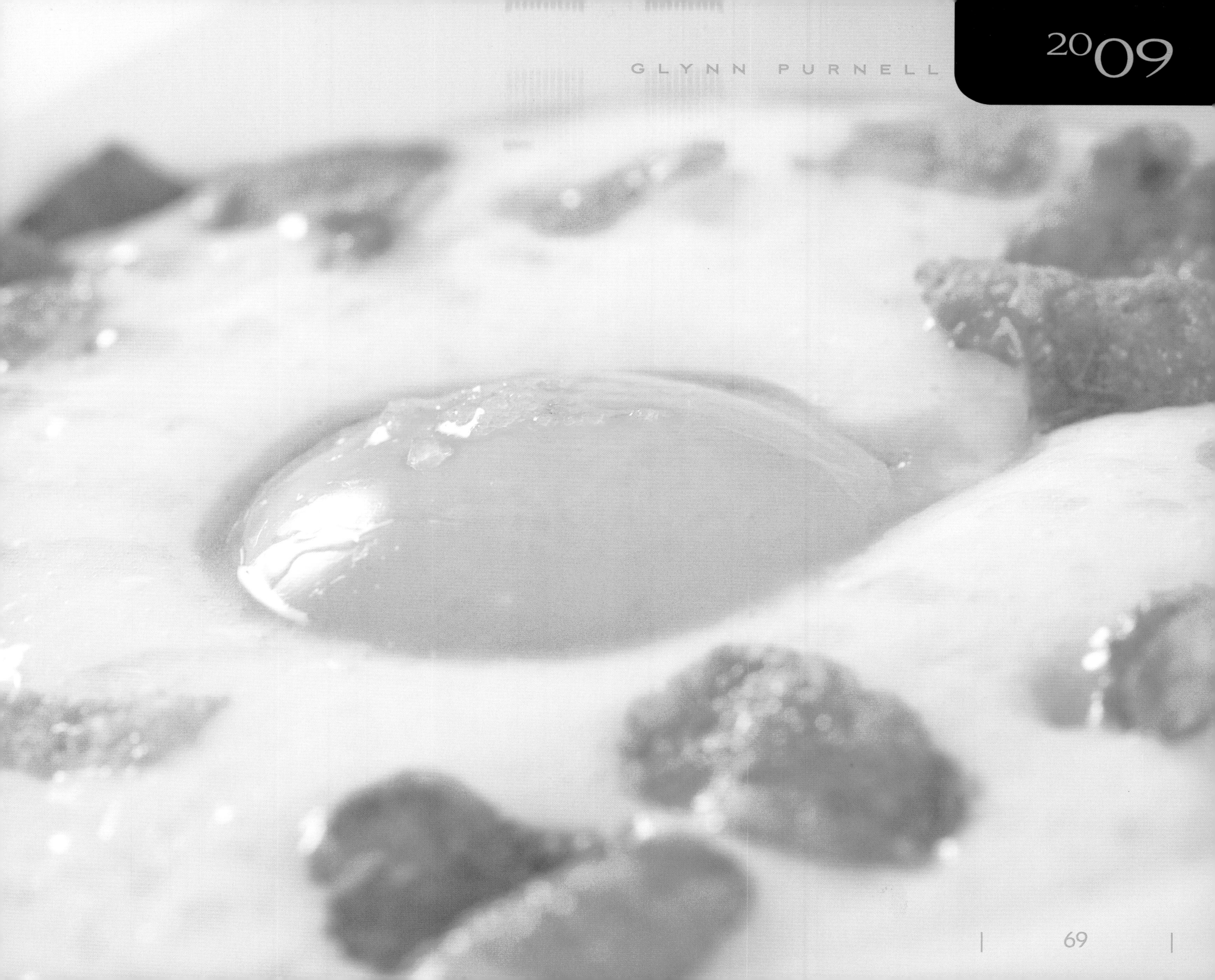

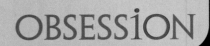

PHIL HOWARD
AND
BRETT GRAHAM

"In 2008 I told Nigel and Craig I would retire from The Festival after 10 years and give way for a more youthful star to shine! I genuinely thought this was the 10th year, so I brought Brett Graham with me to pass the baton to. We shared the dinner and our food dovetails perfectly but it was swiftly explained to me that this was only the 9th year. One more to go then. Quite how local legend Paul Heathcote managed to slip through the net for 9 years, I do not know!"

Phil Howard

"I'm obsessed with the seasonality of the food I cook. I take a very seasonal approach and enjoy sourcing, shooting and preparing some fantastic wild British ingredients."

Brett Graham

Thursday 29th January

PHIL HOWARD
BRETT GRAHAM
*Phil Howard of The Square, London
and Brett Graham of The Ledbury, London*

BRETT
PIGEON TEA WITH WARM GAME CANAPÉS
Don Nuño, Dry Oloroso, Emilio Lustau

PHIL
KEDGEREE
Chardonnay, Hermanus, Walker Bay,
Hamilton Russell, 2007

PHIL
ROAST FOIE GRAS WITH A SWEET AND
SOUR CITRUS GLAZE AND A COMPOTE OF
RHUBARB AND GRANNY SMITHS
Pinot Noir, Beernauslese, Willi Opitz, Illmitz, 2005

BRETT
CARAMELISED SHOULDER
OF PYRENEAN LAMB WITH CREAMED
POTATO,CELERY AND TRUFFLE
Château Leydet-Valentin, St Emilion,
Grand Cru Classé, 2004

BRETT
A TASTING OF COMTE 7 ROQUEFORT
WARM ROASTED PEAR WITH TIRAMISU

PHIL
"DULCE DE LECHE" ICE CREAM
AND SALTED CARAMEL NOUGATINE
Inama, Vulcaia Aprés Vino Dolce,
Veneto Bianco, Verona, 2006

INGREDIENTS

Consommé

10	Wood pigeon carcasses with legs attached (ask your butcher to chop them and save them in the freezer for you)
	Vegetable oil
2 litres	Chicken stock
1	Brown onion, sliced
6	Button mushrooms, sliced
200ml	Madeira
100ml	Oloroso sherry
3	Slices dried ceps

To clarify the consommé

2	Wood pigeon breasts
1	Chicken breast
4	Egg whites
	Pinch of salt

CANAPÉS

Pheasant and quince beignet

1	Pheasant breast with skin sealed in a hot pan, cut into 24 pieces
	Quince paste cut into 12 small squares
100g	Plain flour
100g	Cornflour
	Sparkling water
	Salt
1	ice cube
1	bunch of bay leaves

Wild boar rillette on toast

200g	Confit of boar
1 tsp	Tarragon mustard
25g	Fresh duck fat
	Chopped parsley
	Freshly ground pepper
6	Fingers of Poilâne bread, toasted
	Freshly grated parmesan

Partridge sausage roll

1	White onion
50g	Butter
	Salt & pepper
1	Sprig of sage
1 tbsp	Breadcrumbs
2	Rashers of smoked bacon
200g	Diced fatty pork belly (no skin)
2	Partridges – meat only (no skin, sinew or bones)
3	Rolls puff pastry cut into 10cm squares
	Eggwash

To serve

Herbs (rosemary, thyme, bayleaf, juniper)
Cilass tea pot with fine mesh
Tea cup
Wooden board
Quince paste

METHOD

Consommé

For the consommé, roast off the chopped carcasses in some vegetable oil until golden brown. Remove from the pan. Add the chicken stock, onions and mushrooms and cook until lightly coloured. Deglaze with the Maderia and Oloroso, add the dried ceps and cook for 2 hours, strain through a fine sieve and cool.

To clarify the consommé

Blend the wood pigeon breast, chicken, egg whites and salt in a food processor to make a paste. Whisk this mix into the consommé, place in a heavy bottomed pan and bring up to a light simmer. Pass through a fine cloth and chill.

CANAPÉS

Pheasant and quince beignet

Mix the plain flour, cornflour, sparkling water, salt and ice cube together to make a batter one hour before serving.

Cut the bay leaves into skewer size with a leaf on top and a sharp base. Skewer one piece of pheasant breast, then a quince paste square, then follow with another piece of pheasant. Season lightly, dust in flour, then dip in the batter and deep fry until golden. Drain well. Light the top of the bay leaf, then blow it out so it smokes.

Wild boar rillette on toast

Mix the mustard, duck fat, parsley and pepper together with the confit of boar. Roll this mix between two pieces of greaseproof paper and set in a fridge. Cut to appropriate sizes, place on the toast and warm briefly in the oven. Sprinkle with freshly grated parmesan.

Partridge sausage roll

Sweat the finely diced white onion in the butter with a pinch of salt. When soft add the sage and cool. Add the breadcrumbs and a grind of pepper. Dice all the meat and put through a mincer. Add the meat to the breadcrumbs, mix well. Test for seasoning. Pipe some mix near to one end of each puff pastry square. Fold over the top and crimp with a fork. Eggwash the top lightly and place in an oven for about 12-14 minutes
until crisp.

TO SERVE

Bring the consommé up to the boil and pour it into a herb-filled pot. At the table, pour into the guests' cups and serve on a wooden board with a selection of the canapés and some quince paste.

BRETT GRAHAM

KEDGEREE
Serves 8

This is a modern take on a well known classic. There are many opinions about what constitutes a proper 'kedgeree' and in my opinion the four ingredients which must be present are smoked haddock, rice, eggs and curry. The rest is open to debate. In this version the eggs and the haddock play the star roles and I have added mussels because their affinity with curry is phenomenal. It is not possible to make small quantities of the creams and rice balls, but these items will just have to be enjoyed elsewhere!

INGREDIENTS

8	Quails' eggs
8	Small hens' eggs
1	Long leek
1	Stick celery
24	Mussels, cleaned
2	Granny Smith apples
16	Celery leaves
1 litre	Milk
2	Finnan smoked haddock fillets, skinned, trimmed and cut into 110g pieces – reserve the skin and trim for the stock (see below)
150g	Curry cream (see below)
150g	Mussel cream (see below)
50g	Raisin purée (see below)
24	Smoked haddock rice balls (see below)

Smoked haddock rice balls

450ml	Smoked haddock stock (simply made by covering the smoked haddock skin and trim with water and adding some onion, leek and celery)
3	Shallots, finely chopped
50g	Butter
	Salt
10g	Raz el hanout curry powder
150g	Risotto rice
25g	Parmesan
	Whisked egg
	Flour
	Breadcrumbs

Curry cream

125g	Finely chopped onions
1	Garlic clove, crushed
10g	Raz el hanout curry powder
250ml	Grapeseed oil
	Salt & pepper
200ml	Apple juice
3	Egg yolks
	Squeeze lemon juice

Mussel cream

100ml	Mussel juice (from cooking of mussels)
	Lemon juice
½ tsp	Dijon mustard
3	Egg yolks
	Salt & pepper
200ml	Grapeseed oil

Golden raisin purée

50g	Sugar
250g	Golden raisins
150ml	Apple juice

Mussel beignets

1 x 330ml	Bottle of beer
300g	Plain flour
50g	Yeast
	Pinch of salt and sugar
24	Cooked mussels
	Bunch of celery leaves, to garnish

METHOD

The rice balls and creams can be made the day before.

Cook the quails' eggs in boiling water for 2 minutes and 20 seconds and refresh in cold water. Peel and reserve. Similarly cook the hens' eggs for 9 minutes, peel and reserve. Cut the leek into ½cm rounds, peel the celery and cut into 3mm crescents. Blanch both, separately, in boiling salted water until just tender. Thoroughly drain and chill on a flat tray or plate in a fridge. Do not refresh in iced water – this will leach out flavour.

Briefly cook the mussels by placing in a preheated covered pan with a splash of water, allowing them to steam open. Pick the mussels from the shells and reserve in the fridge along with the juice.

Smoked haddock rice balls

Heat up the smoked haddock stock. Sweat the shallots in a heavy based pan with some butter, a pinch of salt and the curry powder. After 3 or 4 minutes add the rice and cook for a further 2-3 minutes to seal the rice. Now, gradually add the hot smoked haddock stock over a period of about 10 minutes until the rice has just a bit of a bite left. Never swamp the rice with stock – add it gradually as the rice absorbs the previous addition. Finish off the risotto by adding the remaining butter and parmesan. The end result should be a rich, mellow, creamy smoked haddock risotto where the rice is fully, but not over, cooked. Pour this risotto into a shallow dish and chill. Roll into 24 little balls 2.5cm in diameter. Coat them in flour, then egg and finally in the breadcrumbs.

Curry cream

Sweat the onions, the garlic and the curry powder in a splash of the oil with a generous pinch of salt. Once softened and translucent add the apple juice and simmer for 2-3 minutes. Allow to cool, place in a blender, add the egg yolks and blend to a smooth purée. Gradually add oil with the blender running on maximum and you will end up with a smooth curry cream. Check the seasoning and adjust with salt, pepper and lemon juice if necessary. This should be the consistency of a thick pouring cream.

Mussel cream

Place the mussel juice, a squeeze of lemon juice, the mustard and the egg yolks in a blender and blend. Season with salt and pepper. With the blender on maximum add the grapeseed oil until a thick cream is achieved. Check the seasoning and adjust if necessary. This should be the consistency of a thick pouring cream.

Golden raisin purée

Cover the raisins in apple juice and soak overnight. Take the sugar to a caramel in a heavy based pan over a flame. Drain the raisins and add them to the caramel. Stir until the caramel has dissolved, add the drained apple juice and bring to the boil. Place in a blender and purée until smooth.

Place the curry and mussel creams and this purée into plastic 'squeezy' bottles.

Beer batter for mussel beignets

Make a simple batter with the beer, the flour, the yeast, sugar and the salt by whisking all the ingredients together. Set aside in a warm place.

TO SERVE

Bring a pan of vegetable oil to 180°C.

Cut the apple into matchstick-size batons.

Dip the mussels in the beer batter, coating them lightly, and deep fry until golden.

Deep fry the rice balls until golden and deep fry the celery leaves until they are crisp. Reserve and keep warm.

Bring the milk to simmering point in a shallow pan. Remove from the heat and drop in the pieces of smoked haddock. Drain the smoked haddock after 4 minutes, at which point it should break into beautiful translucent flakes. Using an old fashioned egg slicer ideally, slice the hens' eggs into thin slices. Place these onto the plates – do not use the slices with no yolk. Place the flaked haddock on top. Dress this with both the curry and mussel creams and garnish with the leeks and celery. Finish with 'dots' of raisin purée, the mussel beignets, rice balls, celery leaves and julienne of apple and finish each plate with a quail's egg cut in half and seasoned with salt.

ATUL KOCHHAR

"I was fortunate to be born in a family where food and family were the most important things. My dad was a connoisseur in his own right and his values got instilled in me and my siblings right from childhood. Since I've become a professional, I have always worked my food around agriculture and natural cycles. Food is a passion for me and its natural character motivates me to cook with the seasons. I dream of the seasons in terms of their produce and the end products I would create next time. I think of good food markets in terms of fashion show ramps; I imagine food flavours as if they were new perfumes for the season. So if people think I am obsessed, then so be it."

Friday 30th January

ATUL KOCHHAR
Benares Restaurant, London

BEETROOT CUP FILLED WITH
MUSHROOM MOUSSE

CRAB MEAT CAKE
AND CURRY TARTAR SAUCE
Marsanne, Vin de Pays des Collines Rhodaniennes,
Domaine Yves Cuilleron, 2007

CARPACCIO OF SPICED VENISON,
GARLIC CHUTNEY AND SHERRY
VINAIGRETTE
Rose of Virginia, Rosé, Barossa Valley,
Charles Melton, 2008

GOAN SPICED LOBSTER
WITH COCONUT SAUCE AND
YOGHURT RICE
Chenin Blanc, Piekenierskloof, Tierhoek, 2004

ROASTED RUMP OF LAMB WITH CHICKPEA
AND TURNIP STEW
Pinot Noir, Central Otago, Amisfield, 2006

FENNEL BREAD AND BUTTER PUDDING
WITH GINGER AND HONEY CUSTARD
Tokaji Aszú, 5 Puttonyos, Oremus, 2000

GOAN SPICED LOBSTER WITH COCONUT SAUCE AND YOGHURT RICE

Serves 4

INGREDIENTS

4 x 700-800g	Lobster
Salt	
Water	

Goan spice paste

100g	Fresh coconut, grated
3	Dried red chillis
3 tsp	Coriander seeds
1 tsp	Black pepper
4-6	Cloves
1 tsp	Cumin seed

Sauce

Oil	
2	Large onions
1	Green chilli
1 tsp	Ginger and garlic paste
½ tsp	Turmeric powder
1 tsp	Coriander powder
¼ tsp	Red chilli powder
Water	
2	Tomatoes, chopped
40g	Tamarind paste
200ml	Coconut milk
2sp	Finely chopped coriander leaves

Tomato rice

Oil	
½ tsp	Mustard seeds
10	Curry leaves
1 tsp	Garlic clove, chopped
½ tsp	Ginger, chopped
¼ tsp	Green chilli, seeds removed and chopped
1	Onion, chopped
½ tsp	Turmeric powder
1 tsp	Coriander powder
1 tsp	Red chilli powder
10ml	Lemon juice or water, to dilute

100g	Tomatoes, chopped
2 tsp	Tomato paste
200g	Basmati rice (cooked)
Butter	
1 tbsp	Coriander, chopped
¼ tsp	Black pepper

Tail meat and claw

Oil	
50g	Butter

Asparagus

12	Asparagus spears
Water	
Micro cress, to garnish	

METHOD

Lobster

Boil water in a large pan with salt. Add the lobster for 4-5 minutes and simmer. Remove from the pan and immerse in cold water with ice for 30 minutes. Drain the water then split the tail using scissors. Remove the tail meat and pat dry. Wash the tail in running water and dry it using a cloth. Crack the claws and remove the meat. Break the knuckles, remove the meat and set aside. Add most of the spice paste (below) to the tail and claw meat and pack in bags, sealed to make them air tight. Reserve for 30 minutes.

Goan spice paste

Lightly toast the grated coconut, dried red chillis, coriander seeds, black pepper, cloves and cumin seeds in the pan until lightly coloured, remove from the pan and leave to cool. Put the mixture in a food processor with a little water and blend to a smooth paste.

Sauce

Heat the oil in a large pan, add the onions and green chilli and sauté until brown. Stir in the ginger and garlic paste, turmeric powder, coriander powder, red chilli powder, add water and sauté for a few minutes. Add the chopped tomatoes and cook gently. Add any remaining spice paste and cook for 4-5 minutes. Add the tamarind paste and simmer for 3-4 minutes then pour in the coconut milk and simmer for another 10 minutes. Sprinkle in the chopped coriander and remove from the heat.

Tomato rice

Heat the oil in a pan, add the mustard seeds, curry leaves, garlic, ginger, green chilli and stir over a medium heat until the mustard and curry leaves begin to pop. Then add the onion and stir fry until translucent, add the turmeric powder, coriander powder, red chilli powder, lemon juice or water and stir until the moisture evaporates. Add the chopped tomatoes and tomato paste, stirring with a spatula until nicely cooked. Add the cooked rice, a little bit of butter, all of the chopped lobster meat, coriander and mix well. Adjust the seasoning. Remove the pan from the heat and fill the lobster tail with the rice.

Tail and claw meat

Heat the oil in a non-stick pan. Cook the lobster meat from both the tail and claws. Cook until soft and tender, constantly basting with butter. Remove and serve.

Asparagus

Peel the asparagus heads and retain the tips up to 3cm. Blanch in boiling salted water and when crisp, remove and refresh in iced water. Strain and reserve.

TO SERVE

Arrange the different elements of the dish on a round plate. Use some micro cress to garnish.

JASON ATHERTON

"I became obsessed with food from an early age of about 16, so I was lucky I knew I wanted to become a chef and was dedicated to my craft. I came from a modest background and cooking gave me a foot in the door into a world like no other. The smells, the tastes, the most amazing ingredients. I couldn't stop eating, sleeping, breathing my new love which to this very day is still embedded in my soul. I can't walk past a bistro, shop or farm for that matter without getting lost in the romance of our beautiful world which is cooking."

Saturday 31st January

JASON ATHERTON
Maze, London

PRESSED MARINATED FOIE GRAS,
LINCOLNSHIRE SMOKED EEL,
BAKED POTATO FOAM AND DILL
Pinot Gris, Marlborough, Fairhall Downs, 2006

ROASTED HAKE IN PARMA HAM,
CHORIZO AND PIMENTO PURÉE,
SQUID PAINT
Gran Reserva, Blanco "Capellania",
Marqués de Murrieta, 2003

BEEF "TONGUE 'N' CHEEK",
CAPER RAISIN AND GINGER CARROTS
Zinfandel, Sonoma County, Seghesio, 2006

SWEETCORN VANILLA PANNA COTTA
Côteaux du Layon, Chaume,
Domaine des Forges, 2006

BITTER CHOCOLATE AND HAZELNUT
PARFAIT WITH SALTED CARAMEL JELLY
AND MILK MOUSSE
Quinta da Ervamoira, 10 Year Old Tawny, Ramos Pinto

INGREDIENTS

400g	Sweetcorn purée
700g	Cream
120g	Sugar
5g	Salt
4	Vanilla pods
4	Gelatine leaves

Clear caramel jelly

4	Gelatine leaves
400g	Sugar
870g	Water

Popcorn granite

70g	Butter
50g	Popcorn
750ml	Milk
20g	Sugar
2g	Salt

Vanilla powder, to serve
Caramel popcorn, to serve

METHOD

Put the purée, cream, sugar, salt and vanilla into a pan and bring to the boil. Soak the gelatine in ice water. Whisk the gelatine into the mix, pass through a sieve and chill over ice until the vanilla seeds are suspended in the mix and then set in the glasses. When the panna cottas are set put a thin layer of caramel jelly on the top.

Clear caramel jelly

Soak the gelatine in ice water. Make a caramel in a pan by gently melting the sugar and add the water. Measure out 1 litre of this liquid, add the softened gelatine and pass through a sieve.

Popcorn granite

Melt the butter in a large pan and add the popcorn. Cook for 10 minutes on a medium heat, stirring occasionally. Add the milk, sugar and salt. Bring the mix back up to the boil and simmer for 10 minutes. Remove from the heat and cover for 10 minutes. Pass the mix through a sieve, refrigerate until the butter sets on the surface, pass again through a sieve then freeze in a large tray.

TO SERVE

Put the granita on top of the panna cotta. Sprinkle with the vanilla powder and serve with caramel popcorn.

PAUL HEATHCOTE AND NIGEL HAWORTH

"Finding the best piece of meat or fish over and over again is not easy, it is like trying to replicate the right company; ambience; mood – it is a difficult marriage. But when it happens it is magical, and we always want to better this – it is what drives us: for great chefs it is an obsessive pursuit."

Paul Heathcote

"To be obsessed with food is to be obsessed with the fruit of life."

Nigel Haworth

Sunday 1st February

NIGEL HAWORTH
PAUL HEATHCOTE MBE

Nigel Haworth of Northcote, Langho, Lancashire and
Paul Heathcote of
The Longridge Restaurant, Longridge, Lancashire

PAUL
TERRINE "REG JOHNSON",
APPLE COMPOTE, SPICED CHICKEN LIVER,
TOASTED SODA BREAD

Mâcon Village, Quintaine, Domaine de la Bongran,
J. Thévenet, 2001

PAUL
BRAISED TURBOT AND SCALLOPS WITH
LEEKS, WILD MUSHROOMS AND TARRAGON

Hildegard, Bien Nacido, Santa Barbara,
Au Bon Climat, 2004

NIGEL
BEEF TEA,
POACHED FILLET OF RIBBLE VALLEY BEEF
"ROOTS AND HERBS"

Don Nuño, Dry Oloroso, Emilio Lustau

NIGEL
ROAST LOIN AND BRAISED SHOULDER
OF HERDWICK MUTTON,
SMOKED MASH, YELLOW BEETS

Vinha Pan, Beiras, Luis Pato, 2003

NIGEL
TINY MELTING
VALRHONA CHOCOLATE DESSERTS

Recioto della Valpolicella, Corte Sant Alda, 2002

PAUL
HEATHCOTE'S BREAD AND
BUTTER PUDDING,
APRICOT COMPOTE, CLOTTED CREAM

Château Partarrieu, Sauternes, 2005

HEATHCOTE'S BREAD AND BUTTER PUDDING, APRICOT COMPOTE, CLOTTED CREAM

Serves 4

INGREDIENTS

75g	Butter
5	Thin slices of white bread
100g	Sultanas
220ml	Cream
220ml	Milk
50g	Sugar
1	Vanilla pod split and seeds removed
3	Eggs
25g	Icing sugar
50g	Apricot jam
Clotted cream	
8	Dried apricots

METHOD

Butter the bread and remove the crusts. Place one layer of bread in the base of a dish and cover with a layer of sultanas. Place the rest of the bread on top of the sultanas.

Bring the cream, milk, sugar and vanilla to the boil in a pan, place the eggs in a bowl and whisk the hot liquid into them. Pour over the bread and place the dish in a bain-marie, put in a moderate oven for about half an hour until cooked.

Dust with icing sugar and glaze under a grill until golden. Brush with jam.

TO SERVE

Serve with clotted cream and a compote of dried apricots.

TINY MELTING VALRHONA CHOCOLATE DESSERTS

Serves 10

INGREDIENTS

Liquid chocolate

60g	Valrhona 70% chocolate, chopped
40g	33% milk chocolate, chopped
175g	Double cream
75g	Milk
25g	Honey
Seeds of ½ vanilla pod	
Pinch of salt	

Chocolate spray

250g	Valrhona 70% chocolate, chopped
25g	Cocoa butter

Chocolate custard

100g	Full fat milk
190g	Double cream
1	Vanilla pod
10g	Caster sugar
60g	Egg yolks
12g	Caster sugar
25g	Valrhona 55% chocolate (Equatorial Noire)
20g	Demerara sugar
20g	Crackling candy

Pulled sugar

10g	Sugar
200g	Water
30g	Glucose
½ tsp	Lemon juice

Cherry sorbet

200g	Fresh cherry juice
200g	Cherry purée – Boiron
100g	Stock syrup
12g	Sour cherry purée
20g	Lemon juice

Cherry jelly

150g	Cherry juice
50g	Cherry purée – Boiron
5g	Sour cherry purée – MSK
6g	Lemon juice
30g	Stock syrup
2g	Agar agar

Chocolate paint

62g	Sugar
62g	Water
20g	Cocoa powder
62g	Double cream

Kirsch foam

4g	Gelatine leaves (2½ bronze leaves)
150g	Whole milk
40g	UHT 55% whipping cream
30g	Caster sugar
15g	Kirsch

Dipped cherries

10	Cherries with stalks
100ml	Valrhona chocolate 55%

Chocolate swirl

25g	Tempered chocolate

METHOD

Liquid chocolate

Makes 12 portions. Melt the chocolate in a medium heatproof bowl over warm water (or in a microwave). In a pan bring to the boil the cream, milk, honey, vanilla pod seeds and salt. Remove from the heat and pour over the chocolate – leave to stand for 1 minute then blend with a hand blender until fully incorporated. Skim off the foam from the top of the chocolate then strain through a fine chinoise (conical sieve).

Spray a tray approximately 22x13cm and 2cm deep with a non-stick cooking spray to hold a sheet of silicon paper in place – make sure the edges of the silicon paper come up the side of the tray by at least 2cm.

Pour the liquid chocolate into the tray, then place in a blast chiller and freeze until solid. Remove the chocolate from the tray and cut into 4x4cm squares. Then place the chocolate squares carefully on to a tray lined with parchment paper, return to the freezer and reserve.

Chocolate spray

Makes 20 portions. Carefully melt the chocolate and cocoa butter together. Once melted, put into a chocolate sprayer (paint spray gun). Remove the liquid chocolate squares (silicon sheet) from the freezer and place on a silpat then spray with the chocolate taking care to coat evenly. Return the squares to the freezer to set for approximately 10 minutes then turn the squares over and spray the other side, keep the liquid chocolate squares in the freezer until required. N.B. When spraying the chocolate you must protect the area in which you are spraying. One way to protect it is to break up a large cardboard box and remove one side and spray into the v-shaped box.

Chocolate custard

Makes 10 portions. Bring to the boil the milk, cream and 10g sugar. Whisk together the egg yolks and 12g sugar until light and fluffy (to make a sabayon). Once the milk and cream has come to the boil add the chocolate and melt carefully. Then pour the mix onto the egg yolks and sugar, gently whisk until all the mix has been incorporated. Place the mix onto an ice bath and cool.

Line the bottom of 10 stainless steel custard moulds with cling film and put onto a flat tray with acetate on the bottom. Once the mix is cool, fill the mould three-quarters of the way up. Put into a convection oven for 28 minutes at 94°C; when ready remove and allow to cool and refrigerate. To make the caramel top, sprinkle on the sugar and caramelise with a blow torch then, while still warm, sprinkle on the crackling candy and reserve.

Pulled sugar

Boil all the ingredients together to make a golden 'caramel' at 170-175°C then pour onto silicon paper and leave to set. To use, warm in the oven until the sugar is pliable, then pull the sugar as required.

Cherry sorbet

Will make approximately 20 large teaspoons of sorbet. Mix all the ingredients together cold. Pass through a muslin cloth or a fine sieve. Churn in an ice cream machine, remove and reserve until required.

Cherry jelly

Makes 20 jellies. Place all the ingredients, except the agar agar, into a pan, bring to the boil and once boiling whisk in the agar agar and re-boil. Pass through a fine sieve. Pour the mix into a deep tray with acetate on the bottom. Put in the fridge to set. Remove the jelly, carefully cut into 2.5cm squares and reserve.

Chocolate paint

Makes 25 portions. Bring the sugar and water to the boil. Add the cocoa and whisk in well, pour into a small bowl and place on ice water. Once cool, whisk in the double cream, pour into a squeezy bottle and refrigerate.

Kirsch foam

Makes 20 portions. Soak the gelatine leaves in cold water. Bring the milk, cream and sugar to the boil. Dissolve in the gelatine off the heat. Pass through a fine chinoise (conical sieve) and add the kirsch. When cool, load into a kisag gun and load with two cartridges. Keep in the fridge.

Dipped cherries

Simply dip the cherries in the chocolate and then place them on silicon paper to set.

Chocolate swirl

Spread a thin layer of tempered chocolate over a sheet of acetate 21x6cm. Leave for 2-3 minutes until the chocolate is nearly set (still needs to be flexible). Cut into half-width strips (without cutting through the acetate). Take the acetate and roll in opposite directions to form a curl. Place the chocolate covered acetate into a ring to hold the shape, leave until set. Once the swirls are set remove from the ring and carefully peel away the acetate.

TO SERVE

Take an oblong plate and pipe a small round of chocolate paint at the top of the plate and then pull with the nozzle to create a swirl. Put the liquid chocolate square in the middle of the plate and the jelly below. With a blow torch warm the exterior of the stainless steel custard moulds then place onto the plate above the liquid chocolate and remove the mould. Place the pulled sugar on top of the custard. Place the chocolate-dipped cherry to the right of the jelly. Spoon the sorbet onto the liquid chocolate, spoon over the kirsch foam and place the chocolate swirl on top. Serve immediately.

20O8

This was the year when I possibly realised we had created something special; to manage to attract the iconic chef Pierre Koffmann out of retirement for one special evening was truly a remarkable achievement.

Anthony Flinn kicked off on the Monday with his influences of El Bulli where he had spent more time than any other British chef. The first dish of risotto of white onion parmesan air espresso was Antony's signature dish. Other dishes included cured squab, foie gras macaroon, chocolate soy dressing, carton of milk ten different techniques, a truly fascinating dish which had the customers excited, perplexed and intrigued all at the same time. He finished the night with pumpkin cheesecake, a memorable finish to a fascinating start to the festival. The following week we competed against each other in the Great British Menu billed as the War of the Roses.

Next up was Mark Edwards. Mark hails from Wigan and oversees the kitchens for Nobu restaurants worldwide, an incredible job.

Mark cooked an array of Japanese food which included two sashimi dishes which went down fantastically well even though many of our diners had never eaten sashimi or sushi, but they tried it for the first time and loved it. He also served the world renowned blackened cod which is actually sable fish. Wagyu beef was as expected outstanding and he finished on a Suntory Whisky cappuccino, which rounded off the night a real treat.

Pierre's main course on the night was the classic hare royale. Pierre was struggling to get hares in London, so he contacted me to see if we could get the hares. We did and actually ended up with hares from all over the north of England, so many that we were using hare royale for weeks to come. Pierre closed his menu with his famous pistachio soufflé, which is so well known throughout the culinary world, it's a masterpiece. Assisting Pierre came two members of his old brigade at La Tante Claire, his old head chef Eric Chavot and one of my first brigade members Tim Payne, who went on to become Marco Pierre White's right-hand man and of Hell's Kitchen fame.

Angela arrived via Liverpool Lime Street station as I arrived in Preston Station. She had been talking on the phone at Euston and got on the wrong train. I was on the phone saying to her "whereabouts are you, I can't see you?" and she was saying "I'm on the platform!" – I realised she was on the wrong platform at the wrong station. A few hours later we finally got Angela to Northcote. Angela wowed us with white truffle

risotto and everyone wanted an extra bowl so Angela toured the restaurant serving the extra helpings as required. Angela was a little disappointed with the frugal amount of white truffles available as I had miscalculated the cost. To follow was braised halibut with oxtail ravioli, we finished with lemon panna cotta and Grappa granite, a truly memorable night.

Phil arrived for the first time in his Maserati; the old Aston had finally been retired along with its accumulated points. Phil cooked with rock oysters, foie gras and used British White Beef which he absolutely loved; it may not conform but it certainly performs. The night was wrapped up with Bakewell tart and rhubarb ice cream, a simple finish to another brilliant Howard night.

Shane Osborn from Pied à Terre and his family came next and had a fantastic time. Shane prepared an unbelievable scallop ceviche especially for a man who has an intolerance to fish. His pumpkin soup was superb and his herb-crusted venison saddle a real treat. To finish bitter sweet chocolate tart with a stout ice cream was a great dish with a humorous Antipodean twist.

I finished off the year with my first use of goat at the festival; the Boer goat from Sharon and Chris Peacock in Cockerham are superb and the consommé was well received. I finished the evening with Lancashire curd tart which turned out to be not one of Oliver Peyton's favourites on the Great British Menu that year.

ANTHONY FLINN

"I'm obsessed by food because there is no boundary to it, you can do exactly what you want. There are rules to the science of food, but who says you can't put certain things together? It's the playful experimenting that I enjoy."

Monday 21st January

ANTHONY FLINN
Anthony's Restaurant, Leeds

RISOTTO OF WHITE ONION,
PARMESAN AIR, ESPRESSO
Soave Classico, Inama Azienda Agricola, 2006

TONGUE AND CHEEK
ROAST COD TONGUE, BRAISED PIG CHEEK,
SMOKED BRIE AND COCONUT BON BON
Blanc de Blancs, Clos Mireille,
Cotes de Provence-Domaines Ott, 2004

CURED SQUAB, FOIE GRAS MACAROON,
CHOCOLATE AND SOY DRESSING
Terra do Zambujeirio,
Alentejo, Quinta do Zambujeiro, 2002

"CARTON OF MILK"
10 different techniques using milk

PUMPKIN CHEESECAKE,
GINGER, MUSCOVADO ICE CREAM
Botrytis Riesling,
Mellifera, Stellenbosch Jordan, 2006

RISOTTO OF WHITE ONION, PARMESAN AIR, ESPRESSO

Serves 4

INGREDIENTS

Risotto base

50g	Chopped onion
300g	Risotto rice
1 litre	Vegetable stock

Onion purée

2	Onions
100g	Cream
Salt	
Oil	

Parmesan air

500g	Water
500g	Grated parmesan
Pinch of lecithin	

Other ingredients

Chives

Espresso coffee

METHOD

Risotto base

Sweat the onions in a little oil without colour. Add the rice and cook for 1 minute to toast the rice a little. Add the stock a little at a time until three-quarters cooked. You may use all the stock or only half; it all depends on the temperature and speed in which you cook it. Once three-quarters cooked pour on to a tray and cool.

Onion purée

Peel and slice the onions. Place in a pan with a little oil and salt. The salt will start to extract the moisture and sweat them down quicker. Keep cooking them until they are golden brown and fully caramelised. Then add the cream. Blitz to a smooth paste. Store in the fridge.

Parmesan air

Bring the water to the boil and add the parmesan. Simmer for 30 minutes. Strain off the liquid and discard the mass that is left. Chill in the fridge until the fat and liquid separate, then remove the fat from the top. Add the lecithin to the liquid and blitz with a stick blender. Slowly move the blender around to create foam.

TO SERVE

Place the rice in a pan with the purée and some more of the vegetable stock. Mix all together and continue to cook the rice leaving a slight crunch to it. Fold through the chives and season. Sprinkle a little coffee at the bottom of the bowl. Pour the risotto over the coffee and aerate the parmesan foam with the stick blender. Spoon just the froth over the rice and sprinkle with a little more coffee. Serve immediately.

MARK
EDWARDS

"The greatest satisfaction one gets from cooking is other people's enjoyment."

Tuesday 22nd January

MARK EDWARDS
Nobu, London

EDAMAME
NEW STYLE SALMON SASHIMI
Erdener Treppchen Riesling Kabinett,
Dr Loosen, 2005

TUNA SASHIMI SALAD
Pinto Grigio, Ramato, Venezia Giulia, Azienda
Specogna, 2006

BLACK COD WITH SWEET MISO
Chinon, Cuvée de la Cure,
Charles Joguet, 2005

SEARED WAGYŪ WITH
ERINGE MUSHROOMS SOY AND TRUFFLES
Nuits-Saint-Georges, Vieilles Vignes,
Domaine Patrice Rion, 2003

SUNTORY WHISKY CAPPUCCINO
Chambers Rutherglen Muscadelle, Rutherglen

BLACK COD WITH SWEET MISO
Serves 1

The Black Cod (sable fish) with Miso has become one of the most famous dishes at all the Nobu restaurants around the world. Some of our customers like to squeeze some fresh lemon over the top to balance the sweetness out but this is down to your own personal taste.

INGREDIENTS

Den Miso

100ml	Sake
100ml	Mirin
150g	Caster sugar
300g	White Miso paste
200g	Sable fish fillet with the skin intact

Sliced lemon, to serve

Galangal stem

METHOD

Bring the Sake and Mirin to the boil in a thick bottomed, non-reactive saucepan for 2-3 minutes to allow the alcohol to evaporate. Add the sugar and allow to dissolve, slowly mixing in the Miso paste a little at a time using a wooden spoon. Continue to cook on a medium heat stirring constantly so as not to let the mixture burn in the pan for a further 10-5 minutes. Strain the mixture through a sieve to remove any lumps, allow to cool and then refrigerate.

Marinating and cooking

Place the sable fish in a non reactive container and pour over a little of the Den Miso and marinate for 1-2 days in the refrigerator. Preheat the oven to 200°C/400 °F/gas mark 6 and place the fish on to a non-stick baking sheet and cook in the oven for 10-12 minutes until cooked through and golden on the outside.

You can cook the sable fish under a grill or Salamander with the same results but care must be taken that it does not burn before it is cooked through to the centre.

TO SERVE

Place on to a serving dish and dress the plate with a little extra Den Miso and serve with some sliced lemon and galangal stem.

MARK EDWARDS

PIERRE KOFFMANN

"Since early in my childhood I was surrounded by good food and great ingredients – I simply want to carry on the tradition."

Wednesday 23rd January 2008

PIERRE KOFFMANN

AMUSE
CROUSTILLANT DE PIED DE COCHON ET
PETITE SALADE
[PIGS' TROTTERS WITH SALAD]

COQUILLE ST JACQUES, SAUCE ENCRE,
COULIS DE POIVRON
[GRILLED SCALLOPS WITH INK SAUCE AND
RED PEPPER COULIS]
Meursault, "Les Grandes Charrons",
Domaine Michel Bouzereau, 2003

BROCHET CONFIT,
LENTILLES DU PUY ET CHAMPIGNONS EN
ALGRE DOUX
[CONFIT OF PIKE WITH PUY LENTILS AND
SWEET AND SOUR MUSHROOMS]
Chablis, Suzanne Reynard, Domaine J Durup, 2006

LIÈVRE A LA ROYALE, PURÉE DE CELERI
RAVE ET CAROTTE
[HARE ROYALE WITH CELERIAC PURÉE AND
ROASTED CARROTS]
Châteauneuf-du-Pape
Les Vieilles Vignes Domaine de Villeneuve, 1998

TROIS FROMAGES GASCON
[THREE CHEESES FROM GASCONY]
Chateau Romassan, Bandol, Domaines Ott, 2002

SOUFFLÉ A LA PISTACHE ET SA GLACE
[PISTACHIO SOUFFLÉ WITH ICE CREAM]
Côteaux du Layon
Saint-Aubin de Luigné Domaine des Forges, 2003

PISTACHIO SOUFFLÉ

Serves 4

INGREDIENTS

500ml	Milk
½	Vanilla pod
120g	Egg yolks
100g	Caster sugar
50g	Plain flour
40g	Pistachio paste
25g	Butter, softened
25g	Dark chocolate, grated
4	Egg whites
1 tbsp	Caster sugar

Icing sugar, to serve

METHOD

Boil together the milk and vanilla pod. Simultaneously whisk together the egg yolks and caster sugar, whisk until the mixture slightly thickens and turns light in colour.

Sieve the flour and add into the mixture, whisk until smooth. Add half of the milk to the base, whisk until there are no lumps. Sieve through a fine strainer, remove the vanilla pod and return the mixture back to the pan and add the remaining milk. Using a whisk, stir the mixture. When it comes to the boil, bring the temperature down to a simmer. Continue to stir and cook out for 8-10 minutes and mix in the pistachio paste.

Pour the pastry cream onto a shallow tray, wrap with cling film and cool rapidly.

Generously butter 4 individual soufflé dishes. Put the grated chocolate inside and rotate the moulds so that the chocolate completely covers the inside, sticking to the softened butter.

Beat the egg whites until firm, add the tablespoon of caster sugar and whisk until stiff. Add a small quantity of the whites to the pistachio mix to soften it, then fold in the rest of the egg whites and pour into the soufflé dishes.

Bake in a hot oven 240°C/475°F/ gas mark 9 for 15 minutes or until well risen.

TO SERVE

Dust the top with icing sugar and serve with ice cream of your choice.

ANGELA HARTNETT

"I'm obsessed with food because I like to eat – simple as that. I was fortunate as a kid to grow up in a household that cared a lot about what we ate, and when you have that as a child it spoils you and becomes a part of what you want to do. I love my job, and I love cooking, end of story."

Thursday 24th January

ANGELA HARTNETT MBE
Murano, Mayfair, London

PRESSED RABBIT MOSAIC
WITH PICKLED BABY VEGETABLES,
PRUNE JAM
Châteauneuf-du-Pape,
La Bernardine M. Chapoutier, 2005

WHITE TRUFFLE RISOTTO
Verdicchio di Matelica, La Monacesca, 2005

BRAISED HALIBUT WITH OXTAIL RAVIOLI
Sancerre Rouge, Pascal Jolivet, 2005

ROASTED WINTER FRUITS WITH
WARM ZABAGLIONE
Moscato d'Asti, Pio Cesare, 2006

LEMON PANNA COTTA WITH
GRAPPA GRANITÉ
Sauvignon Blanc, Late Harvest,
Semi-Dulce, Bornos, 2004

GLAZED HALIBUT WITH OXTAIL RAVIOLI

Serves 4

INGREDIENTS

Pasta dough

600g	Pasta flour '00'
Salt	
5-6	Large Italian eggs
Extra virgin olive oil	

Braised oxtail

1	Carrot
1	Onion
1	Stick celery
1	Stick leek
½	Head garlic
Thyme	
Bay leaf	
Peppercorns	
2 bottles Red wine	
1 bottle Port	
1	Oxtail, chopped
½ litre	Veal stock
½ litre	Chicken stock
Parsley, chopped	
2	Shallots, chopped

Parsnip purée

1kg	Parsnip (peeled and chopped)
1 litre	Milk
Thyme	
Bay leaf	
50ml	Double cream
Butter	

Halibut

4	120-130g piece halibut
Olive oil	
Butter	
Chopped chervil	
Fish stock	
1	Bunch baby spinach
8	Baby leeks

METHOD

Pasta dough

Mix the flour with a pinch of salt in the Robot Coupe (food processor).

Mix the eggs with a squirt of olive oil and start adding into the Robot Coupe slowly.

When the crumble starts to climb the walls and does not collapse any more, the dough should be ready to knead.

Turn the dough onto a work surface and start kneading.

Knead for 10 minutes or until it is smooth. Cover with cling film and let it rest in the fridge for at least 1 hour.

Braised oxtail

Dice the vegetables (all except the shallots) into a bowl, add the oxtail together with the aromats (herbs), port and wine, and leave to marinate overnight.

Once marinated, drain off the liquid and separate the oxtail from the vegetables.

In a hot pan, colour off the oxtail on all sides and set aside.

In the same pan, colour off the vegetables and add the oxtail back in.

Deglaze with all the alcohol from the marinade and reduce until sticky and glazed.

Add the stocks and simmer for approximately 2 hours or until the meat is coming off the bone.

Leave to cool then pour into a colander over a bowl.

Discard the vegetables and let the oxtail slightly reduce in temperature.

Pick the meat off the bone and shred it down and pass the juices through a chinoise (conical sieve). Divide into 2, keep half as it is to be used later as a sauce. Reduce the remaining half down until sticky and add to the meat. Add the chopped parsley. Cook down the chopped shallots in olive oil and butter until golden brown and almost sweet, then season and also add to the meat.

Let the farce cool down until it is possible to shape into balls, and leave to set in the fridge.

Roll out the dough and make into ravioli with the oxtail as a filling.

Parsnip purée

Bring the milk together with all the ingredients to the boil and simmer for 30 minutes or until the parsnip is soft.

Pass through a chinoise (conical sieve), keeping the milk and the parsnip.

Place the parsnip in Vitamix and blend, adding the milk as needed so as to get a smooth purée.

Season, add a few cubes of butter and pass mixture through a chinoise (conical sieve). Add a touch of cream if it isn't runny enough.

TO SERVE

Season the fish, and colour in olive oil on both sides. Once coloured, with presentation side up, add a spoonful of butter, chopped chervil and a ladle of fish stock.

Cover and finish cooking in boiling salted water.

Cook the baby leeks until a knife can go through the centre then shock in ice water. Once cold trim so that they all have the same shape.

Warm the baby leeks in foaming butter.

Warm the parsnip purée.

Boil the ravioli.

Cook the spinach in butter, season and drain on kitchen paper.

Finish with the oxtail cooking juices as a sauce.

PHIL HOWARD

"Over the years of visiting Northcote and Lancashire in general, I have come to appreciate how much they love their food. I always try to propose a menu that not only showcases what we do at The Square but includes dishes that will have a natural affinity with what local folk will want to eat. The field mushroom veloute is a classic example of this. The great old master Pierre Koffman was "in the house" this year – always a pleasure to see him delivering his well honed classics!"

Friday 25th January

PHIL HOWARD
The Square, London

FIELD MUSHROOM VELOUTÉ,
ENGLISH BREAKFAST GARNISH

POACHED IRISH ROCK OYSTER
WITH A MOUSSELINE OF CORIANDER
–AND LIGHT CURRY
Albarino, Lagar de Cervera, Rias Baixas, 2005

PARFAIT OF FOIE GRAS
AND CHICKEN LIVERS WITH SALTED
PEANUT BRITTLE AND GRAPE CHUTNEY
Pinot Gris, Marlborough, Mudhouse, 2005

FILLET OF HALIBUT WITH TRUFFLE PURÉE
AND CROQUETTE OF CAULIFLOWER
Rully, l'er Cru "Les Clous", Olivier Leflaive, 2006

FILLET OF BRITISH WHITE BEEF WITH AN
OXTAIL RAVIOLI
AND A VELOUTÉ OF PEPPERCORNS
Gloria Reynolds, Alentejo Julian Cuellar Reynolds, 2002

RHUBARB "BAKEWELL" TART
WITH VANILLA AND RHUBARB ICE CREAM
Essensia, Orange Muscat, Andrew Quady, 2006

FIELD MUSHROOM VELOUTÉ, ENGLISH BREAKFAST GARNISH

Serves 4

INGREDIENTS

100g	Butter
1	White onion, finely sliced
Salt & pepper	
6	Large field mushrooms, finely sliced
500ml	Chicken stock
100ml	Double cream
1	Bay leaf
Garnish	
2	Cumberland sausages
1 tbsp	Grapeseed oil
4	Small eggs
4	Lambs' kidneys, quartered

METHOD

Place a large, heavy based pan over a medium heat, melt 50g of the butter and add the onion with a generous pinch of salt. Cook until the onions are soft and translucent. Turn the heat up, add the mushrooms and cook, stirring frequently for 5 minutes, or until all the moisture has evaporated.

Add the chicken stock, cream and bay leaf, bring to the boil and cook at a bare simmer for 15 minutes. Remove from the heat, lift out the bay leaf and blend to a smooth, homogeneous soup. Adjust the seasoning, chill over ice and set aside in the fridge.

Garnish

Colour the sausages in half a tablespoon of grapeseed oil and finish in an oven at 160°C/325°F/gas mark 3 for 15 minutes. Remove from the oven, take the sausages out of the pan and keep warm.

Place the same pan over a gentle heat, add 50g of butter and crack the four small eggs into it and gently cook. Remove from the pan, season the eggs and cut the yolk out with a pastry cutter, slightly larger than the yolk itself. Set aside in a warm place, covered. Finally, sauté the lambs' kidneys in a hot pan with the remaining grapeseed oil. Season with salt and pepper.

TO SERVE

Into each of 4 prepared soup bowls, place an egg yolk, two slices of sausage and some kidney. Heat up the soup to near boiling point and serve it in a jug on the side.

SHANE OSBORN

"There are so many reasons for my Obsession. I've loved my job since I was 15 and being an Australian working in the UK, the seasonality is fantastic. Every season offers exciting ingredients – from game to chervil; that's what keeps me inspired and engaged, and the changing of the seasons gets me excited. Being immersed in food, meeting producers and finding out where it comes from is a part of that. I'm very lucky to have a talented and enthusiastic young team with a thirst for knowledge who keep me on my toes so I have to keep pushing the food and not resting on my laurels. It's always moving forward."

Saturday 26th January

SHANE OSBORN
Pied à Terre, London

CHILLED PUMPKIN AND GINGER VELOUTÉ,
TOASTED PUMPKIN SEEDS,
BROWN SHRIMPS
Sylvaner, Vieilles Vignes
Organic-Domaine Ostertag, 2006

SCALLOPS MARINATED
WITH BLACK TRUFFLE, JERUSALEM
ARTICHOKES, BRANDADE MOUSSE
Gavi di Tassarolo "Terrarosa", La Zerba, 2006

PAN FRIED TURBOT, ROASTED CARROT OIL,
BEURRE NOISETTE,
LETTUCE AND CARAMEL SAUCE
Condrieu, Invitare, M. Chapoutier, 2006

VENISON WITH CELERIAC
AND CHANTERELLES
Zinfandel, Sonoma County, Seghesio, 2004

BITTER SWEET CHOCOLATE TART,
MACADAMIA MOUSSE AND STOUT
ICE CREAM
Pedro Ximénez, San Emillio, Lustau

113

INGREDIENTS

1 tbsp	Butter
½	Celeriac, peeled and diced
Salt & pepper	
4 x 120g	Boneless venison loin portions
50g	Pasteurised egg white
8 tbsp	Green herb crumb (see below)
1 tbsp	Olive oil
100g	Butter
150g	Chanterelles
200g	Shallot stock

Green herb crumb

2	Sprigs of thyme
2	Sprigs of rosemary
1	Garlic clove
300g	Japanese breadcrumbs (Panko)
2	Bunches of flat leaf parsley

Shallot stock

2	Large shallots, peeled
30g	Butter
2	Garlic cloves
1 tsp	Fresh thyme, chopped
Salt	
500ml	White chicken stock
8	Pomme soufflés, to serve

METHOD

Heat a frying pan and add the butter, when golden brown add the celeriac and a pinch of salt. Sauté over a medium heat until the celeriac is golden brown and soft. Drain the butter and add water to cover the celeriac. Bring to a simmer and cook for 5 minutes. Pour into a blender and purée until smooth. Adjust seasoning

Heat the oven to 140°C/275°F/gas mark 1.

Season the venison well with salt and pepper. Roll through the egg white then through the green crumb.

Warm a non-stick frying pan and add the oil. Place the venison in the pan and gently fry the meat on all sides for 30 seconds.

Place in the oven and turn after every 30 seconds. The meat should take between 6-8 minutes for medium rare. Allow to rest for 5 minutes in a warm place.

For the mushrooms heat a frying pan over a high heat and add 30g of butter. When golden brown add the mushrooms and sauté until all the water has evaporated. Add the shallot stock and reduce by two-thirds. Add the remaining butter and stir in well. Adjust seasoning and keep warm.

Green herb crumb

Pick the leaves off the thyme and rosemary and place in the Robot Coupe (food processor) with the garlic and breadcrumbs. Blend for 3 minutes.

Pick the leaves off the parsley then add slowly to the breadcrumbs while the machine is on.

Blend until the crumbs are bright green. Pass over a fine sieve.

For the shallot stock

Chop the shallots finely. Melt the butter in a small pan. Then add the garlic, thyme and shallots and a sprinkle of salt. Sweat without colour until soft. Add the stock and simmer for 20 minutes.

TO SERVE

Swipe a spoonful of celeriac purée on a plate. Cut the venison in half. Spoon the chanterelles over the meat and top with the pomme soufflés.

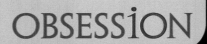

N I G E L
H A W O R T H

"To be obsessed by the seasons is to
capture the moment."

Sunday 27th January

NIGEL HAWORTH
Northcote, Lancashire

LOCAL GAME BAKED IN BUTTER PUFF
PASTRY, CELERIAC PURÉE
Gewürztraminer, les Folastries, Josmeyer, 2005

CONSOMMÉ OF GOAT, CURRY FLAVOURS
Marismeno Fino, Sanchez Romate

LINE CAUGHT COD ON TROTTERS,
TRIPE AND PULSES
Puligny Montrachet, Domaine Louis Carillon, 2005

CANNON OF MEY-SELECTION BEEF,
SMOKED MARROWBONE,
YOUNG CAULIFLOWER AND WATERCRESS
Pinot Noir, San Antonio, Leyda Valley,
Amayna, 2005

LANCASHIRE CURD TART,
YORKSHIRE RHUBARB
Château Lafaurie-Peyraguey l'er Cru Classe,
Sauternes, 1995

LOCAL GAME BAKED IN BUTTER PUFF PASTRY, CELERIAC PURÉE

Serves 4

INGREDIENTS

Game roll

160g/9	slices (1mm thick) Sliced rindless streaky bacon (must be 28cm long, slice while frozen)
2 x 100g	Pheasant breasts (skinless)
2 x 100g	Wild duck breasts (skinless)
4 x 50g	Partridge breasts (skinless)
10g	Salt
400g	Chicken mousse (see below)
500g	Puff pastry
Egg wash	

Celeriac purée

20g	Butter
200g	Celeriac, diced
100ml	Milk
100ml	Cream
Salt to taste	

Madeira sauce

50g	Shallots
100g	Mushrooms, sliced
35g	Unsalted butter
200ml	Strong Madeira
400ml	Brown chicken stock
Salt & pepper, to taste	

Chicken mousse

200g	Chicken breasts, diced
250ml	Cream
1	Egg white
4g	Salt
10g	Chives, chopped
5g	Chervil, finely chopped

METHOD

Game roll

Place a sheet of cling film flat onto the table, line it with streaky bacon to form a square 25x25cm.

Check the game breasts for lead shot then season lightly with salt.

Place the pheasant breasts exactly in the middle of the bacon, overlap slightly, spread a layer of chicken mousse 1cm thick on top of the pheasant breasts.

Place the wild duck breast on top of the chicken mousse then spread another even layer of the chicken mousse on top of the duck breasts.

Place the partridge breast on top of the chicken mousse, fold the bacon over to wrap completely around the game.

Wrap the cling film around the game roll and refrigerate. Remove the cling film before using.

To complete the game roll, roll out the puff pastry on a clean surface to a 3mm thick 25x25cm square. Place onto a flat tray lined with parchment paper and put in the blast chiller for 20 minutes (this is to ensure a perfect shape for the pastry).

Once chilled place back onto a clean surface and allow to semi defrost, then cut the pastry with a lattice cutter width ways. Carefully open the lattice, then fold the pastry over and around the game roll. Place onto the tray lined with parchment paper and put into the fridge and chill for 20 minutes.

Once chilled again completely egg wash the pastry and put into the oven at 200°C/400°F/gas mark 6 for 14 minutes. Remove from the oven, place on a wire rack and rest for 5-8 minutes. It is now ready to serve.

Celeriac purée

In a heavy bottom pan, melt the butter then add the diced celeriac. Sweat for 2-3 minutes then cover with cling film, cook for a further 10-15 minutes without colouring and until the celeriac is tender. Remove the cling film, add the milk and cream, season with salt and bring to the boil. Remove from the pan, place into a Thermomix and blitz until smooth, pass through a fine sieve, check seasoning and reserve.

Madeira sauce

In a heavy bottom pan, sweat off the shallots and mushrooms in 25g of butter for 2-3 minutes. Add the Madeira and reduce by two-thirds, once reduced add the chicken stock and reduce by half. Pass through a fine sieve, add the remaining 10g knob of butter and whisk well, check seasoning.

Chicken mousse

Place the diced chicken, 100ml of cream, egg white and salt into a Pacojet beaker and freeze to -20°C. Once frozen Pacojet three times (a food processor can be used). Place

into a metal bowl over ice and beat in the remaining 150ml of cream until smooth and shiny. Mix in the chives and chervil, check the seasoning and reserve.

TO SERVE

Put a medium sweep of celeriac purée on the plate, add the hot butter puff pastry wrapped game, finish with the lightly foamed Madeira sauce.

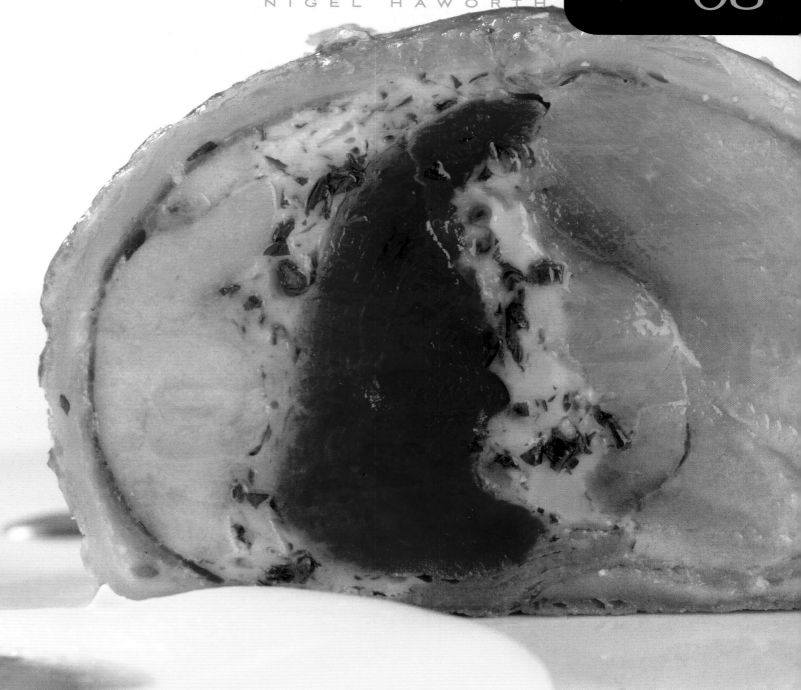

20O7

Andrew Pern arrived with his brigade from Yorkshire with the biggest bottle of Rhubarb Schnapps I have ever seen in my life; needless to say, most of it was drunk on the night, and many of the chefs were a little the worse for wear. Andrew cooked his signature dish of black pudding and foie gras that later became the title of his award-winning book. His main course was a selection of Yorkshire beef with Hambleton ale and root vegetables and he finished with a magnificent plate of various desserts using Yorkshire rhubarb – rhubarb and custard, my favourite.

Raymond Blanc had already sent an advanced posse led by his development chef, Adam, and a team of three; all was well. The great man himself arrived late afternoon checking everyone from top to bottom in his flamboyant and exacting style; the team had done a great job and approval was given. There was a moment of anxiety when he asked to taste the wines alongside the food. Raymond questioned some choices but, after Craig had advised him that he had chosen alongside his then sommelier Xavier, he was reassured. It turned out to be another amazing Blanc night with classics from the Le Manoir stable. The turbot with cucumber and seaweed was sensational and the squab pigeon classically brilliant, one of my favourite ingredients.

Michel Roux Jr arrived and Craig organised flowers, hair and spa for his wife Giselle. Michel was happy and is a true gent, which reminds me of the time Craig, Paul Heathcote and I came back from a trip to France, penniless, and Michel rescued us, feeding us and putting us up over night at Le Gavroche. Michel cooked along classical lines, making the legendary lobster cassoulet with pigs' trotters – a combination perhaps you wouldn't normally put together but ate incredibly well. He did a lovely veal and morel dish, and finished with the most perfect chocolate tart with pears and lashings of cream.

Paul Cunningham was introduced to me through Sat Bains, two great characters who typify the phrase that genius is close to insanity – their energy and humour is always endless. Paul has been in Copenhagen for a number of years and has established a fantastic reputation at The Paul in Tivoli Gardens. He cooked some extraordinary food – the rabbit dish will live with me forever, probably one of the most surprising combinations that was truly outstanding, in terms of favour and balance the star of the show. What a character, what a night! Paul took loads of photos and brought a ridiculously expensive Danish wine that no one drank or liked, and that is still in this cellar today.

Michael Caines cooked solid food from the Gidleigh Park repertoire, a classic ballontine of foie gras with Madeira jelly – perfection – and the slow poached sea bass with Thai purée and lemongrass foam was exquisite and the fillet of beef and smoked belly pork was to die for. We drank rum and coke into the early hours by the roaring fire in the bar, reminiscing about time spent at Robuchon, Ramsay and the like, a fascinating night.

Phil cooked on Saturday night in his own formidable style. He broke all records that night with 108. Phil kicked off with a warm game jelly with chanterelles, bacon foam and frazzles which was a fantastic start to the night followed by pan roast foie gras – perfection with the raisin pain d'epice one of our ultimate favourite ingredients. Finishing off with a pave of bitter chocolate and roast madadamias. A rich evening, not for the faint hearted.

Life was difficult following Phil that particular festival. All the extra staff had gone and the place was crammed with 105 on a Sunday night. But hey, that's life. I cooked game for the first time at the festival and the partridge went down incredibly well.

Obsession07
FOOD
of the Gods

FESTIVAL OF FOOD & WINE 22ND - 28TH JANUARY 2007

ANDREW PERN

"I've always been obsessed with food from an early age. I was born and brought up on a farm in the Esk Valley and many of my childhood memories are the tastes and smells from the farm. I can instantly recall the waft of bacon frying; the aroma of roasting beef; the gamey scent of partridge in the oven; the smell of warm straw as I gathered eggs and the tang of blackberries plucked — purple-fingered — from the hedgerows. The North Yorkshire moors was, and still is, an idyllic place to live and learn about nature's larder — be it seafood from the north sea or lamb, beef and pork reared by people with pride in their produce. This in turn makes my Obsession a very nice reality."

Monday 22nd January

ANDREW PERN
The Star Inn, North Yorkshire

A TASTE OF THE NORTH SEA...
Alvarinho Soalheiro, Vinho Verde, Minho,
António Esteves Ferreira, 2005

GRILLED BLACK PUDDING WITH
PAN-FRIED FOIE GRAS,
SALAD OF PICKERING WATERCRESS,
APPLE AND VANILLA CHUTNEY,
SCRUMPY REDUCTION
Gewürztraminer, Domaine Albert Mann, 2005

PEPPERED PINEAPPLE SORBET WITH AGED
YORK HAM

PAN ROAST TAIL FILLET OF BEEF WITH
BRAISED SHIN, FRESH HORSERADISH
RISOTTO, HAMBLETON ALE JUICES AND
ROOT VEGETABLES
Pera Manca Tinto, Fundação Eugénio de Almeida, 1998

A PLATE OF YORKSHIRE RHUBARB...
Essensia, Orange Muscat, Andrew Quady, 2005

GRILLED BLACK PUDDING WITH PAN-FRIED FOIE GRAS, SALAD OF PICKERING WATERCRESS, APPLE AND VANILLA CHUTNEY, SCRUMPY REDUCTION

Serves 1

INGREDIENTS

10g	Washed and trimmed watercress

Salt & pepper
A dash of vinaigrette
Apple and vanilla chutney
(see below)
Sprigs of thyme for garnish
Scrumpy reduction – made with apple juice and a splash of cider vinegar.

2	Slices black pudding

Knob of butter

1	Slice caramelised apple
1	Decent slice of duck or goose foie gras

Apple and Vanilla Chutney

1k	Granny Smith apples with skin, ½ - 1cm diced
3	Medium shallots, finely diced
200ml	Cider vinegar (or white wine, if you wish)
1	Fresh vanilla pod – split and de-seeded
400g	Caster sugar

Pinch of salt

METHOD

Place five small piles of apple chutney at intervals around the plate; garnish each pile with a sprig of thyme. In the centre of the plate dress a few seasoned leaves with vinaigrette to form a little 'salad'. Drizzle the reduction around the side of the plate.

Lightly brush the slices of black pudding with melted butter and grill for 3 to 4 minutes. While this is cooking heat a frying pan and pan-fry the foie gras for 1½ minutes each side.

When cooked, stack alternatively: black pudding, foie gras, black pudding. Top with the slice of caramelised apple. Serve immediately. Drizzle the scrumpy reduction.

Apple and Vanilla Chutney

Place everything into an ample-sized thick-bottomed pan and reduce down until thickened and starting to caramelise. Cool down and tub up ready for using. Keep in a cool place.

RAYMOND BLANC

"My earliest learning in the kitchen was as chef's apprentice to Maman Blanc. I worked as a minion, with the tasks of peeling and preparing vegetables, plucking chickens and so on, all ready to give to my mother for her to perform the simple creative act of cooking. These were truly my formative years with food, because I am totally self-taught and have never worked under a chef in my life. I learned the seasons of the garden and the nobility of produce; I connected with the woods and fields, which were full of delightful wild produce, and partook in the feast of cooking and sharing around the table. This training formed the basis of the simple food philosophy which permeates
Le Manoir aux Quat' Saisons: seasonality; simplicity; fresh produce; cooking and giving. As children we would mostly eat only seasonal food which came either from our garden or from the farms around us. Everything we grew was organic – although the word didn't exist back then. This is why food is my Obsession."

Tuesday 23rd January

RAYMOND BLANC OBE
Le Manoir Aux Quat' Saisons, Oxfordshire

TERRINE D'ANGUILLE AUX PARFUMS DU
JAPON [EEL AND MOOLI TERRINE]
Mercurey "Meix Foulot", Paul de Launay, 2005

CONFIT DE FOIE GRAS ET PURÉE DE
COINGS; GELÉE DE MONBAZILLAC ET
VINAIGRE BALSAMIQUE
[CONFIT OF FOIE GRAS, QUINCE PURÉE;
MONBAZILLAC AND AGED BALSAMIC
VINEGAR JELLY]
Château Bouscaut Blanc, Pessac Léognan,
Grand Cru Classé, 2003

FILET DE TURBOT POCHÉ, COQUES
PALOURDES, HUITRE ET ALGUES DES
CORNOUAILLES, CONCOMBRE ET WASABI
[BRAISED FILLET OF TURBOT, OYSTER;
CUCUMBER AND WASABI JUS]
Menetou–Salon, Clos des Blanchais,
Domaine Henry Pellé, 2005

PIGEONNEAU D'ANJOU RÔTI CHOUCROUTE
DE CELÉRI RAVE ET SAUCE AU VIN ROUGE
PARFUMÉE AU GÈNIEVRE
[ROASTED AND JUS SQUAB, CELERIAC
CHOUCROUTE AND
RED WINE JUNIPER SAUCE]
Gigondas, Domaine les Palliéres, H. Brunier, 2001

CHARLOTTE AUX POIRES WILLIAMS,
GLACE A LA CANNELLE ET VANILLA
[CARAMELISED WILLIAMS PEAR BAKED IN
A THIN BRIOCHE;
CINNAMON AND VANILLA ICE CREAM]
Goldackerl, Beerenauslese, Willi Opitz, 2005

BRAISED FILLET OF TURBOT, OYSTER; CUCUMBER AND WASABI JUS

Serves 4

It has been a classic dish at Le Manoir for many years. But as with all Le Manoir dishes it is about details which are not always easy to duplicate in your own home. I have 40 chefs in my kitchen. Maybe the best way to enjoy it is at Le Manoir.

INGREDIENTS

Fish

50g	Shallots, peeled and sliced
20g	Butter, unsalted
120g	Button mushrooms, washed and sliced
100ml	Dry white wine eg. Chardonnay
4	150g each turbot, filleted and portioned, brushed with melted butter, lemon, salt & pepper. Can be prepared a few hours in advance and refrigerated
2g	Sea salt
0.5g	Pepper, freshly ground white
80ml	Water

Vegetable garnish and oysters

20g	Butter, unsalted
30ml	Water
200g	Spinach, washed
85g	Cucumber ribbons
60g	Samphire grass
Salt	
120g	Native Colchester oysters, size 2, opened and kept in their juices in a small saucepan

To finish the sauce

200ml	Strained cooking liquor, see above
60g	Cucumber skin
12g	Wasabi paste
1g	Lecithin, soya based (optional)
40g	Butter
1g	Lemon juice

METHOD

Sauce and fish

Preheat the oven to 190°C/375°F/ Gas mark 5.

In a sauté pan on a medium heat, sweat the shallots in the butter for 2 minutes.

Add the sliced mushrooms and sweat for a further minute. Add the wine and water and bring to the boil.

Place the fillets of fish on the mushrooms and cover with a lid.

Cook in the preheated oven for approximately 5 minutes. Remove from the oven, spoon out the fish on to a large buttered serving dish and keep warm. Strain the juices into a large jug blender, pressing on the shallots and mushrooms to extract as much juice as possible. Reserve.

Finishing the sauce

In a large jug blender, blitz together the hot cooking juices, cucumber skin, wasabi paste, lecithin, butter and lemon juice. Strain and reserve.

Cooking the vegetable garnish and heating the oysters

Divide the butter and water into two saucepans. Place the spinach in one and cucumber and samphire in the other. Add a tiny pinch of salt to the spinach. Cover with a lid. On a high heat bring the pans of vegetables to a quick boil. The spinach will take 1 minute, the cucumber and samphire 30 seconds. Just barely warm the oysters in their own juices. Place the turbot back in the oven for 1 minute. Bring your sauce to the boil.

TO SERVE

Place the spinach in the middle of each plate, with the cucumber and samphire spread around. Top with the fish and oyster, spooning the sauce over and around.

MICHEL ROUX JR

"Food is my life. There isn't a moment in the day or night that it isn't on my mind. Cooking or eating gives me equal amounts of pleasure; I suppose you could call it an Obsession, though I prefer to call it my life."

2007

Wednesday 24th January

MICHEL ROUX JR
Le Gavroche, London

OXTAIL AND FOIE GRAS TERRINE,
LITTLE GEM SALAD AND
TRUFFLE DRESSING
Condrieu, Invitare, M. Chapoutier, 2005

LOBSTER CASSOULET WITH
PARSLEY AND GARLIC BREADCRUMBS
Auxey-Duresses Blanc, Domaine du Comte Armand, 2002

FILLET OF VEAL WITH MORELS,
CREAMY MASHED POTATOES AND SPINACH
"CHARTREUSE"
Chassagne-Montrachet, Domaine Louis Carillon, 2003

CASHEL BLUE CREAM WITH GRAPES
AND GRAPPA

BITTER CHOCOLATE AND PEAR TART,
WHITE CHOCOLATE ICE CREAM
Rasteau, Vin Doux Naturel,
Domaine des Escaravailles, 2003

BITTER CHOCOLATE AND PEAR TART, WHITE CHOCOLATE ICE CREAM

Serves 8-10 cold and on the day it is made, otherwise the pastry will go soft.

INGREDIENTS

300g	Caster sugar
2	Cinnamon sticks
400ml	Water
4	Williams pears, peeled, cored and halved

Sweet pastry

120g	Butter, softened
250g	Plain flour
60g	Caster sugar
1	Egg yolk
½ tbsp	Double cream

Chocolate filling

120ml	Double cream
60g	Butter, cut into small pieces
250g	Extra-bitter dark chocolate, chopped

White chocolate ice cream

½ litre	Milk
6	Egg yolks
50g	Caster sugar
350g	White chocolate, broken into pieces

METHOD

Put the sugar and cinnamon in a pan with the water and bring to the boil. Add the peeled, cored and halved pears. Cover and simmer for 10 minutes or until the pears are tender. Leave to cool in the syrup.

Sweet pastry

Mix the soft butter, flour and sugar together using your fingertips. Gradually add the yolk and cream until the pastry comes together. Do not overwork. Wrap in cling film and refrigerate for at least a couple of hours.

Preheat the oven to 180°C/350°F/gas mark 4. Butter a fluted tart tin, 22cm in diameter. Roll out the pastry on a lightly floured surface and line the tin. Cut the edges flush with the sides and prick the base with a fork. Line with greaseproof paper and dry beans, then bake for 15 minutes. Remove the paper and beans and put back in the oven until golden and fully cooked, about another 10 minutes. Leave to cool in the tin.

Chocolate filling

Bring the cream to the boil. Add the chopped butter and chocolate and whisk well until completely melted Pour the chocolate filling into the tart.

Drain the pears on a tea towel until completely dry. Slice them across, fan out and place on the tart, keeping their shape. Refrigerate for 45 minutes before taking out of the tin and serving.

White chocolate ice cream

Boil the milk. Meanwhile whisk the yolks and sugar together until pale, add to the boiling milk and cook as an 'Anglaise' then pour onto the chocolate, mix well and pass through a sieve. Churn in an ice cream machine or freeze overnight.

TO SERVE

Serve each slice with the ice cream.

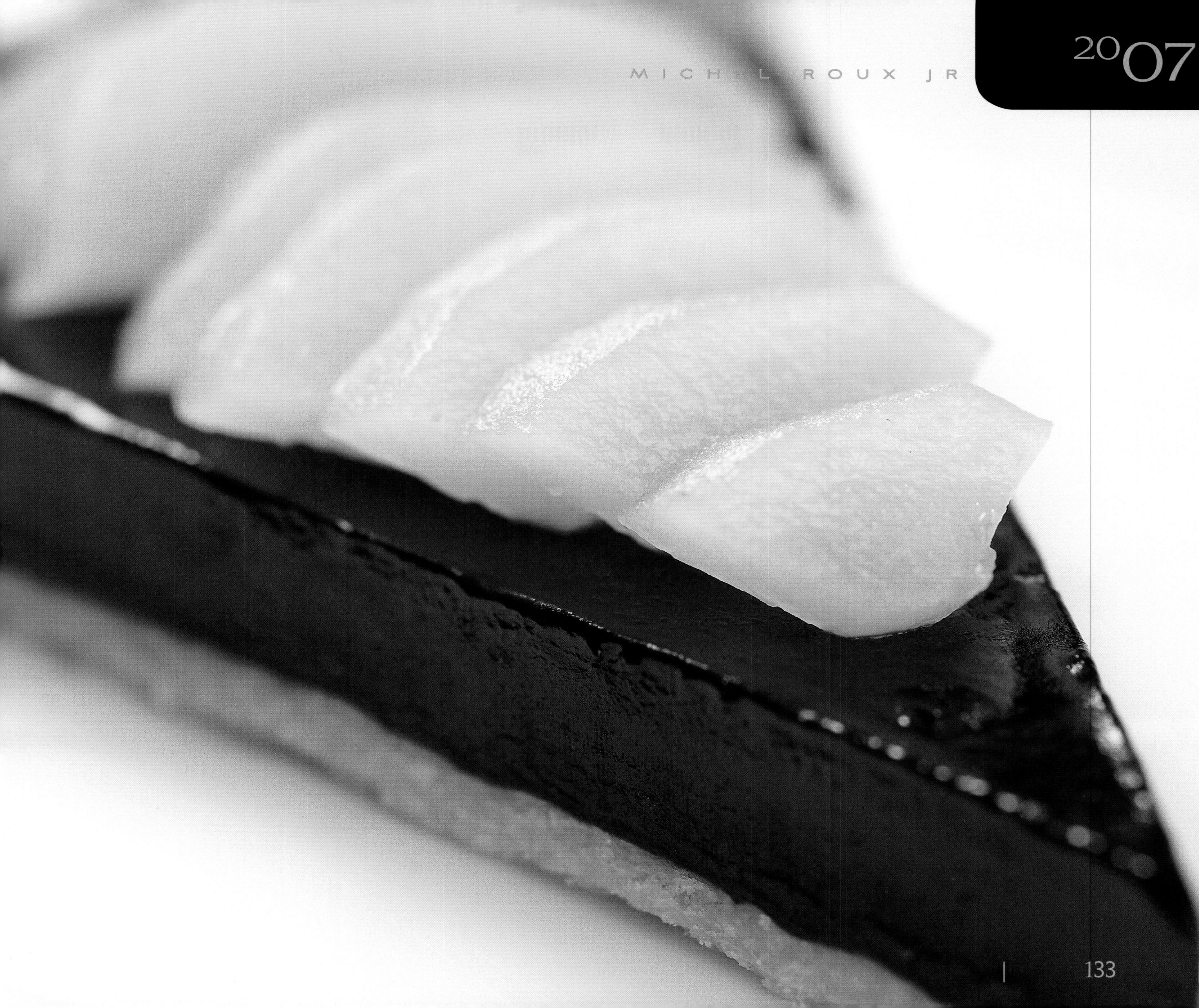

PAUL CUNNINGHAM

"I wouldn't really say that I am obsessed. It's more of a passion, and not only for food. For me food, and in particular cooking, is more of an artistic expression – an extension of my creative self. The only wish that I have for my children, apart from obvious good health and happiness, is that their chosen professions are creative and that they are able to use their hearts as well as their heads. I photograph as much as I cook nowadays. My photography enables me to keep a more permanent record of my emotions. Our problem as creative chefs is the fact that our art is displayed, destroyed and digested within minutes – seconds even. Not really a problem – as long as we move our guests with what we do. As long as they understand and appreciate the reference point and where we're coming from.

I am driven, inspired by everything I am in contact with. Every day at the restaurant I cook within a glass pavilion, within a private garden. Wooden floors, white walls and glass ceilings surround my chefs and I – we are constantly inspired by the change of light, temperature and the weather. Using each other as catalysts for inspiration is also a most important factor. We are all moved and inspired in very different ways. We work as a team, but are very much inspired as individuals – for me it is most important to pick up on this.

I love what I do; I love to create ... if love is an Obsession then, yes, I am obsessed."

Thursday 25th January

PAUL CUNNINGHAM
The Paul, Copenhagen

A SELECTION OF THE PAUL'S SNACKS, SPOONS AND APERITIVOS

JOMFRUHUMMER VARMEDE MED LARDO.
BLØD GRAPEFRUIT, RISTET HAZELNØDDER AND ESTRAGON BLADE.
RAPSOLIE FRA BORNHOLM
[LANGOUSTINE WARMED WITH LARDO, RUBY GRAPEFRUIT,
ROASTED HAZELNUT AND TARRAGON LEAF
RAPESEED OIL FROM BORNHOLM]
Grüner Veltliner, Kamptal, Fred Loirmer, 2005

SMØR RISTET PIGHVARRE-RØGET OKSEMARV.
KNOLDSELLERI, TRØFFEL AND MARCONA MANDLER,
APPELSIN AND KLIPPET PURLØG
[BUTTER ROASTED TURBOT – SMOKED BEEF MARROW,
CELERIAC, TRUFFLE AND MARCONA ALMOND, ORANGE AND
SNIPPED CHIVE]
Meursault, Domaine Henri Boillot, 2001

'BLOC DE FOIE GRAS AUX ANANAS', MERCI JÖEL
ANANAS SLIK, PURE AND GASTRIQUE, RISTET MACADAMIA AND
ENGELSKE TOFFEE GEL
[FOIE GRAS, PINEAPPLE 'SLIK', PURÉE AND GASTRIQUE
ROASTED MACADAMIA AND ENGLISH TOFFEE GEL]
Vino Dolce, Veneto Bianco, Inama, 2001

KANIN, PLANCHA RISTET MED ROSMARIN BLADE AND HVIDLØG,
HJERTEMUSLINGER, POCHERET MED SMØR, KNOLDGALTETAND,
[LOCAL RABBIT GRILLED WITH LANGOUSTINES FROM LÆSØ]
Pinot Noir, Geelong and Yarra Valley, Shadowfax, 2003

ISCREME PÅ ØKOLOGISK DANSK GEDEOST, BABY FIGNER I RØDBEDER,
SHERRYEDDIKE AND RUGBRØD
[ICE CREAM OF ORGANIC DANISH GOATS CHEESE, BABY FIGS IN BEETROOT.
SHERRY VINEGAR AND RHUBARB]
Chateau Ålsgårde, 2005, Denmark

MØRK CHOKOLADE CREME GEL, ØKOLOGISK CHOKOLADE FRA
SCHARFFEN BERGER
SORT OLIVEN AND OLIVE OIL SORBETTO, CAVIARE
[DARK CHOCOLATE CREAM GEL, ORGANIC CHOCOLATE FROM
SCHARFFEN BERGER
BLACK OLIVE AND OLIVE OIL SORBETTO, CAVIAR]
Banyuls, Vin Doux Naturel, M. Chapoutier, 2004

FINANCIER, PEAR AND CRANBERRY GEL,
LAVENDER FLOWER TRUFFLE TO THE COFFEE

LOCAL RABBIT GRILLED WITH LANGOUSTINES FROM LÆSØ

Serves 4

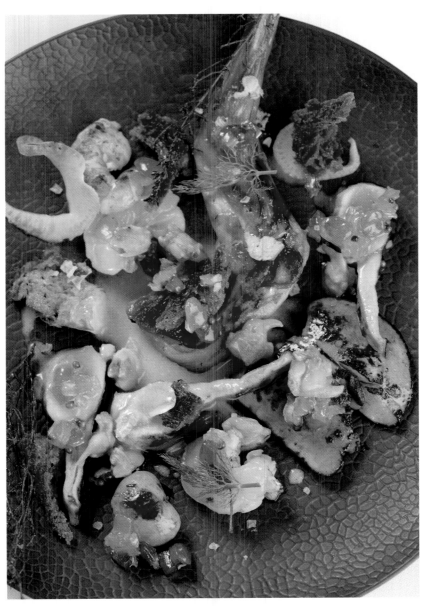

INGREDIENTS

4   Gigantic fresh langoustines
       from the Danish island of
       Læsø
2   Saddles of medium-sized
       local rabbit
1 tsp Roasted, crushed
       fennel seed
Poul's Læsø sea salt

Chutney

4   Green tomatoes, diced
2   Green apples, diced
2   Gotland shallots,
       finely diced
100g   Sugar
100ml Lilleø apple vinegar
1 tsp Roasted, crushed fennel
       seed plus more to serve

Aioli

4   New potatoes
1   Fennel
Water
Olive oil
100ml Olive oil mayonnaise
2   Garlic cloves
Lemon juice
1tbsp Pastis
Garlic salt from Læsø

Salad

1   Bunch fennel
1   Bunch wild rocket leaf from
       Gotland
Rapeseed oil from Bornholm
1   Lemon

METHOD

Chutney

Boil the tomatoes, apples and shallots together with the sugar, vinegar and the fennel seed for about 10 minutes until thick and well reduced.

Aioli

Braise the potatoes with the fennel in a touch of water and olive oil. Blend together with the mayonnaise until smooth. Finish with a little lemon juice, pastis and fresh garlics salt from Læsø.

TO SERVE

Dress the rabbit and the langoustines with the crushed fennel seed and sea salt. Grill rare over hot coals.

Dress the finished dish with the salad ingredients and a little roasted fennel seed to enhance the aromas.

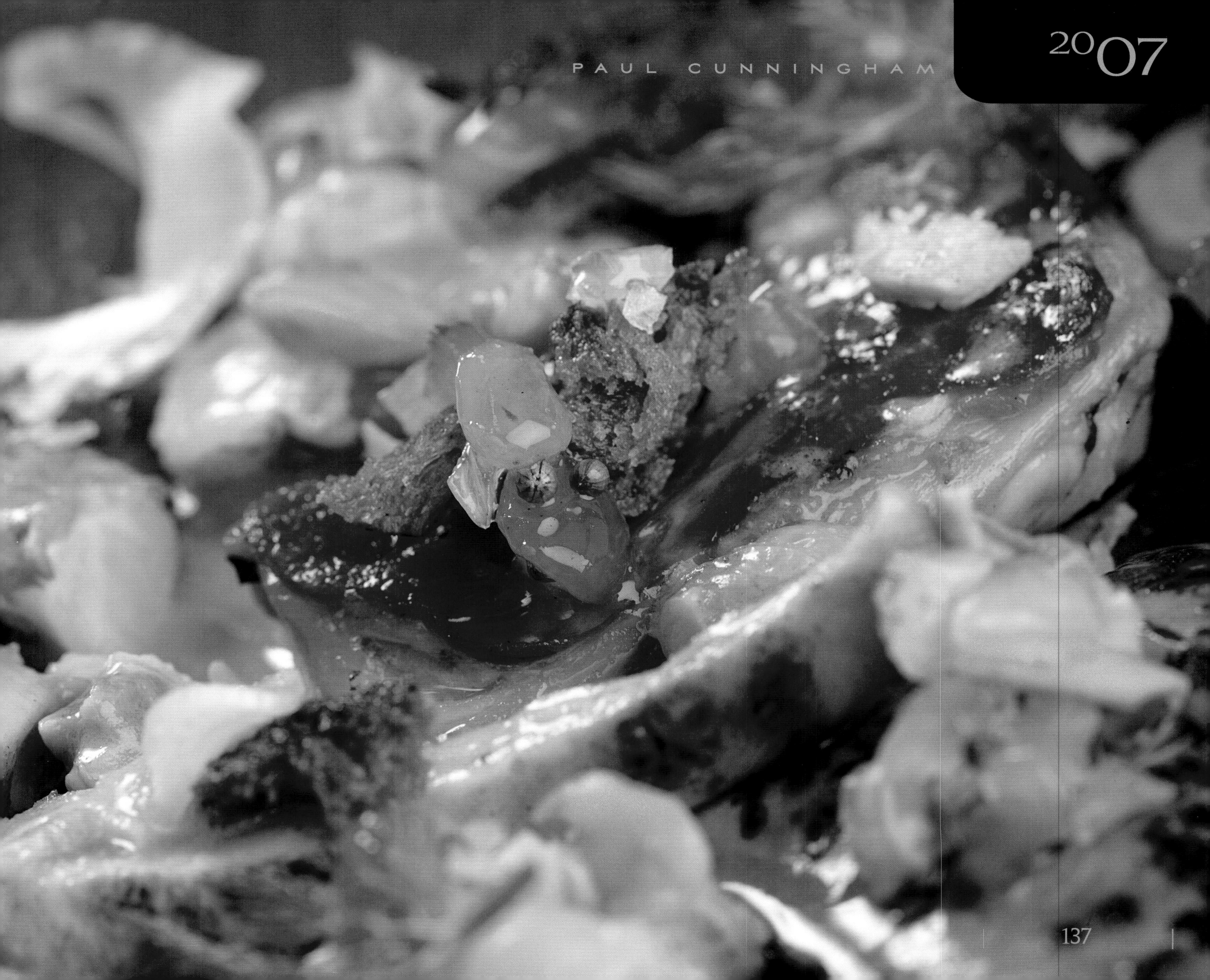

MICHAEL CAINES

"My love for food came from being within a large family and enjoying meals around the table. My time was spent helping my mother cook for these occasions using the crops that father lovingly tended from our garden. So the love came from here and the Obsession grew from my desire to cook to the best of my ability, using the best ingredients. By the nature of the trade that we are in, food becomes an Obsession and a quest for excellence in all you do. I'm lucky to have found my Obsession in food for others to enjoy!"

Friday 26th January

MICHAEL CAINES MBE
Gidleigh Park, Devon

PAN FRIED SCALLOPS WITH CELERIAC
AND TRUFFLE
Verdicchio de Matelica Riserva, Mirum,
La Monacesca, 2005

BALLOTTINE OF FOIE GRAS WITH MADEIRA
JELLY AND A GREEN BEAN SALAD
Gewürztraminer, les Folastries, Josmeyer, 2005

SLOW POACHED SEA BASS WITH THAI
PURÉE AND A LEMON GRASS FOAM
Sauvignon Blanc, San Antonio-Leyda Valley,
Amayna, 2005

ROAST FILLET OF BEEF, SMOKED BELLY
PORK, RED CABBAGE, FIG AND
CHESTNUT PURÉE
Le Cigare Volant, Bonny Doon Winery, 2002

PASSION FRUIT MOUSSE WITH EXOTIC
FRUIT SALAD, RICE PUDDING AND
COCONUT ICE CREAM
Domaine des Forges, Coteaux de Layon,
Saint-Aubin de Luigné, 2004

PAN FRIED SCALLOPS WITH CELERIAC PURÉE AND TRUFFLE VINAIGRETTE

Serves 4

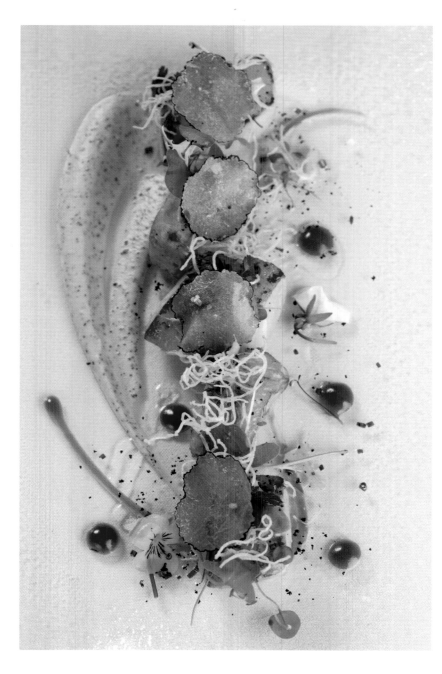

INGREDIENTS

| 12 | Scallops |
| Olive oil |
| Mixed salad |
| Chopped chives |

Celeriac Purée

| 15g | Onions, chopped |
| 15g | Celery, chopped |
| Salt and pepper |
25g	Unsalted butter
150ml	Milk
150ml	Chicken stock
150ml	Water
200g	Celeriac, chopped
25g	Unsalted butter
Pinch of salt & pepper to season

Soy & truffle vinaigrette

| 25g | Shallots sliced |
| 130ml | Olive oil |
| Salt & pepper |
| 50g | Button mushrooms |
| 2 sprigs of fresh thyme |
10ml	Soy sauce
20ml	Truffle juice
25g	Veal glace
5ml	Truffle oil

French vinaigrette

| 300ml | Vegetable oil |
| 100ml | White wine vinegar |
| Salt & pepper |
| Sprig of thyme |
| Clove of garlic |

Deep fried celeriac straw

4 celeriac fondants, cut in half
16 slices perigord truffle
8 edible flowers

METHOD

Celeriac purée

In a saucepan sweat the onions, celery and salt with the butter, add the milk, chicken stock and water then the celeriac and pepper. Bring to the boil and reduce to a simmer. Cook for 30 minutes and then allow to cool. Drain through a colander and then place into a Robot Coupe (food processor) and blend until fine. Remove from the Robot Coupe and then place into a blender and blend to a very fine purée.

Soy & truffle vinaigrette

Sweat the shallots in 30ml of the olive oil, add a pinch of salt and lightly colour.

Add the mushrooms and thyme and sweat for a further 2 minutes. Add the soy sauce and reduce to nothing, then add the truffle juice and reduce by half. Add the veal glace and bring to the boil, place into a blender and blend to a fine purée. Warm 100ml olive oil and add to the pulp followed by the truffle oil. Adjust the seasoning and pass through a fine sieve. Place into a plastic bottle and use at room temperature.

French vinaigrette

Mix all together in a bottle and shake before using.

TO SERVE

Pan fry the scallops in a non-stick pan in olive oil.

Dress some celeriac purée onto the plate, then some soy vinaigrette.

Now place 3 scallops and 2½ celeriac fondants onto the plate. Top with the salad flowers and chives dressed in French vinaigrette then add the truffle slices and celeriac straw.

PHIL HOWARD

"One of the great benefits of participating in an event such as Northcote Food Festival is the fact that you get to see what is happening outside your own world. It is so easy to be too introspective in this industry. For me, Paul Cunningham's menu was one of the greatest displays of cooking I have witnessed at Northcote over the years. A larger than life Lancashire lad cooking world class food."

Saturday 27th January

PHIL HOWARD
The Square, London

WARM GAME JELLY WITH CELERIAC,
CHANTERELLES,
BACON FOAM AND "FRAZZLES"
Blanc de Blancs, Clos Mireille,
Cotes de Provence-Domains Ott, 2004

SEARED SCALLOPS WITH ENDIVE, VANILLA,
SAUTERNES AND BAY
Pouilly-Fumé, Cuvée d'Eve Vieilles Vignes
Jean Claude Dagueneau, 2003

ROAST FOIE GRAS WITH RAISIN PURÉE,
PAIN D'ÉPICE
AND A SWEET AND SOUR GLAZE
Pinot Noir Beerenauslese-Willi Opitz, 2005

BRAISED VEAL CHEEK WITH A FRICASSEE
OF HAND ROLLED MACARONI,
CAULIFLOWER AND TRUFFLE
Chianti Classico Riserva, Berardo,
Castello di Bossi, 2001

PAVÉ OF BITTER CHOCOLATE WITH
CARAMELISED MACADAMIAS,
HONEYCOMB AND PEAR
Boal, Colheita Cask 81A, Vinhos Barbeito, Maderia

PHIL HOWARD

BRAISED VEAL CHEEK WITH A FRICASSEE OF HANDROLLED MACARONI, CAULIFLOWER AND TRUFFLE

Serves 8

INGREDIENTS

Veal

16	Veal cheeks
Salt & pepper	
100g	Plain flour, on a plate
100ml	Grapeseed oil
100g	Butter
500ml	Veal stock
1	Onion, peeled and quartered
1	Carrot, peeled and quartered
1	Leek, peeled and quartered
1	Celery stick, peeled and quartered
250g	Button mushrooms, washed and cut in half
1	Calf's foot – split in half lengthways
1	Bay leaf
10	Peppercorns
2	Stems of thyme

Macaroni

2	Eggs
6	Yolks
Splash of olive oil	
300g	'00' pasta flour
Salt	
Couscous	
50ml	Grapeseed oil

Cauliflower cheese

1	Onion, finely sliced
1	leek, finely sliced
70g	Butter
Salt	
450ml	Milk
1	Bay leaf
1	Large, firm, luxury cauliflower
80g	Flour
50g	Beaufort cheese, grated
50g	Parmesan, grated

To finish the sauce

2	Shallots, finely sliced
150g	Button mushrooms, washed and finely sliced
50g	Butter
Salt	
100ml	White wine

Vegetables/other ingredients

8	Salsify pieces, 10cm long
8	Swiss chard leaves
1	Perigord truffle, finely grated on a microplane.
100ml	Crème fraîche

METHOD

Veal

The back bone of flavour in a braised dish comes from the initial caramelisation of the meat and vegetables. The extent to which you do this varies from dish to dish but it is a critical point, the importance of which can not be underestimated.

Place a hot, large, heavy based, oven proof dish on the stove over a high heat and leave for 5 minutes. Trim any skin and membrane off the cheeks and dry them on a cloth. Transfer to a plate, season with salt and pepper, and press each side onto the flour.

Pour grapeseed oil into the pan and add the cheeks. Veal goes a rich golden colour when browned. Do not take it past this point. Turn the cheeks and at the point when the second side is just golden add the butter. Turn the cheeks over a couple more times to ensure a thorough colouring is achieved. If at any stage it looks like the butter is going to burn, turn down the heat.

Remove the cheeks from the pan, add all the vegetables, a pinch of salt and, while stirring occasionally, caramelise them until lightly coloured all over. Return the meat to the pan, add the calf's foot, the bay leaf, peppercorns and thyme and cover with water. Bring to the boil, skim off any scum and tick over for 5 minutes. Skim.

Add the veal stock, cover with a lid or disc of parchment paper and cook in an oven at 110°C/225°F/gas mark ¼ for an hour. Check the veal at this point. It should feel supple and tender. Check two or three pieces. If it is still firm, place back in the oven and check every 15 minutes, until you feel the meat 'give'. While it should have some bite to it, it must be tender.

Remove from the oven and allow to cool to room temperature. Carefully lift out the 16 cheeks, season with a pinch of salt and cover with cling film. Drain the stock through a colander, discard the vegetables, and pass the stock through a fine sieve. It can be chilled at this point or processed into the finished sauce (see below).

Macaroni

The hand-rolled macaroni are a fantastic refinement, but bought macaroni would more than suffice. Make a firm pasta dough in a food processor by adding the eggs, yolks and olive oil to the flour and salt. Rest, well wrapped, for 2 hours.

Roll it out into sheets 2mm thick. Now cut this sheet quickly so it does not dry, into rectangles 2x5cm and cover with cling film. You will need 80 pieces.

At this point recruit a partner to put the pasta through the machine while you roll them into tubes – this will save both time and excessive ageing! Place the long edge of the rectangle between the rollers of the pasta machine, set 1 notch finer than when you rolled the sheets. Now roll it through, short side first, at the finest setting. Each piece will vary slightly but you are aiming to make these pasta sheets 10x5cm.

Now dip a pencil into a bowl of flour to completely coat with a film of flour. Have the rectangles of pasta horizontally in front of you, sitting on a wooden butter ball pat. Place the pencil on the long edge closest to you and in one move roll the pasta sheet into a tube. Slip it off the pencil and place on a tray covered in a layer of couscous. This will stop the pasta from sticking and ensure it dries easily. As with all pasta work, there is a knack to this. Work as a pair and do not let the pasta dry out. When you have finished, blanch them all in boiled salted water for 1 minute, drain through a colander, toss in the grapeseed oil and store, covered in the fridge.

Cauliflower cheese

Sweat the onion and leek in 50g of butter and a pinch of salt for 2-3 minutes, until softened. Add the milk and the bay leaf, bring to the boil, simmer for 10 minutes, allow to cool for 15 minutes, pass through a sieve and set aside.

Break the cauliflower down into large florets and boil in a large pan of salted water for 5 minutes. Drain and place in an ovenproof dish.

Melt 20g butter over a high heat and, at the point where it starts to smell nutty, add the flour and cook, stirring constantly, for 2 minutes. Now, gradually add the set-aside milk, stirring all the time, until you have a smooth white sauce. Return to the boil and cook for 1 minute. Add the Beaufort and Parmesan and stir until smooth. Spoon generously over the cauliflower and bake, covered with foil, in an oven at 160°C/325°F/gas mark 3 for 25 minutes, removing the foil for the last 5 minutes. Remove from the oven and leave to cool to room temperature.

Finishing the sauce

Sweat the shallots and button mushrooms in butter with a pinch of salt over a medium heat in a heavy based pan. After 2-3 minutes add the white wine and continue to cook until it has completely evaporated. Add the cheek braising liquor, bring to the boil, skim and reduce by half.

Pass through a fine sieve, return to the heat and taste the sauce. The sauce should have a beautiful rounded flavour and enough body to coat the back of a spoon. If it lacks body, make a paste with 1 teaspoon of cornflour and 1 tablespoon of water and add, bit by bit, to the sauce until it has the desired consistency. Set aside

Vegetables

If you have a professional waterbath refer to the cooking times and temperatures for the salsify and swiss chard. If not, whisk 25g of plain flour into 50ml water and pour into a large pan containing 6l of cold water. This is called a blanc and will keep the salsify and chard white during cooking. Season with salt and bring to the boil.

Peel the salsify and place it in a bowl of water with the juice of half a lemon. Remove the green top from the swiss chard by snapping at the top and remove any 'strings' from the stem in the process. Cut into pieces approximately 10x3cm. Place the salsify in the blanc, turn the heat right down and cook until just tender, approximately 10-15 minutes. Lift out the salsify and allow to cool to room temperature. Similarly cook the swiss chard. Once the vegetables are cooked, cut the chard across into 3mm pieces and the salsify into little rounds about 3mm thick. Set aside in the fridge.

TO SERVE

Reheat the veal by putting all but 200ml of the sauce into an ovenproof pan, adding the cheeks, covering with a lid and placing in an oven at 110°C/225°F/gas mark ¼ sfor 30 minutes. Turn the cheeks from time to time. Reheat the cauliflower cheese in the same oven. When hot, remove from the oven and, using a fork lightly crush the cauliflower to give rise to a coarse, textured mix. Cover with foil and keep hot in the oven.

Reheat the macaroni by plunging them for 15 seconds into boiling salted water. Transfer them to a large pan and add the remaining 200ml of sauce, crème fraîche and grated truffle. Stir carefully to coat the pasta. Taste and adjust the seasoning if necessary. Add the salsify and swiss chard.

Into each of 8 large preheated bowls, place a spoon of the cauliflower. Cover with some of the macaroni mix. Place two cheeks on top of this and coat generously with sauce. Serve immediately.

NIGEL HAWORTH

"To be obsessed by perfection and its demands is unrelenting and never ending."

Sunday 28th January

NIGEL HAWORTH
Northcote, Lancashire

SHAVINGS OF GOOSNARGH DUCKLING
AND SMOKED FOIE GRAS
ORANGE CAVIAR, WATERCRESS
Gewürztraminer, les Folastries, Josmeyer, 2005

WARM LOIN OF HERDWICK MUTTON,
JERUSALEM ARTICHOKES,
HONEY AND MINT DRESSING
Pinto Grigio, Ramato, Venezia Giulia,
Azienda Specogna, 2005

POTATO WRAPPED LANGOUSTINE,
YELLOW BEET, PAK CHOI, SPICES
Mâcon-Village, Quintaine, Domaine de la Bongran,
J. Thévenet, 2001

ENGLISH GREY LEG PARTRIDGE BAKED
IN PUFF PASTRY, BUTTERNUT SQUASH,
CHESTNUTS, CRANBERRIES AND
BUTTON ONIONS
Nuits St Georges Clos de Forêts St Georges Domaine
de L'Arlot, 2001

SHORROCK'S TASTY LANCASHIRE CHEESE
ON TOAST WITH SMOKED STREAKY BACON
Thwaites Lancaster Bomber

CARPACCIO OF RHUBARB, PASSION FRUIT
GRANITE, CUSTARD PARFAIT
Late Harvest Orange Muscat and Flora,
Brown Brothers, 2005

WARM LOIN OF HERDWICK MUTTON, JERUSALEM ARTICHOKES, HONEY AND MINT DRESSING

Serves 4

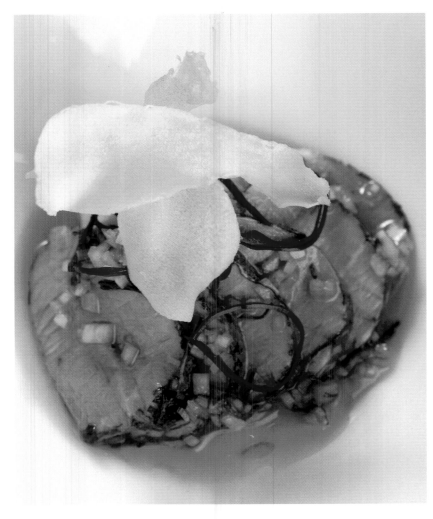

INGREDIENTS

250g	Boneless loin of mutton (silverskin removed and trimmed)
Salt	
4g	Mint leaves, finely shredded
10g	Mutton ham, finely diced
10g	Pickled red cabbage
	Artichoke purée (see below)
	Artichoke crisps (see below)
	Honey & mint dressing (see below)

Artichoke purée

100g	Jerusalem artichokes, peeled
2g	Butter
Salt to taste	
100ml	Whipping cream

Artichoke crisps

1 x 100g Large artichoke, peeled

Honey and mint dressing

50ml	L'Estornell vinegar
1 tsp	English heather honey
12g	Shallots, finely chopped
1 dstspn	Shredded mint
40ml	Extra virgin olive oil
Salt & pepper	

METHOD

Mutton

Season the loin of mutton with salt then roll the mutton in the mint, completely covering it. Wrap the loin tightly in cling film. Steam for 8 minutes, allow to rest (serve pink and keep warm).

Artichoke purée

Finely slice the artichokes on a mandolin.

In a medium pan, melt the butter then add the sliced artichokes, season with salt and cook for 3-4 minutes without colouring. Add the cream, cling film the pan and cook for a further 10-15 minutes until the artichokes are tender. Once tender place into a Thermomix and blend until smooth. Pass through a fine sieve, check the seasoning, leave to cool and reserve.

Artichoke crisps

Slice the artichoke lengthways as thinly as possible on a mandolin. Deep fry at 160°C until golden and crispy. Remove from the fryer and season with salt.

Honey and mint dressing

Bring the L'Estornell vinegar, honey and shallots to the boil, add the mint and olive oil, season with salt and pepper and allow to cool.

TO SERVE

Take a deep bowl and place a good spoonful of artichoke purée in the middle. Remove the mutton from the cling film and carve into 6 pieces per person. Put the mutton ham on top of the artichoke purée and pour over a spoonful of honey and mint dressing. Place the warm mutton loin carefully on the artichoke purée, garnish with red cabbage and spoon over a little more dressing. Finally, put the crisps on top and serve.

20O6

This was the year of the infamous game pie, when Phil Howard chose to cook individual game pies. The story goes that this was a simple dish but – two days later – at 7.18pm, minutes before service, we were still making game pies.

Claude Bosi stormed in with typical French passion, he started the festival with the delicacy of baked potato soup and melilot flower; the precision of the monkfish and complexity of the venison with his combination of marmalade, chocolate and chicken liver pâté blew everyone away.

David Thompson arrived in with partner Tanongsak Yordwai and the extraordinary flavours he conjured from his time spent in Thailand had to be tasted to be believed – the red curry of duck with santol made with Reggie's Goosnargh cornfed ducks was exceptional and the lobster braised with sugar cane and steamed curried scallops were not to be missed.

Fergus Henderson arrived bringing the flavours of St John, a simple dish of shrimps and cabbage, the famous roast marrow bone and parsley salad, finishing with St John's Eccles cake and Lancashire cheese, a real taste of British heritage. He was absolutely fantastic and his mum and dad came to support him and were very proud of a brilliant evening full of northern appreciation. Fergus is a great character, charming and modest who has championed the best of British throughout his career, wise and thoughtful who certainly liked a tipple of Fernet Branca in the early hours.

Andoni Luis Aduriz arrived with his team of six and everyone had a bespoke job – one was even in charge of looking after garden products. Andoni's very special food was so interesting and stimulating, I don't think the Northcote clientele really knew what to expect. Particularly striking was the vegetable coal, which was yucca plant cooked with aubergine skin to make the flesh go deep purple, to imitate charcoal. His cod and tripe stew even for Lancastrians was challenging and he finished the menu with his version of pain perdu served with raw sheep's milk ice cream – brillante!

I remember they had a late night after service where they sat around the roaring log fire in the bar on a late January morning (2 am). I asked them if they wanted something to eat and their eyes lit up. So I went and knocked up a few rounds of rare roast beef butties and two pots of tea, a real culture change with real British comfort food and they absolutely loved it – wholesome British fare for the team from molecular Mugaritz. This Spanish invasion would not have been possible without the patient help and translation of my great friend and fellow foodie, Alain Mols, who flew from Spain to Northcote at the drop of a hat after we realised that Andoni and his team did not speak English. Alain passed away in October of 2006 and is sadly missed.

Mark cooked razor clams and wild garlic, a marriage made in heaven. He also reintroduced us to Carlings – not the lager but those wonderful peas that we all ate around bonfires with a splash of vinegar in the depth of winter in our youth. Nevertheless we had a couple of late nights with Mark (or Hixy, as I like to call him); he doesn't know how to go to bed and it's very difficult to get him away from the bar. He is a true legend in every sense.

Bruce Poole biked up from Wandsworth having accepted my invitation during the Young Chef of the Year in the northern heats. Bruce loves northern hospitality and his football – he is yet another foreign Manchester United supporter. He cooked some truly wonderful dishes, turbot on tartar sauce with the largest turbots to grace the Northcote kitchens and a pithivier of quail, the essence of simplicity.

The Sunday morning was a very cold, crisp day in Lancashire and Paul Heathcote popped by in his running gear. He'd been at Northcote on Bruce's evening as a guest of Reggie Johnson the night before and had left his car, and decided just to jog over (nine miles) and pick it up, as you do! Andy Lynes the journalist couldn't get over the fact he'd just popped in for a bacon butty. That evening while Phil was preparing his chicken wings, I was still rolling out the game pies and the pastry was getting harder, my arms were dropping off. For the first time on that Sunday evening I saw a twinkle of fear in Phil's eyes that we might not get there. He certainly didn't go out for a run that year, which, as far as I can remember, was the first year ever. To add to our problems Aunty Sandra (Craig's adopted aunty) and regular supporter was reluctant to leave the restaurant after lunch. So we couldn't lay up the restaurant for dinner – this all culminated in us promising to never, ever do lunch again throughout the festival, which just made things so much easier from then on in.

C L A U D E
B O S I

"Food and cooking has been part of my life for as long as
I can remember. There are no boundaries with food, meaning
you can always develop and evolve existing dishes, while
creating others. You have to be passionate about this
industry especially, as positive results only come from
hard work and determination."

Monday 23rd January

CLAUDE BOSI
Hibiscus, London

OEUF COCOTTE, BAKED POTATO SOUP,
MELILOT FLOWER
Pinot Gris, Marlborough,
South Island- Kim Crawford, 2005

CARPACCIO OF HAND DIVED SCOTTISH
SCALLOPS AND BLACK RADISH,
ALMOND OIL AND BLACK
TRUFFLE VINAIGRETTE
Auxey-Duresses Blanc, Domaine du Comte Armand, 2002

MONKFISH POACHED IN COFFEE AND
CARDAMOM, SPICED QUINCE PURÉE
Chardonnay, "Wild Boy", Santa Barbara,
California-Au Bon Climat, 2003

SAVOURY ICE CREAM OF FOIE GRAS, WARM
EMULSION OF BRIOCHE,
BALSAMIC CARAMEL
Château Partarrieu, Sauternes, 2001

ROAST MORTIMER FOREST VENISON,
CHERVIL ROOT PURÉE, CLEMENTINE
MARMALADE, SMOKED CHOCOLATE,
CHICKEN LIVER PARFAIT
Châteauneuf-du-Pape, Cuvée Etienne Gonnet,
Domaine Font de Michelle, 1996

MEADOWSWEET PANNA COTTA,
GOLDEN DELICIOUS PURÉE, SHORTBREAD
Plantagenet off the Rack,
Chenin Blanc-Great Southern, 2003

MEADOWSWEET PANNA COTTA, GOLDEN DELICIOUS PURÉE AND SHORTBREAD

Serves 6 - 8

INGREDIENTS

Meadowsweet panna cotta

600g	Whipping cream
200g	Full fat milk
8g	Meadowsweet
120g	Caster sugar
2.5	Gelatine leaves

Shortbread

(Makes 15-20 biscuits)

150g	Butter
150g	T55 flour
75g	Cornflour
38g	Caster sugar
1	Egg yolk

Golden delicious purée

12	Golden delicious apples

METHOD

Meadowsweet panna cotta

Combine the milk and cream in a saucepan, and bring gently to the boil. Pour over the meadowsweet and infuse for one hour.

Soak the gelatine in cold water until it becomes soft. Strain the milk and cream and add the sugar. Bring back to the boil and cool slightly. Add the soaked gelatine and pass through a sieve.

Pour into glasses and place in the fridge to set overnight.

Shortbread

Mix all the dry ingredients then slowly add the egg yolks.

Roll until level, with a 1cm height. Use a circular cutter to portion. Place on a baking tray and cook at 180°C/350°F/gas mark 4 for 15 minutes. When cool dust with icing sugar.

Golden delicious purée

Cook the apples over a medium heat, with no added sugar or liquid, until soft. This will take 10-15 minutes. Take them out and purée them. Each serving should be 40g per person. Spoon on top of the panna cotta and serve with the shortbread.

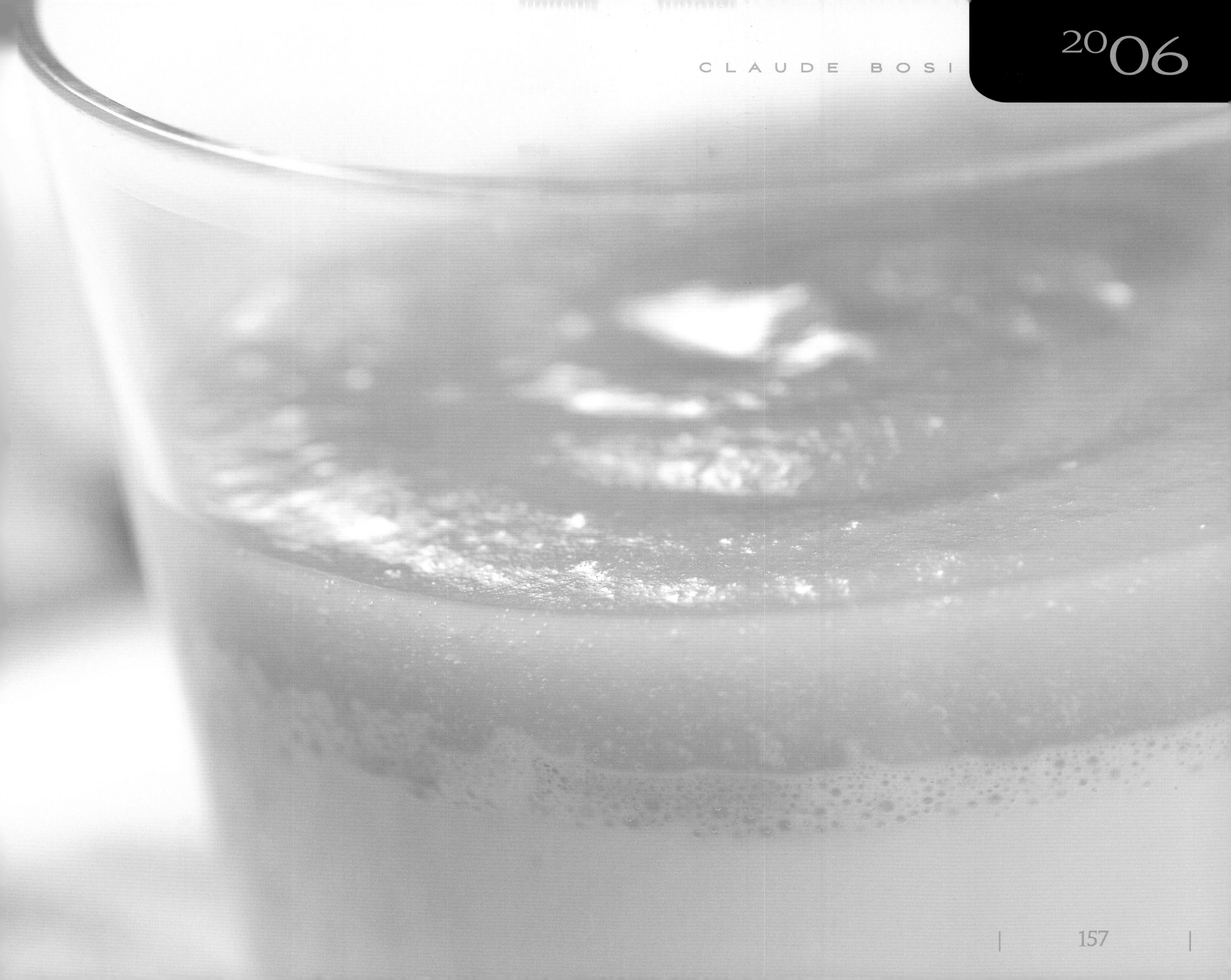

DAVID THOMPSON

"Food is a happy and wholesome diversion. When I was about twenty-one I became obsessed, it was as if a genetic time bomb went off. I read and ate voraciously, anything and everything to do with food enthralled me. It was during this time I first went to Thailand and it all fell together: the food, the culture and the people. I have been a captive ever since."

Tuesday 24th January

DAVID THOMPSON
Nahm, London

MA HOR
MINCED PRAWNS AND CHICKEN SIMMERED
IN PALM SUGAR WITH DEEP FRIED
SHALLOTS AND PEANUTS
SERVED ON PINEAPPLE AND MANDARIN

STEAMED SCALLOP CURRY SERVED WITH
STEAMED RICE
Gewürztraminer, les Folastries, Josmeyer, 2002

CHICKEN AND GRILLED BANANA BLOSSOM
SALAD WITH CHILLI JAM AND
COCONUT CREAM
Viognier, Rapel Valley Special Reserve, Anakena, 2004

CLEAR SOUP OF PAK WARN WITH CRAB
AND SHIITAKE MUSHROOMS
RED CURRY OF DUCK WITH SANTOL
Juliénas, Domaine Gérard Descombes, 2003

SPICY PORK AND GREEN PEPPERCORN
RELISH WITH STEAMED EGGS, WHITE
TUMERIC AND GREEN BEANS
Pinto Grigio, Ramato, Venezia Giulia,
Azienda Specogna, 2003

LOBSTER BRAISED WITH SUGAR CANE AND
STAR ANISE
BABY CORN SIMMERED IN COCONUT
CREAM WITH GINGER AND THAI BASIL

A SELECTION OF THAI DESSERTS, SUCH AS
BLACK SESAME SEED DUMPLINGS IN
GINGER SYRUP
CARAMELISED COCONUT AND
COCONUT PUDDING
DEEP FRIED BANANA FRITTERS
Mâcon-Clessé-Quintaine, Sélection de Grains
Cendrés, Guillemot-Michel, 1992

Or

A PLATE OF FRESH THAI FRUIT
Sauvignon Blanc, Late Harvest, Semi-Dulce Bornos, 2002

INGREDIENTS

Curry Paste

8	Dried long red chillies, deseeded, soaked and drained
	Large pinch of salt
1 tbsp	Chopped galangal
4 tbsp	Chopped lemongrass
1 tsp	Finely chopped kaffir lime zest
1 tsp	Scraped and chopped coriander roots
3 tbsp	Chopped red shallots
3 tbsp	Chopped garlic
	A little gapi (optional)
4	Pla salit (salted fish from Thailand)

Duck and santol

1	Large santol (tropical fruit from southeast Asia, available from specialist suppliers)
	Salt
2	Duck breasts

Fish sauce

1 cup	Separated coconut cream
2 tbsp	Palm sugar
1-2 tbsp	Fish sauce (to taste)
1 tbsp	Tamarind water
3	Kaffir lime leaves, torn
118ml	Coconut milk or stock
2	Large red or green chillies, halved

METHOD

Curry Paste

First, make the paste by grinding all the ingredients apart from the pla salit together in a pestle and mortar or blender. Lightly grill the pla salit, fillet, skin and grind before adding to the paste.

Duck and santol

Clean the santol, score the skin and steep in salted water.
Trim the duck breast and marinate briefly in the fish sauce. Grill the duck breast to medium then rest.

Meanwhile, heat the coconut cream over a medium heat, add 3 tablespoons of the paste and fry until the paste is smoky and fragrant from the fish. Season the curry with palm sugar, fish sauce – not too much – and then the tamarind water. Do not cook the paste for more than a minute or so after adding the tamarind or it will burn. Squeeze the santol to extract as much water as possible and add to the curry with the kaffir lime leaves before moistening with coconut milk or stock and simmer for a few minutes until the santol has softened. Remove the seeds.

Slice the duck breast finely then add to the curry but do not simmer, remove the curry from the heat. Add the chillies and check the seasoning – it may need more fish sauce. The curry should be reasonably light, salty, smoky, sweet and sour.

FERGUS HENDERSON

"I've always been a gutsy soul and a big believer in the table and white tablecloths. They've held my family together through thick and thin and we all still gather at the table. The power of eating is extraordinary. I trained to be an architect, but all my buildings became feasts and my course was otherwise destined. Genius loci expresses the magic of the moment and place, and never is this stronger than in restaurants – those two moments in the day when wonderful organised chaos takes place. There's something very magical and special about restaurants that's hard to put your finger on, but that's why I like them."

Wednesday 25th January

FERGUS HENDERSON MBE
St John, London

CANAPÉS
GRILLED OX HEART AND HORSERADISH
DEEP FRIED TRIPE WITH PICKLED ONION
VINEGAR

BROWN SHRIMP AND WHITE CABBAGE
Pinot Gris Grand Cru Brand, Cave de Turckheim, 2001

ROAST BONE MARROW AND
PARSLEY SALAD
"R" Rosé Côtes de Provence,
Domaine de Rimauresq,2004

WHOLE FISH ON GREEN AND
WHITE VEGETABLES
Rimauresq Blanc Côtes de Provence,
Domaine de Rimauresq, 2004

POT ROAST GLOUCESTER OLD SPOT,
PRUNES AND TROTTERS
Beaune l'er Cru Epenottes, Vallet Frères, 2001

ST JOHN ECCLES CAKE AND
LANCASHIRE CHEESE
Vin de Paille Hermitage Gambert de Loche,
Cave de Tain, 1999

ROAST BONE MARROW AND PARSLEY SALAD

Serves 4

INGREDIENTS

7-8cm   Pieces of middle veal
marrowbone (available from
any good butcher)
Healthy bunch of flat parsley, picked
from its stems
2   Shallots, peeled and very
thinly sliced
Modest handful of capers (extra fine
if possible)

Dressing

Juice of 1 lemon
Extra virgin olive oil
Pinch of sea salt & pepper
Good supply of toast to serve
Coarse sea salt to serve

METHOD

Put the bone marrow in an
ovenproof frying pan and place in
a hot oven. The roasting process
should take about 20 minutes
depending on the thickness of
the bone. You are looking for the
marrow to be loose and giving, but
not melted away, which it will do if
left too long (traditionally the ends
would be covered to prevent any
seepage, but I like the colouring and
crispness at the end).

Meanwhile, lightly chop the
parsley, just enough to discipline it,
mix it with the shallots and capers,
and at the last moment dress it with
the lemon juice, extra virgin olive oil,
sea salt and pepper.

Using a teaspoon or long thin
implement scrape the marrow out of
the bone onto the toast and season
with coarse sea salt. Put a pinch of
parsley salad on top and eat.

FERGUS HENDERSON

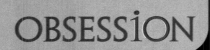

ANDONI LUIS ADURIZ

"Obsession is the transformation of an apparently unnecessary,
or not so unnecessary, idea into a priority need.

Nourishment is not exactly superfluous, although what can
be superfluous is the mandatory consumption of culture,
practices, styles and original and private visions in addition
to nutrients, which is what comprises the essence of
gastronomy today.

Strip life of poetics, inspiration and curious gazes and
you'll succeed in suppressing passion; but you'll also put an
end to the human being."

Thursday 26th January

ANDONI LUIS ADURIZ
Murgaritz, Spain

ROASTED SCALLOPS AND TUBERS
COVERED WITH AMARANTH AND WINTER
PURSLANE, WITH A CLAY AND TRUFFLE
JUICE DRESSING
Albariñō, Lagar de Cerveza, Rias Baixas, 2004

CRUSHED POTATOES, BROKEN EGGS AND A
"VEGETABLE COAL"
DRESSED WITH "A GARLIC PROTEIN"

COD CHEEK AND TRIPE STEW
CROUTON-LIKE SOPAKO, TOMATO AND
SPICY PARSLEY PISTOU SOUP
Blanc de Blancs, Clos Mireille,
Cotes de Provenance-Domaines Ott, 2001

TOASTED FOIE GRAS ESCALOPE
FRESH SOYA AND THYME CREAM SKIMMED
YEAST EMULSION
Jurançon, Vendanges Tardives, "Symphonie de
Novembre", Domaine Cauhapé, 2002

REPRODUCING AN AROMA FROM OUR
ENVIRONMENT: ROASTED LAMB SHOULDER,
SHREDDED SWEET GARLIC,
CHROLOPHYLL WHIPPED WITH HAZELNUT OIL
[OXALIS ACETOSELLA],
AND TOASTED HAZELNUTS
San Vincente, Tempranillo-San Vincente, Rioja, 1994

FRENCH TOAST SOAKED IN EGG YOLK,
SAUTÉ BROWNED AND CARAMELISED
ACCOMPANIED BY AN ICE CREAM
HANDMADE WITH RAW SHEEP'S MILK

A CYLINDER OF CHOCOLATE ICE CREAM
ACCOMPANIED BY A CREAM OF ALMONDS,
ANOTHER CHOCOLATE AND LIME
Rasteau, Vin Doux Naturel,
Domaine de Trapadis, 2001

OBSESSiON

FRENCH TOAST SOAKED IN EGG YOLK, SAUTÉ BROWNED AND CARAMELISED ACCOMPANIED BY AN ICE CREAM HANDMADE WITH RAW SHEEP'S MILK

Serves 4

A homemade brioche is not absolutely essential for this recipe. Brioche may purchased at a good bakery, however, it must be made with butter.

INGREDIENTS

Confectioner's custard

250ml	Milk
25g	Cornflour
40g	Sugar
60g	Egg yolks
25g	Butter, cubed

Almond custard

125g	Butter
1	Egg
1	Egg yolk
150g	Confectioner's custard
125g	Ground almonds
1	Capful of rum
1	Vanilla pod

Brioche

250g	Flour
4	Eggs
10g	Yeast
190g	Butter
25g	Sugar
5g	Salt

French toast marinade

720g	Liquid eggs
440g	Sugar
2l	Milk
2l	Cream

To marinade the Torrija French toast

1	Brioche
1	Batch French toast marinade

Sheep's milk ice cream

1.3 litre	Sheep's milk
200g	Sugar

60g	Powdered glucose
20g	Invert sugar
35g	Powdered milk
7g	Anti-crystallising agent
Salt	

Lemon zest confit

Rind of ½ lemon	
100ml	Water
100g	Sugar

To finish

50g	Butter
100g	Sugar
Apricot jelly	

METHOD

Confectioner's custard

Boil 150ml milk in a saucepan.

In a separate bowl, mix the cornflour, sugar and the remaining milk.

Once the milk has boiled, combine it with the milk mixture and cook for 15 minutes.

In a separate bowl, beat the egg yolks and add a little of the cooked mixture to the beaten egg yolks. Mix quickly and pour over the mixture in the saucepan. Once everything is blended well, remove from heat. Allow the temperature to go down to 60°C and add the cubed butter. Spread out the mixture on a baking sheet. Cover with plastic wrap, ensuring that the plastic touches the custard, to prevent it from forming a skin.

Almond custard

Soften the butter by leaving it out at room temperature or whipping it with a whisk or spatula until creamy. Mix in the rest of the ingredients. Cover and refrigerate. Because this recipe is prepared with raw eggs, it cannot be stored for long and must be used quickly.

Brioche

Combine all the ingredients except for the butter, to form a dough. Knead the dough for approximately 10 minutes, until it no longer sticks to the sides of the bowl. Next, gradually add the butter, only as fast as the dough can absorb it. Once all of the butter has been added, knead the dough until you can form a very fine film with your hand, measuring approximately 20cm (there should be fine lines on the film). A 'dough starter' may be added to this dough if necessary.

Place the dough in a bowl with cellophane at a lukewarm temperature for half an hour and then transfer to the refrigerator for 3 to 4 hours more. Next, knead the dough, shape it and allow it to ferment very slowly for 3 hours in a warm place, between 25°C and 30°C. Once the dough has risen, place in the oven at 180°C for 15 to 20 minutes. If the baking tin is small, bake at 220-230°C/425-450°F/gas mark 7-8 for 6 to 7 minutes.

French toast marinade

Carefully break the eggs and mix them with the sugar. Add in the milk and the cream.

Beat until the liquid is smooth. Strain the mixture through a fine sieve or mesh.

To marinade the Torrija French toast. Cut the brioche into 60g slices. Submerge the slices in the marinade and allow them to soak for at least 4 to 6 hours.

Sheep's milk ice cream

Prepare a cold double boiler with water and ice cubes, and a saucepan with a strainer inside. Boil the sheep's milk in a saucepan if it is home produced and cool immediately.

Reheat the milk to 40°C and add the sugar, the powdered glucose and the anti-crystallising agent. Use a whisk to dissolve the mixture completely. Add the invert sugar and the powdered milk and mix again. Heat the entire mixture to 85°C. At this time, strain the contents of the saucepan into the other saucepan, where you have set up the double boiler with the strainer. Shake and cool the ice cream base.

Lemon zest confit

Use a vegetable peeler to remove the rind from the lemon. Remove all excess skin and the inner white pith. Cut the lemon rind into fine julienne strips. Place the lemon rind strips

into a saucepan with cold water, and bring to the boil. Strain the strips and repeat the process two more times.

In another saucepan, mix the water with the sugar and bring to a boil.Once the mixture has cooled, add in the lemon rind strips which you have already blanched three times, and bring to a boil one last time. Store in its own syrup in the refrigerator.

TO SERVE

Use an ice cream maker to whip up the ice cream, following the manufacturer's instructions. Store the ice cream in a freezer at approximately -13°C.

Cut the butter into cubes. Melt the cubed butter in a skillet until it is golden brown in colour. At this time, strain the marinated brioche slices, coating each side with sugar, and sauté them until golden brown on both sides. Once fried, ensure that the crust retains the liquid inside the brioche, keeping it moist while still hot.

In a safe place, prepare a blow torch or similar gadget.

Heat the brioche slices in the oven for several minutes and spread the almond cream on one side of each. With a spoon, sprinkle sugar on the surface with the almond cream, until completely covered. Quickly and carefully, torch the sugar. The sugar will burn slowly as it turns to caramel.

Streak a cool flat plate with the apricot jelly. Place the hot brioche Torrija on top of the jelly, with the caramelised side face up. Spoon a ball of the ewe's milk ice cream onto the plate, next to the brioche slice. Finish by placing a strand of the lemon zest confit on top.

MARK HIX

"I grew up on the coast with a good ethic of home-cooking
ingredients that were on our doorstep. I remember my gran
cooking my mackerel straight out of the water, and eating
my grandfather's tomatoes fresh from the greenhouse with
Sarson's malt vinegar. I think if you work in, own or run
restaurants and kitchens you need to be slightly obsessed
with food or it just ain't worth doing."

Friday 27th January

MARK HIX

*Caprice Holdings, including The Ivy and
Le Caprice, London*

ROASTED BEETS WITH WILD HERBS,
LEAGRAM'S ORGANIC SHEEP'S
MILK CHEESE
Riesling, Eden Valley, Rockford, 2001

BAKED RAZOR CLAMS WITH CHORIZO
AND WILD GARLIC
Cartuxa Branco de Évora, Reserva, Alentejo, Fundação
Eugénio de Almeida, 2001

FARMER SHARP'S MUTTON BROTH
WITH CARLINGS
Napoleon, Oloroso Abocado, Vinicola Hidalgo

ROAST GOOSNARGH DUCK, SERVED
THREE WAYS, BRAISED, ROASTED AND A
TRUFFLED SALAD OF ITS OFFAL
Pinot Noir, San Antonio, Leyda Valley, Amayna, 2003

RHUBARB TART, LITTLE TOWN DAIRY
CRÈME FRAÎCHE
Late Harvest, Three Choirs Vineyard, 2002

BAKED RAZOR CLAMS WITH CHORIZO AND WILD GARLIC

Serves 4

INGREDIENTS

1kg	Live razor clams
½	Glass dry white wine
Few sprigs of thyme	
3	Wild garlic cloves
1 tsp	Salt
1 tbsp	Chopped parsley, reserving the stalks
250g	Broad beans
4 tbsp	Olive oil
115g	Cooking chorizo. sliced
60g	Butter
Pepper	

METHOD

Rinse the razor clams in cold running water for about 10 minutes, discarding any that don't close when handled.

Put them in a pot with the wine, thyme, garlic, salt and parsley stalks. Cover with a lid and cook over a high heat for a few minutes, stirring occasionally until all the shells open. Drain in a colander and leave to cool.

Preheat the oven to 150°C/300°F/gas mark 2. Carefully remove the clams from the shells, keeping the shell intact (discard any that haven't opened). Cut away the central dark-looking intestinal sac and discard. Cut each clam into 4 or 5 pieces, place back in the shell and arrange the shells on a baking tray. Keep warm in the low oven.

Meanwhile, cook the broad beans in boiling salted water for 2 minutes, then drain in a colander.

Heat the olive oil in a pan and cook the chorizo on a low heat for 1-2 minutes. Add the broad beans, butter and chopped parsley, season lightly with salt and pepper.

Put the clams in their shells on warmed serving plates and spoon the chorizo mixture over.

BRUCE POOLE

"I am obsessed with all aspects of running a restaurant in which, naturally, the food plays a major part. I have strong views about what makes a meal enjoyable, or even great, and striving to achieve the latter while in practice having to settle for the former is what moves us onwards as chefs. I wish there were more skilled cooks attempting to simplify their food by taking ingredients away, rather than adding them."

Saturday 28th January

BRUCE POOLE
Chez Bruce, London

DEEP FRIED TURBOT WITH TARTARE SAUCE
Montagny l'er Cru, Château de la Saule,
Alain Roy, 2004

PITHIVIER OF QUAIL WITH CELERIAC PURÉE
Pinot Noir, Marlborough South Island, Isabel, 2002

COD, CRAB AND ARTICHOKE BARIGOULE
WITH SAFFRON AND PARSLEY
Riesling, Les Princes Abbés,
Organic-Domaine Schlumberger, 2001

FILLET AND DAUBE OF BEEF WITH ONION
DUMPLING, PEARL BARLEY, RED WINE
AND THYME
Cartuxa de Évora Reserva,
Fundação Eugénio de Almeida, 1999

GRIOTTINE CHERRY AND VANILLA CUSTARD
WITH BISCUITS
Maury Vins Doux Naturels, Domaine Pouderoux, 2003

DEEP FRIED TURBOT WITH TARTARE SAUCE

Serves 4 generously as a starter or as a light main course

This dish is simple but very special indeed. However, the cost of turbot may well put you off which is a great pity, as prepared in this way, it is a blindingly good thing to eat. Cheaper white fish such as lemon sole or plaice will substitute well, but for that added luxury, you simply can't beat turbot – it is in my opinion the king of fish.

INGREDIENTS

1 small (900g)	Fresh turbot, filleted and skinned to make 4 fillets

Plain flour

4	Eggs, beaten

Half a loaf of white slice bread turned into coarse breadcrumbs. Enough vegetable or sunflower oil to half fill a pan big enough to deep fry the fish. You will need more than you think – depending on the size of your pan, at least one litre – and the oil can be filtered and re-used. Remember that the more oil you start with, the easier and quicker it will be to fry the fish.

Tartare sauce

1 heaped tsp	Dijon mustard
1 tsp	White wine vinegar
2	Egg yolks

Half a pint of vegetable or sunflower oil
Salt & pepper
Fresh lemon juice to taste

1 dstspn	Chopped capers
1 heaped dstspn	Chopped cornichons

A small handful of chopped fresh parsley
Lemon wedges, to serve

METHOD

Cut the turbot fillets into long even strips about 1cm wide. This cut is called a goujon. Fill three separate, roomy containers with the flour, beaten eggs and breadcrumbs. Toss the goujons in the flour, shake off the excess and add a few at a time to the egg. Completely submerge in the egg, again shake off the excess egg and finally add to the breadcrumbs. This is a messy and rather enjoyable process – you could make it into the kind of cookery lesson kids love. Make sure the goujons are thoroughly and generously coated in the breadcrumbs and leave the fish in with the crumbs. This can be done an hour or two (but no longer) in advance of cooking. Now wash your hands!

Tartare sauce

Make a mayonnaise in the normal way. Add the mustard and vinegar to the egg yolks. Slowly beat in the oil and taste for seasoning adding salt, pepper and lemon juice. Stir in the capers, cornichons and parsley. Add more of any of these ingredients if you like – I like a lot of cornichons in my tartare sauce (minced anchovies are another welcome addition if you like them).

Bring up a large pan of oil to about 180°C. A sugar thermometer is useful here, or simply test the temperature of the oil by dropping in one goujon which will sizzle and float pleasingly when the oil is at the right temperature. Please take great care when deep frying food – on no account should the oil become smokingly hot and never leave the pan unattended. Fry all the goujons, but take care not to overcrowd the pan or the temperature of the oil will drop quickly and significantly and the fish will not fry to a beautiful, golden crispness.

Drain the goujons on paper towels and reserve in a warm place if frying in batches. Divide the goujons onto four plates and serve with the tartare sauce and lemon wedges.

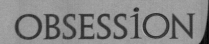

NIGEL HAWORTH
AND
PHIL HOWARD

"To be obsessed with creativity has no boundaries, a brush stroke to infinity."

"I aged as many years as I spent days at Northcote that year! I made many poor decisions – stuffing chicken wings, making 100 pies and 10 cheesecakes. I went down like a bag of crap! The problem with these events is that the menu is always prized out of me mid December, when The Square is so busy and I don't give it the attention I should – not in terms of quality but more in terms of practicality. I got it all horribly wrong this year but for once, I saw Nigel roll up his sleeves and bail me out!"

Sunday 29th January
PHIL HOWARD
NIGEL HAWORTH
of The Square, London and Northcote, Lancashire

NIGEL
SEARED DEXTER BEEF, WILD HERB AND SALSIFY SALAD,
LIME CARAMEL, ROAST MARROWBONE
Pinot Grigio, Ramato, Venezia Giulia, Azienda Specogna, 2005

PHIL
GLAZED CHICKEN WINGS WITH PARMESAN GNOCCHI,
FIELD MUSHROOM PURÉE AND BLACK TRUFFLE JELLY
Sauvignon Blanc, San Antonio-Leyda Valley, Amayna, 2003

NIGEL
DUBLIN BAY PRAWN TAILS, SMOKED SHALLOTS,
ESPUMA OF ROUILLE, WOODALLS HAM
Riesling Mount Barker, Plantagent, 1998

PHIL
GAME PIE WITH SWEDE AND CARROT MASH, SAVOY CABBAGE,
CELERIAC PURÉE AND LARDONS
Gevrey Chambertin, Les Sevrees, Vieilles Vignes, Domaine Michel Magnien, 2000

NIGEL
SAGO AND MULLED PEAR SHOT

PHIL
BRILLAT-SAVARIN AND PASSION FRUIT CHEESECAKE
WITH BANANA AND PASSION FRUIT SORBET
De Bortoli, Noble One Botrytis Semillon, Riverina 2000

GLAZED CHICKEN WINGS WITH PARMESAN GNOCCHI, FIELD MUSHROOM PURÉE AND BLACK TRUFFLE JELLY

Serves 8

INGREDIENTS

24	Chicken wings
1 tbsp	Grapeseed oil
Salt & pepper	
50g	Butter
4	Shallots, finely sliced
10	Button mushrooms, sliced
1	Bay leaf
600ml	Chicken stock
150g	Chicken breast, chilled and trimmed of all sinew
1	Egg
150ml	Double cream
1	Sprig of tarragon
3g	Sosa elastic gel or agar
1	Small black truffle, finely chopped
½ tsp	Cornflour
1 tbsp	Water
100g	Butter
50g	Trompettes de la mort (horn of plenty mushroom)
3 tbsp	Olive oil

Gnocchi

3	Large baking potatoes
250g	Rock salt
70g	'00' pasta flour
1	Egg
10g	Parmesan, finely grated
Salt & pepper	

Field mushroom purée

50g	Butter
1	White onion, finely sliced
Salt	
6	Large field mushrooms, finely sliced
250ml	Double cream

METHOD

Prepare the chicken wings by trimming the wing tip and first bone away from the prime middle bone. Heat a heavy based pan over a medium heat, add 1 tablespoon of grapeseed oil, season the chicken wings and place them in the pan in a single layer. Brown the first side, turn the wings, add 50g butter and brown the second side. Remove the wings from the pan, add the shallots, button mushrooms and bay leaf and a pinch of salt. Gently cook until all the moisture has evaporated then return the wings to the pan. Add the chicken stock, cover with a lid and cook in an oven preheated to 110°C/225°F/gas mark ¼ for 1 hour.

Remove from the oven, allow to rest for half an hour, lift out the wings, pass the stock through a fine sieve. Remove the prime middle bone from each wing by pulling it out carefully.

Place the chicken breast in a food processor with a generous pinch of salt and blend until thoroughly puréed. Add the egg and briefly blend again. Transfer to a round bottomed bowl, sit over iced water and vigorously beat in 150ml of double cream, adding it gradually. Pick, wash and chop the tarragon leaves and add to the mix. Transfer to a piping bag with a fine nozzle and carefully pipe the chicken mousse into the chicken wings (where the bone was).

Now place each chicken wing on a piece of cling film approximately 20cm x 10cm, roll it up tightly and tie a knot at each end of the wing. Steam the wings for 8 minutes, refresh in iced water, chill for half an hour, unwrap and set aside, covered, in the fridge.

You should have about 400ml of stock left from the cooking of the chicken wings. Divide this in two and check the seasoning. Add 2.5g of Sosa elastic gel or agar to one half, whisk thoroughly, bring to the boil, add half the truffle and tip onto a flat baking sheet or surface. It will set quickly. Using a 2cm diameter pastry cutter, cut 24 small discs and lift off the sheet and set aside in the fridge.

To the other half of the stock add a paste of the cornflour mixed with a tablespoon of water and bring to the boil. Whisk 25g of potato into this until thoroughly combined. Then whisk in 100g of butter and add the remaining truffle. You should have a delicious, rich, coating truffle butter emulsion. Reserve warm.

Sauté the trompettes in 1 tablespoon of olive oil. Season and set aside.

Gnocchi

Bake the potatoes on a bed of rock salt until completely cooked, in an oven at 160°C/325°F/gas mark 3.

Scoop the potato out of the skin and pass through a fine ricer or drum sieve. You will need 300g for

the gnocchi and 25g for the sauce. Place 300g into a large bowl, add the flour, 1 egg, parmesan, salt, pepper and knead briefly into a homogenous dough. Turn out onto a floured surface and roll into a long sausage. Cut 24 2.5cm lengths, lightly press down on each one with a fork and transfer to a tray lined with parchment paper. Bring a large pan of salted water to the boil and cook the gnocchi for 2 minutes. Drain, refresh in iced water and set aside in the fridge on a tray lined with a tea towel.

Field mushroom purée

To make the field mushroom purée, place a heavy based pan over a medium heat, add 50g of butter and allow it to melt, add the onions, a pinch of salt and sweat until soft and translucent. Add the field mushrooms and cook until any moisture has evaporated. Add the 250ml double cream, bring to the boil, cover with a lid and cook gently for 10 minutes. Transfer to a blender, purée until smooth and pass through a fine sieve. Check the seasoning and set aside in the fridge.

TO SERVE

Place two large non-stick pans on the stove over a medium heat. Add s1 tablespoon of olive oil to each. Place the chicken wings into one and the gnocchi into the other and gently brown on both sides. Warm the purée, sauce and trompettes de la mort.

Onto each of 8 preheated plates place a spoon of purée, dragging it swiftly across the plate. Place three gnocchi onto each plate, top each with a chicken wing. Spoon a small quantity of sauce over each wing, top with a disc of jelly and finish with a couple of trompettes. Serve immediately.

SEARED DEXTER BEEF, WILD HERB AND SALSIFY SALAD, LIME CARAMEL, ROAST MARROWBONE

Serves 4

INGREDIENTS

Beef

400g	Sliced sirloin of Dexter beef
5g	Salt
Black pepper	
10g	Icing sugar

Roast marrowbone and toast

1	Slice of white bread 1.25cm thick
50ml	Clarified butter
Salt	
4	Middle cut marrowbones (soaked for 24 hours in cold water to remove all the blood – refresh the water regularly)
8	Shallot rings
2 tsp	English curly parsley, finely chopped

Lime and caramel syrup

Juice of ½ lemon
Juice of 2 limes

50g	Sugar

Herb dressing

15g	Parsley, chopped
½	Egg yolk
¼ tsp	English mustard
25ml	Sunflower oil
25ml	Olive oil
5g	Chives, chopped
5g	Tarragon, chopped
	Chervil
5g	Basil, chopped
2.5g	Parmesan cheese
Salt, to taste	

Pickled salsify

1	Stick of salsify
300ml	Water
Salt, to taste	
3	Drops of lemon juice

Pickling liquor

50ml	White wine vinegar
25g	Sugar
25ml	Water

Deep-fried salsify

Stick of salsify

Salsify fritter

2 x 80g	Salsify sticks, washed and peeled
5g	Butter
1g	Lemon juice
2g	Salt

Tempura

40g	Fecule
40g	Self raising flour
40g	Cornflour
150ml	Sparkling water
2g	Salt

Celeriac and horseradish purée

10g	Butter
100g	Small diced celeriac
15g	Small diced fresh horseradish
100ml	Cream
Salt to taste	

Salad garnish

Bronze fennel
Ruby red streak cress
Garden chervil

METHOD

Beef

To get the 400g piece of beef for this dish you need to strip a sirloin of all its fat, remove all sinew, cut in half across the sirloin then in half lengthways. You will then have 4 fillet-like pieces which you can cut again depending on the amount of meat you require.

Take the 400g piece of Dexter beef, cling film it tight and place into a vacuum pack bag and seal tightly. Put into a water bath at 60°C for 1 hour. Remove from the bath and place in a blast chiller. Once cool, remove from the vacuum pack and wrap in cling film. Dry on absorbent kitchen roll then dust with salt, black pepper and icing sugar.

Seal straight on to the stove top to get a deep dark crust all around the beef, allow to cool then cling film tightly and chill.

Slice the Dexter beef 2cm thick on a slicing machine. Serve at room temperature.

Roast marrowbone and toast

Remove the crust from the slice of bread, cut the bread to a square 9x9cm, place it in the chiller to semi freeze. Once semi frozen cut the bread into fingers 1cm thick, repeating this 8 times to get 8 fingers. In a small pan heat the clarified butter and shallow fry the fingers for 3-4 minutes until golden. Remove from the pan on to absorbent kitchen paper, season with salt and keep warm.

Scrape clean the marrowbones to remove any excess sinew. Put in the oven at 190°C/375°F/gas mark 5 for 8-10 minutes until the marrowbone is soft. Remove from the oven.

Serve hot with two shallot rings mixed with the finely chopped parsley on the top of each marrowbone with two warm fingers of toast.

Lime and caramel syrup

In a heavy bottomed pan add the lemon juice, lime juice and sugar then reduce on a gentle heat until a syrup is able to coat the back of the spoon. Leave to cool. Once cool place into a squeezy bottle.

Herb dressing

In a Thermomix blitz the parsley, egg yolk, English mustard, sunflower oil and olive oil to make a rustic purée. Remove the purée and put it into a bowl, add the chopped chives, tarragon, chervil, basil, parmesan, mix well and season.

Pickled salsify

Peel the stick of salsify and cut into 8cm long sticks, then slice lengthways on a mandolin, as thinly as possible – try to make them look transparent. Bring the water, salt and lemon juice to the boil, add the salsify and cook until tender, then refresh in iced water and drain well.

5 minutes before serving marinate the salsify in the pickling liquor.

Pickling liquor

In a small pan bring all the ingredients to the boil. Remove from the heat and cool. Reserve for the pickled salsify.

Deep-fried salsify

Peel and cut the salsify into 2 batons 8cm long. Slice the salsify long ways on a mandolin 1mm thick, so that they become matchstick size. Deep fry at 180°C for 1-2 minutes until golden. Remove from the fryer and place onto a sheet of absorbent paper and season with salt.

Salsify fritter

Cut the salsify into 4 batons 3cm long, cutting each end at a slight angle. Place into a small pan and just cover with water. Add the butter, lemon juice and salt and bring to the boil. Cook the salsify until tender, remove from the boiling liquor and place into a blast chiller to immediately cool. Once cool reserve for the batter.

Tempura

Mix together all the ingredients and place into a iSi gun and charge with 3 canisters. Take the 4 pieces of salsify and flour lightly. Eject the batter into a bowl, place the salsify into the batter and cover completely. Fry at 180°C for 2 minutes until light and crispy. Keep warm.

Celeriac and horseradish purée

In a medium pan melt the butter, add the celeriac and horseradish, cook for 3-4 minutes without colouring. Add the cream and cling film the top of the pan and simmer until soft. Place into a Thermomix, blitz until smooth and pass through a fine chinoise. Check the seasoning and cool. Once cooled, place into a piping bag and reserve.

TO SERVE

Place a slice of beef onto the plate, pipe on 3 cones of celeriac and horseradish purée and a dessertspoon of herb dressing. Place on the pickled salsify and salsify fritter. Garnish with salad leaves and deep-fried salsify, finish with a small amount of lime and caramel syrup. Place the warm marrowbone and toast onto a side plate and serve.

20O5

We had another great line up for 2005. Eric Chavot started off the festival with Sat Bains and Dieter Koschina – is it possible to start a festival with three bigger characters? Two two stars and a one star. Dieter came to us from Vila Joya in the Algarve through a family connection with Craig, whose cousin Zoe is married to Bruce Hawker who edits Essential Algarve magazine and is bon viveur and great gastronome of some reputation. Bruce introduced us to Joy and Gebhard whose family owns Vila Joya. They asked Dieter if he would cook at the festival. Dieter was so inspired by the event he started his own festival in Portugal that is now a great event in its own right.

A great start with Eric, a man who I have known and eaten with throughout his career in his many venues, always cooking with precision and flair. Eric's sea bass on the confit of lemon and tomatoes was very special and his more-than-spectacular chocolate and orange pudding was a great finish.

I managed to get hold of Sat Bains through judging the Catey Awards prior to the festival. When I asked him if he would be willing to cook at the festival he accepted without hesitation. Then there was Mr Bains' 12-hour slow cooked beef, which proved really interesting from a customer point of view. He also did langoustines with back fat and passion fruit which was so memorable.

Dieter's sauces – which he'd laboriously worked through the night to reduce down – had incredible flavours and you could see how he'd built up his reputation through this kind of cooking. That was a long night. All Dieter's dishes were outstanding, none more so than the ravioli of black sausage and goose liver, and the lobster dish. Then, at four in the morning, he

decided to make fillet steak and foie gras butties, which after lots of wine, went down decidedly well among the other chefs.

Dieter's quote of the festival was his characteristically Austrian "Full Power!" catchphrase, which Eric Chavot also picked up on. The following morning I took him to the Three Fishes and he developed a liking for the Thwaites beer there, and it turned out to be a long and fascinating lunch.

Roy Brett, Rick Stein's executive chef, arrived from Padstow – we'd met when taking my son Kirk down to Rick Stein's for a stagiaire. Roy cooked a truly memorable meal of fish, fish and more fish. He did langoustines, sea bass, brill, smoked salmon and a shellfish soup among other things, which showcased his incredible flair for cooking seafood.

Phil Howard made a delightful Mediterranean dish with red mullet sardine chantilly and anchovies which, with the Pera Manca Blanco, was a marriage made in heaven. His pud was the best rice pud ever with raisins and tangerines – yet another great Howard night.

Richard Corrigan made two superb dishes, a butter poached haddock with caviar, langoustine and champ followed by a spectacular crubeens with Jabuga ham and woodland salad which was characteristically robust yet refined, Irish style rivalling any French imitation. Richard who is forever a true Irish gent certainly had a few drinks that night.

It was my first introduction to Farmer Sharp's mutton which I cooked with Ascroft's yellow beets, infamously known as Lancashire pineapple; mutton is a truly great British product. To finish the evening I chose Queen of pudding soufflé with a lemon and crème fraîche ice cream, reminding me of influences from Granny Ish, a true cook of her generation.

Bravura

NORTHCOTE MANOR
FESTIVAL OF FOOD & WINE 2005

ERIC CHAVOT

"This is what I do. I wish I could turn it off but I just can't."

Monday 24th January

ERIC CHAVOT
The Capital, London

SNAIL BOURGUIGNON WITH SEARED
QUEEN SCALLOP
Grand Millésime, Champagne Gosset, 1996

PAN-FRIED LANGOUSTINE
WITH SLOW COOKED PORK BELLY,
LANGOUSTINE FOAM
Dry Furmint, "Mandolas", Tokaji-Oremus, 2002

SEA BASS WITH TOMATO AND
LEMON CONFIT
Menetou-Salon, Clos des Blanchais,
Domaine Henry Pellé, 2002

ROAST QUAIL WITH FOIE GRAS BOUDIN
AND MUSCAT JUS
Chambolle Musigny, Frédéric Mugnier, 1998

GIANDUJA AND ORANGE CRUMBLE WITH
ICED NOUGAT
Muscat de Rivesaltes, Domaine Piétri Géraud, 2003

GIANDUJA AND ORANGE CRUMBLE WITH ICED NOUGAT

Serves 8

INGREDIENTS

Nougat glace

125g	Acacia honey
25g	Caster sugar
25g	Liquid glucose
120g	Egg whites
20g	Caster sugar
500ml	UHT cream
125g	Caramelised hazelnuts
100g	Marmalade

Crumble

50g	Caster sugar
50g	Ground almonds
50g	Butter
50g	Flour
3g	Maldon salt
150g	Orange zest

Feuillantine (chocolate thins)

100g	Praline paste
150g	Tanariva chocolate
10g	Cocoa butter
150g	Eclats d'or

Orange coulis

200g	Orange juice
20g	Mango purée
20g	Orange concentrate
30g	Caster sugar
15g	Vitpris (pectin)

Gianduja mousse

250ml	Milk
25g	Caster sugar
80g	Egg yolks
15g	Cornflour
½ sheet/2g	Gelatine
300g	Gianduja noir (a finely ground smooth mixture of chocolate and nut butter, such as hazelnut, almond or pistachio eg. Nutella)
200g	Praline
260ml + 60ml UHT cream at room temperature	
Dried orange, to decorate	

METHOD

Nougat glacé

Whisk the cream and refrigerate.

Boil the honey, glucose and 25g sugar to 121°C. Pour on to the egg whites. Whisk up to a thick meringue and whisk slowly until cool. Fold in the rest of the ingredients and cream. Pipe into moulds and freeze.

Crumble

Mix the zest with the sugar and then the rest of the ingredients and form the mix into little nuggets. Bake in the oven at 170°C until golden brown.

Feuillantine (chocolate thins)

Melt the cocoa butter and tanariva and incorporate the praline paste and éclats d'or. Roll out between sheets of greaseproof paper to the desired thickness and freeze. Break to required size.

Orange coulis

In a pan warm the orange juice, mango purée and orange concentrate then add the vitpris (pectin) and sugar. Cook for 2 minutes and pass through a fine sieve. Cool down.

Gianduja mousse

Soften the gelatine in ice cold water. Whip 260g cream slowly to a soft peak. Melt the Gianduja and keep at 35°C. Make a crème pâtissière with the milk, sugar, egg yolks and the cornflour. Add the gelatine to 200g pâtissière. Add that mix to the melted Gianduja and the praline. Beat in a blender using the paddle until it reaches 28°C and incorporate slowly the 60g of cream as if you are making mayonnaise. When the mix is smooth, fold the whipped cream in gently.

TO SERVE

Swirl some orange coulis on a plate. Loosen each nougat glacé from its mould and place on the plate. Add the crumble nuggets, feuillantine, mousse and dried orange as pictured.

SAT BAINS

"At first it was a flirtation; then seduction; after that a passion which led to Obsession ... my accidental journey into gastronomy."

Tuesday 25th January

SAT BAINS
Restaurant Sat Bains, Nottingham

CANAPÉS
LANGOUSTINE "AU LARD" CARROT,
CARDAMOM FROGS LEGS,
PEAR, LIQUORICE
PEANUT MILK, SESAME OIL

CELERIAC SOUP, CHICKEN OYSTERS,
APPLE CHESTNUTS
Quincy, Domaine des Ballandors, 2003

ROAST SCALLOP, INDIAN SPICES,
TEXTURES OF CAULIFLOWER,
CORIANDER, SALT
Viognier, Podere di Montalupan, Ascheri, 1997

DRY AGED SCOTCH BEEF, "TEXTURES"
OF THE ONION FAMILY
Château de Fonsalette, Jacques Reynaud, 1993

"CHEESE ON TOAST"
Boal, Colheita Cask 81A, Vinhos Barbeito, Madeira

"BANOFFEE PIE"
Château Partarrieu, Sauternes, 2001

RAW AND COOKED PINEAPPLE, VANILLA
SET YOGHURT, MINT SUGAR
Jurançon, Vendanges Tardives,
"Symphonie de Novembre"
Domaine Cauhapé, 2001

DRY AGED SCOTCH BEEF, "TEXTURES" OF THE ONION FAMILY

Serves 4

INGREDIENTS

Braised oxtail

1kg	Chopped oxtail
2pt	Guinness
6	Sprigs thyme
6	Peppercorns
6	Juniper berries
236ml	Brown chicken stock

Salt and pepper
Olive oil

Caramelised shallot purée

8	Chopped shallots
25g	Butter
25g	Olive oil

Salt
Brown chicken stock

Braised baby onions

| 12 | Peeled baby onions |

Salt
Sprig of thyme
15ml Olive oil
Emulsion (25g butter, salt, 200g white chicken stock)

Roast shallots

4 peeled shallots
Salt
Sprig of thyme
15ml Olive oil plus a little extra for re-heating
Butter

Crispy onion rings

| 1 | Shallot cut into rings about 0.5cm thick |

Plain flour
Egg wash
Panko breadcrumbs

Raw shallot salad

| 1 | Shallot sliced wafer thin |

Pickling juice (50g white wine vinegar, 25g sugar, pinch of salt)

Spring onions

| 4 | Large spring onions |

Olive oil
Butter
Salt

METHOD

Marinade the oxtail in the Guinness and aromats (thyme, peppercorns and juniper berries) for 7 days, strain and pan roast the oxtail until browned all over, reduce the Guinness down by half and add the brown chicken stock, season. Place the oxtail and the sauce in a pressure cooker, bring up to full pressure and cook for 45 minutes. Allow to cool slightly and then pick off the meat, discarding the bones. Fold in the sauce and roll into cylinders, allow to set. To reheat the oxtail place in a pan of olive oil, fry both sides of the cylinder and finish off in the oven at 180°C/350°F/gas mark 4 for 6-8 minutes.

Caramelised shallot purée

Start sweating off the shallots in the butter and olive oil; when all the moisture has evaporated lower the heat and gently caramelise, this should take around 2 hours. When caramelised, deglaze the pan with a little brown chicken stock and blend to a purée. Season if necessary.

Braised baby onions

Place the onions in a sous vide bag along with the rest of the ingredients, place in a pan of boiling water until soft and then into a tub of iced water. Reheat in the emulsion.

Roast shallots

Place the shallots in a sous vide bag along with the salt, sprig of thyme and olive oil, place in a pan of boiling water until soft and then into a tub of iced water. When reheating caramelise the shallots in a little butter and olive oil and warm through in the oven.

Crispy onion rings

Dip the shallot rings in the flour followed by the egg wash and the breadcrumbs, fry at 180°C until crispy and golden brown.

Raw shallot salad

Season the shallot with the pickling juice just before serving.

Spring onions

Blanch the spring onions in boiling salted water until soft. Reheat in a little olive oil and butter then season with salt.

TO SERVE

Assemble the dish as illustrated.

DIETER KOSCHINA

"Cooking and food are so important for me because of having this endless possibility of being creative, and the creativity goes hand in hand with the enjoying. First comes the pleasure of being creative, second the joy of finalising the creation and third the delight with all the human senses. We chefs have the gratification of being able to satisfy all the senses of the guests with one single dish. My biggest Obsession with food is to find the best products to create the perfect dish. This sounds easy, but is maybe the most difficult challenge in my life."

Wednesday 26th January

DIETER KOSCHINA
Vila Joya, Portugal

CANAPÉ
COMPOSITION OF DUCK AND QUAIL
WITH KUMQUATS

FILLET OF RED SEA BASS ON BRAISED
TOMATO, ONION PURÉE AND OLIVES
Bairrada Reserva, Casa de Saima, 1996

RAVIOLI OF BLACK SAUSAGE WITH
SAUTÉED GOOSE LIVER
Quinta do Bom-Retiro, 20 Year Old Tawny, Ramos Pinto

MEDALLION OF LOBSTER, WITH MASHED
POTATOES AND CEPS
Alvarinho Soalheiro, Vinho Verde,
António Esteves Ferreira, 2001

SADDLE OF VENISON WITH
PORT WINE SAUCE
Cartuxa de Évora Reserva,
Fundação Eugénio de Almeida, 1999

CRISPY CHOCOLATE WITH RASPBERRIES
AND CHAMPAGNE, ICE CREAM
Opitz One, Vin de Paille, Willi Opitz, 2000

MEDALLIONS OF LOBSTER WITH MASHED POTATOES AND CEPS

Serves 4

INGREDIENTS

2 x 500g   Lobsters
300g   Potatoes, peeled
20g   Chives
250ml   Fish nage
8   Ceps
Salt & Pepper
Olive Oil
Lemon Juice

Fish nage

250ml   White wine
125ml   Noilly Prat
125ml   White dry port wine
500ml   Chicken soup clear
250ml   Clear fish soup
400ml   Cream
Salted butter

METHOD

Fish nage

Reduce white wine, Noilly Prat and port wine to a third. Reduce chicken and fish soup to a third. You should cook them in two different pots very slowly to achieve this. When the reductions are done, put the white wine, Noilly Prat and port wine into the soup. You should have around 400ml of that mixture. Put the same amount of cream into it and bind with a little salted butter.

Lobsters

Put the lobsters in water heated to 60°C for 8 to 10 minutes. Remove the pincers and return the lobster without the pincers to the water for another
6 minutes. Remove the lobster from the water and peel it. Cut into 1cm slices, cover with foil and keep warm.

Clean the ceps, cut them in a half and roast with olive oil.

Cook the potatoes in salted water. When they are well cooked mash with a fork. Mix in the chives, lemon juice, salt and some fish nage.

TO SERVE

Put the mash on a plate, place the warm lobster slices on top. Heat the rest of the fish nage then pour it over the lobster.

ROY BRETT

"When you open a restaurant at 41 you have to be driven to go back to the 16-hour days. It's a never-ending journey, and you can never be bored. It's a privilege to be able to work with the produce we work with and I never feel it's a chore. The day you do is the day you should stop cooking."

Thursday 27th January

ROY BRETT
Seafood Restaurant, Padstow

CANAPÉ
FRANK HENDERMAN'S SMOKED SALMON
ON MELBA TOAST

LANGOUSTINES GRILLED WITH PERNOD
AND OLIVE OIL DRESSING
Mud House Sauvignon Blanc, Marlborough, 2004

FISH AND SHELLFISH SOUP WITH ROUILLE
AND PARMESAN
Gran Reserva Rioja Blanco, Marqués de Murrieta, 1998

CHARGRILLED FILLET OF SEA BASS WITH A
TOMATO, VANILLA VINAIGRETTE
Mercurey Blanc, Clos Rochette, Domaine Faiveley, 2001

A CASSEROLE OF BRILL WITH SHALLOTS
AND WILD MUSHROOMS
Sancerre Rouge, Pascal Jolivet, 2003

SEVILLE ORANGE TART
Quinta da Ervamoira, 10 Year Old Tawny, Ramos Pinto

FISH AND SHELLFISH SOUP WITH ROUILLE AND PARMESAN

Serves 12

INGREDIENTS

Fish Soup

50 ml	Olive oil
50g	Butter
1	Red pepper, finely chopped
1	Orange, zest removed, remainder chopped
1	Onion, finely chopped
100g	Celery, finely chopped
100g	Leeks
20g	Chopped garlic
1	Bay leaf
Sprig of thyme	
250g	Atlantic prawns
50g	Tomato purée
½ litre	Reduced fish stock
1	Pinch saffron
400g	Tinned tomatoes
1kg	Pollock, diced
1	Pinch smoked paprika
Seasoning	

Rouille

12	Roasted red peppers
2 tsp	Tomato purée
2 tsp	Ground coriander
1	Pinch saffron
1	Red chilli, finely chopped
10 tsp	Cayenne pepper
Seasoning	

25g	Crusty white bread
100ml	Fish stock
4 tsp	Harissa paste
2	Egg yolks
2	Garlic cloves, peeled and finely chopped
200ml	Olive oil

Garlic croutons

250g	Baguette, sliced into rounds
100g	Clarified butter
1	Garlic clove, peeled
Seasoning	
Grated parmesan, to serve	

METHOD

Fish soup

Heat the oil and butter in the pan, add the mirepoix (red pepper, orange zest and chopped pieces, onion, celery, leeks, garlic, bay leaf and thyme) and cook for 10 minutes. Add the prawns and tomato purée, and cook with the mirepoix for a further 10 minutes. Then add half the fish stock along with the saffron and tinned tomatoes. Bring to simmer for 5 to 10 minutes before adding the pollock. Simmer for a further 5 minutes then liquidise, adding the smoked paprika. Season to taste.

Rouille

Mix the roasted red peppers, tomato purée, ground coriander, saffron, chilli, cayenne pepper and seasoning, and blend until smooth.

Soak the bread in fish stock, then squeeze out the excess. Put the bread in a processor with the harissa paste, egg yolks, garlic and seasoning. Blend again until smooth. Finally, add the olive oil to make a mayonnaise.

Garlic croutons

Heat up the clarified butter in a pan. Cook the croutons until golden brown in small batches. Season well and rub with a little garlic.

TO SERVE

Serve the soup with the rouille, croutons and parmesan.

ROY BRETT

PHIL
HOWARD

"2005 was the high octane year with some of the country's
most flamboyant cooks descending on Northcote. Eric, Sat,
Dieter and Richard set the place alight with cracking
banter. In fact, my son still takes the mick out of Dieter
who launched into service with yet another glass of fizz
shouting "full power, full power - I drink champagne all
night and go - crazy!!"
Mad man, fantastic food."

Friday 28th January

PHIL HOWARD
The Square, London

ROAST SCALLOP WITH PUMPKIN PURÉE,
BUTTERED CHANTERELLES AND
RED WINE SAUCE
Pinot Grigio, Ramato, Venezia Giulia,
Azienda Specogna, 2002

ESCABECHE OF RED MULLET WITH
SARDINE CHANTILLY AND ANCHOVIES
Pera Manca Branco, Alentejo-Fundação Eugénio de
Almeida, 2001

ROAST COD WITH RAVIOLI OF POTATO,
VELOUTE OF CHICKEN AND
BLACK TRUFFLE
Montagny, l'er Cru, Château de la Saule, Alain Roy, 2003

LOIN OF PORK WITH SAVOY CABBAGE,
PANCETTA AND PRUNES
Pinot Noir, Yarra Ranges and Geelong, Shadowfax, 2002

WARM RICE PUDDING WITH TANGERINE,
MARINATED RAISINS AND PALMIERS
Essensia, Orange Muscat, Andrew Quady, 2003

ESCABECHE OF RED MULLET WITH SARDINE CHANTILLY AND ANCHOVIES

Serves 8

INGREDIENTS

Escabeche

300ml	Extra virgin olive oil
2	Large white onions, peeled and finely sliced
2	Large carrots, peeled and finely sliced
1	Leek, finely sliced
2	Sticks of celery, peeled and finely sliced
8	Garlic cloves, finely sliced
4	Star anise
1 tsp	Coriander seeds
1 tsp	Fennel seeds
1 pinch	Saffron
300ml	White wine vinegar
100ml	Water
2	Strips orange zest
¼	Bunch coriander, picked and washed
Salt & pepper	
100g	Plain flour
4 x 14oz	Red mullet, filleted and pin boned

For the sardine chantilly

100ml	Olive oil
1	Red onion, finely sliced
2	Garlic cloves, finely sliced
½	Red pepper, finely sliced
Salt & pepper	
100ml	Tomato passata
4	Plum tomatoes, roughly chopped
Pinch of sugar	
50g	Flour for the sardines
8	Sardine fillets
100ml	Whipping cream
100ml	Double cream

Other ingredients

1	Head of fennel, very finely shredded
Zest of ¼ orange	
100g	Black olive tapenade
16	Top quality anchovies (optional)

METHOD

Escabeche

The idea here is to make a hot 'pickle' with all the vegetables and pour it over sealed but uncooked red mullet. The residual heat will cook the fish and, left to sit for 24 hours, this develops into a phenomenal dish, full of flavour.

Place a large heavy based pan on high heat for 2 minutes. Add half the olive oil, followed by the onions, carrots, leek, celery, garlic, star anise, coriander seeds, fennel seeds and saffron. Cook for 5 minutes, stirring frequently and without seasoning. Adding salt too early will make all the vegetables soften which is not what is wanted. At this point, add the vinegar and cook, still over a high heat, until completely evaporated. If you do not reduce the vinegar away completely, the final product will simply be too sour. You can always add a bit more vinegar at the end if the dish is lacking a 'tang'.

Now add the water, the remaining olive oil, orange zest and the coriander. Bring back to the boil and simmer over a low heat for 5 minutes. Set aside at room temperature. When it has cooled, season with salt and pepper – this is a key to the dish's success and bear in mind you are seasoning something warm which will be served cold.

Now reheat this mix, flour the mullet fillet on the skin side and fry, skin side down, in a splash of olive oil for 30 seconds, turn over and seal for 5 seconds, then transfer to a shallow dish. Pour the hot vegetable marinade over the fish. Leave to cool and place in the fridge.

Sardine chantilly

Heat a heavy based pan over a medium heat, add half of the olive oil, the onions, garlic and red pepper and a generous pinch of salt. Sweat for 5 minutes, stirring frequently. Once softened, add the tomato passata and fresh tomatoes and a generous pinch of sugar. Cook very gently for a further 5 minutes.

Now flour the sardine fillets, on the skin side, season them with salt and pepper and pan fry, skin side down in olive oil – 1 minute each side will do. Add to the tomato mix, stir gently, cover with a lid or disc of parchment paper and cook in an oven at 110°C/225°F/gas mark ¼ for half an hour.

Remove from the oven, stir briefly and pass through a coarse sieve. This should give rise to a delicious oily, sardine vinaigrette. Adjust the seasoning if necessary, place in a small container, spoon off any excess oil and chill.

TO SERVE

Remove the mullet from the fridge half an hour before serving. Pour the whipping and double cream into a large bowl, season with salt and pepper and whip until peaks form. Add a tablespoon of the sardine paste and fold in with a rubber spatula. Whisk further if it is not thick.

Season the fennel, add the orange zest, mix briefly and divide among 8 plates. Place a fillet of red mullet on top, along with plenty of the vegetable marinade. Put 3 small spoons of tapenade on each plate and garnish with a quenelle of sardine chantilly (spoon it onto the plate using a hot dessert spoon) and 2 anchovies, if desired.

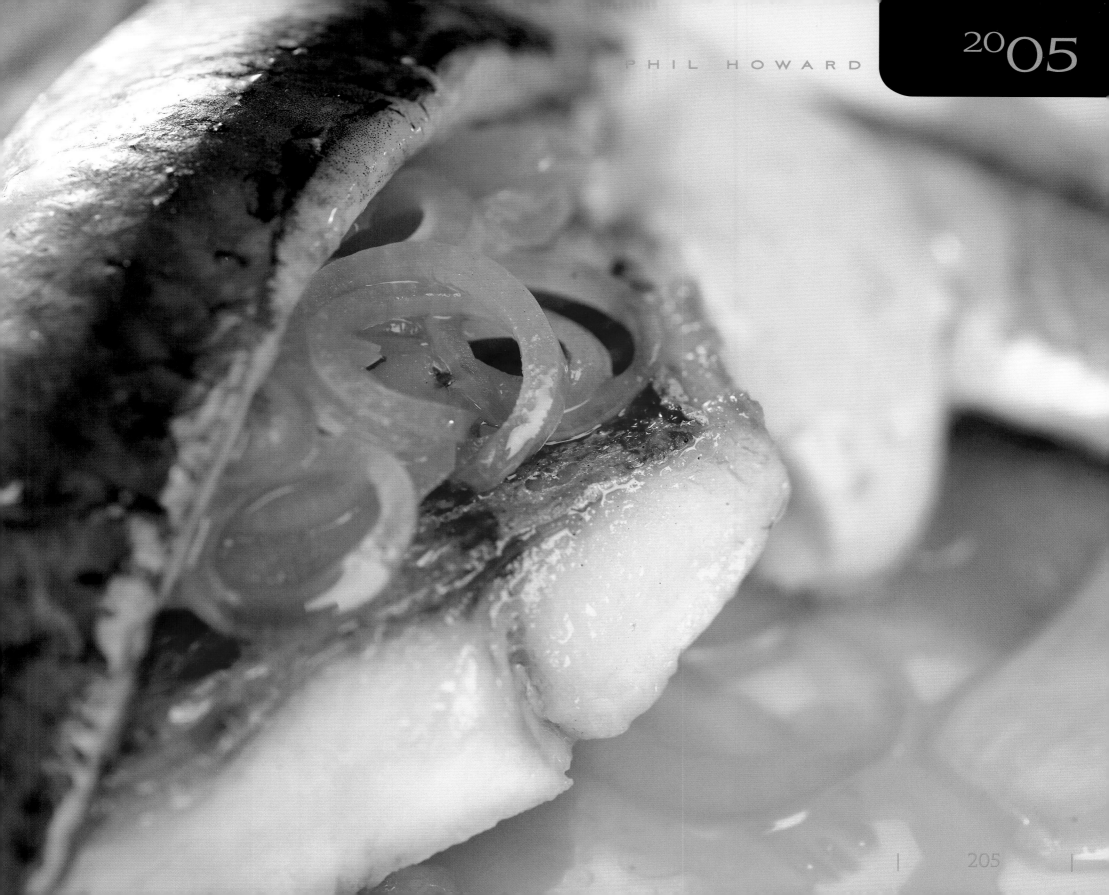

RICHARD CORRIGAN

"Like everyone who has entered the hospitality profession, in order to stay in it you need to be obsessed and quite possibly mad. I'm both."

Saturday 29th January

RICHARD CORRIGAN
Lindsay House Restaurant, London

BUTTER POACHED HADDOCK WITH CAVIAR,
LANGOUSTINE AND CHAMP
La Bernardine M. Chapoutier,
Châteauneuf-du-Pape Blanc, 2003

CRUBEENS, JABUGA HAM WITH
WOODLAND SORREL,
BEETROOT AND HORSERADISH
REMOULADE
Tokay Pinot-Gris, Le Fromentau, Josmeyer, 2002

ROAST FILLET OF WEST CORK BEEF,
PARSNIP AND WATERCRESS,
PÉRIGORD TRUFFLE
Château Marsac-Séquineau,
Cru Bourgeois-Margaux, 1996

CROZIER BLUE SOAKED IN BANYULS
Côteaux du Layon, Saint-Aubin de Luigné,
Domaine des Forges, 2003

ENGLISH RHUBARB WITH
ORGANIC YOGHURT

CHOCOLATE SOUFFLÉ WITH SEVILLE
ORANGE AND ALMOND TART
Maury Domaine Pouderoux, 2001

CRUBEENS, JABUGA HAM WITH WOODLAND SORREL, BEETROOT AND HORSERADISH REMOULADE

Serves 4

INGREDIENTS

4	Pigs' trotters, soaked in brine overnight
1	Onion, chopped
2	Carrots, chopped
1	Garlic bulb
1	Bouquet garni
1	Ham hock
	Mustard
	Parsley
	Flour
1	Egg (beaten)
	Breadcrumbs
40g	Parmesan, grated

To serve

Woodland sorrel or watercress

Beetroot and horseradish remoulade (grated beetroot and horseradish)

Jabuga/Serrano ham

METHOD

Wash brine off pigs' trotters, cover them with water, add chopped onion, chopped carrots, a bulb of garlic and bouquet garni. Bring to the boil and skim. Simmer for 3 hours until the meat falls off the bone. After one hour of cooking add the ham hock (the ham hock will only need cooking for 2 hours).

Remove from the pot, lay all the meat on a tray and separate fat, gristle, meat and bones.

Shred the ham hock off the bone, mix with nuggets of trotter meat, add a little gristle and half of the fat, mustard and parsley.

Line out the four trotter skins and spoon in the ham mix. Roll each trotter into the shape of a ballotine and refrigerate.

When cold cut each ballotine into quarters length ways, then cut into even-sized pieces, the size of a thumb nail.

Dip into flour, beaten egg and breadcrumbs.

Deep fry until crispy and serve with beetroot and horseradish remoulade, woodland sorrel/ watercress, Jabuga/Serrano ham and sprinkle with the parmesan.

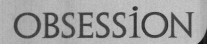

NIGEL HAWORTH

"To be Obsessed with regionality is to love your roots and express your belonging."

Sunday 30th January

NIGEL HAWORTH
Northcote, Lancashire

REG JOHNSON'S SEARED CORNFED
DUCKLING, SPICY RED CABBAGE, MEAD
Gewürztraminer, les Folastries, Josmeyer, 2002

CORNISH CRAB RAVIOLI, WHITE LEEK
BROTH, TRUFFLE
Malvasia, Colheita Cask 3, Vinhos Barbeito, 1993

FARMER SHARP'S HERDWICK MUTTON,
MATURED FOR 3 WEEKS, BRAISED SLOWLY
WITH ENGLISH ONIONS,
HERB DUMPLINGS, BUTTERED ROOTS
Rasteau, Cuvée Prestige, André Roméro, 2000

LEAGRAM'S ORGANIC LANCASHIRE CURD,
ONION MARMALADE, QUAIL EGG
Sauvignon, Late Harvest, Semi-Dulce, Rueda 2001

QUEEN OF PUDDINGS SOUFFLÉ,
LEMON AND CRÈME FRAÎCHE ICE CREAM
Elysium, Black Muscat Quady, 2003

GOOSNARGH CORNFED DUCKLING BREAST, DUCK STRAWS, SPICY RED CABBAGE, MEAD

Serves 4

INGREDIENTS

1 x 2.5kg	Cornfed Goosnargh duck
50ml	Duck fat
Salt & pepper	
100ml	Duck sauce
4	Duck straws (see below)
4	Baby turnips (see below)
Mead syrup (see below)	
Red wine syrup (see below)	
Turnip purée (see below)	
Spicy red cabbage (see below)	

Mead syrup

350ml	Mead

Red wine syrup

250ml	Shiraz wine
60g	Sugar

Duck straws

100g	Flaked slow cooked duck (leg meat)
20g	Duck fat
8	Green peppercorns, crushed
Pinch of salt	
2	Spring rolls sheets
50g	Plain flour with a few drops of water (to make a thick paste to stick the pastry down)

Spicy red cabbage

½ head	Red cabbage
15g	Coarse sea salt
100ml	Sesame oil
50g	Icing sugar
50ml	Sherry
50ml	White wine vinegar
1	Red chilli, finely chopped
10g	Fresh ginger, grated

Turnip purée

200g	Unsalted butter
200g	Turnip, peeled and diced
100ml	Whipping cream
Pinch of salt	

Baby turnips

4	Baby turnips
100ml	Water
40g	Butter
Salt	
Sugar	

METHOD

Take the duck and remove the legs (reserve for the slow cooked duck straws). Remove the excess duck fat and break off the undercarriage. Render the duck crown in a medium-size frying pan with the 50ml of duck fat – this should be done slowly until the fat is golden and will take about 10 minutes.

Remove the duck breasts from the crown and allow to cool. Wrap them individually in cling film and then into a vacuum pack bag and seal. Cook off the breasts in a water bath at 68°C for 27 minutes and reserve.

When you are ready to assemble the dish, place the duck breasts skin side down in a little of the remaining duck fat and fry the duck breasts carefully until golden brown and crispy. Season with salt and pepper. Remove from the pan and allow to rest on a cooling rack for at least 2 minutes.

Mead syrup

Reduce down to approximately 50ml. Pour into a small pipette bottle and allow to cool.

Red wine syrup

Reduce the ingredients down to 50ml, place into a small pipette bottle and allow to cool.

Duck straws

In a mixing bowl add the duck, duck fat, green peppercorns and pinch of salt. Mix all the ingredients together carefully until a rough mixture is formed, then roll the duck into pencil thickness strips approximately 18cm long.

Cut the spring roll sheets into half lengthways and then brush each sheet down the sides and along one end with the paste.

Place the rolled duck on the opposite end, roll the pastry tightly around the duck mix and crimp at both ends, Repeat with the other straws. When you are ready, fry in a deep fat fryer at 180°C for 2-3 minutes until golden. Remove from the fryer and reserve (cut off one end on a slant before serving).

Spicy red cabbage

Finely slice the red cabbage and mix with sea salt, leave for 4 hours. Wash off all the salt thoroughly and drain well.

Preheat a large heavy bottom pan, add the sesame oil and quickly fry off the cabbage without colour for a few minutes. Push the cabbage to one side of the pan, sprinkle the other side with icing sugar, allow to caramelise then add the sherry, white wine vinegar, ginger and chilli, mix the red cabbage in well and continue to fry for approximately 2 minutes. Remove from the pan and reserve.

Turnip purée

Melt the butter in a thick bottom pan, sweat off the turnips carefully without colour, add the cream and reduce until the cream almost splits. Blitz in a Thermomix until it makes a smooth purée, season with salt, pass through a fine sieve and then place into a piping bag ready for use.

Baby turnips

Cook the turnips in the water and butter, add a pinch of salt and a large pinch of sugar. Boil carefully and leave al dente.

TO SERVE

Reheat the duck sauce, red cabbage, turnip purée and baby turnips. Deep fry the duck straws. Reserve. Place the red cabbage in the middle of the plate, remove the fillet from the duck and place to the side of the cabbage. Carve the duck breast in half lengthways and place onto the cabbage. Garnish with the duck straws, turnip purée and baby turnips, then sauce over with the duck sauce and finish with the two syrups.

20O4

Year four: Peter Gordon came in short long pants. John Campbell kicked all the staff out of the kitchen, his usual focused self. Rowley Leigh wasn't happy with Craig's wines, and changed some of them on the day. Darina Allen arrived from Ireland and promptly sent us out for Kerrygold butter, a taste of home and some decent organic cider vinegar because she said that ours was too harsh.

Peter Gordon's flavours in the smoky coconut and tamarind laska were just incredible and to finish – a stunning chocolate cake with cranberry and rose-water compote. John's menu was technically astute, executing some excellent dishes none better than the turbot braised with oxtail and slow cooked veal cheeks – the mandarin parfait and espuma was a knock-out.

Rowley Leigh cooked a favourite of ours with his partridge with pigs' trotters, chestnuts and lentils, a dish with influences from France; he also brought a fantastic truffle brie which was sensational.

It was an honour to have Darina Allen cooking with all the flair of the Irish dynasty of Ballymaloe, ably assisted by a former student Breda Murphy, who now runs Food by Breda Murphy Deli Bistro in Whalley, Lancashire. Her potato, parsley and chorizo soup with her famous soda bread was simplicity itself. Darina's husband Timmy spent the whole day preparing the breads and cheese biscuits alongside our own team, sharing his knowledge which we still use today.

Phil Howard pulled the rabbit out of the hat with a great monkfish dish that was on the bone. I can't imagine anyone else cooking monkfish on the bone like that – especially not for 90 people.

This was the year Giorgio Locatelli walked in to the kitchen with his right-hand man Frederico. Phil and I were getting ready for the evening service at the side of the fish corner when suddenly we noticed a large presence. Giorgio walked in wearing a full-length moleskin coat, trilby and all. The Italian mafia had arrived. A man of great presence, Giorgio brought his family and it was a joy to have Plaxy and his daughter Margherita so involved in the festival. Margherita was a little star full of fun and mischief – she stole the show in many ways.

Giorgio cooked risotto with Barolo wine and he finished the dish with Castelmagno cheese. He told an epic story about this cheese, which was a mark of his roots from his home village where it had been hung and dried for three years: the story lasted for days and was long and passionate.

This was the year I made treacle salmon for the first time. I was looking to do a regional salmon dish, which I marinated and cured with treacle. I used to tell the customers that there was a very famous treacle mine in Sabden – Lancashire legend has it that it was mined by 'The Treacle Miners' – and a surprising amount of people believed me!

PETER GORDON

"I am obsessed by the 'new' of discovering new flavours, tastes and textures from around the world. I can't think of a healthier Obsession as it also encourages exploration of other cultures and an understanding of other people. At the moment I'm obsessed with tapioca and tofu (recurring Obsessions I have to say) and it's a fun Obsession."

Monday 26th January

PETER GORDON

The Providores and Tapa Room, London

A GRILLED SCALLOP AND GREEN
PLANTAIN CRISPS WITH SWEET CHILLI
SAUCE AND CRÈME FRAÎCHE
Tokay Pinot-Gris, Le Fromentau, Josmeyer, 2002

SMOKY COCONUT AND TAMARIND LAKSA
WITH GREEN TEA NOODLES, MORELS AND
A PRAWN HIJIKI DUMPLING
Chardonnay, Barossa Vines, Grant Burge, 2001

GRILLED HALIBUT ON CHORIZO MASH
WITH SNAILS, EDAMAME AND YUZU
POMEGRANATE DRESSING
Cartuxa Branco de Évora, Reserva-Fundação Eugénio
de Almeida, 2000

ROAST GOOSNARGH DUCK BREAST ON
SWEET POTATO MISO MASH
AND CAVOLO NERO WITH SHERRY AND
CHILLI POACHED QUINCE
Zinfandel, Sonoma Country-Pedroncelli, 1999

CHOCOLATE CAKE WITH SALTED ALMOND
CREAM AND CRANBERRY
ROSEWATER COMPOTE
Recioto di Soave-Anselmi, I Capitelli, 1995

CHOCOLATE CAKE WITH SALTED ALMOND CREAM AND CRANBERRY ROSEWATER COMPOTE

Serves 10

This flourless cake is always a winner – rich and mousse-like, you don't need too large a portion. I team it with a lovely fragrant cranberry compote and give it an edge with the salted Marcona almond cream. These are the best almonds in the world and the saltiness really brings the dish together.

INGREDIENTS

Chocolate mousse cake

300g	Dark chocolate (minimum 65% cocoa butter)
150g	Unsalted butter
6	Eggs
60g	Caster sugar

Cranberry rosewater compote

100g	Caster sugar
30ml	Lemon juice
2	Strips lemon peel
½ tsp	Pure vanilla extract
200g	Fresh cranberries
20ml	Rosewater

Almond cream

100ml	Double cream
50g	Mascarpone
1 tsp	Caster sugar
12	Salted Marcona almonds, crushed

METHOD

Chocolate mousse cake

Preheat the oven to 180°C/350°F/gas mark 4.

Wrap tin foil around the base of 10 ring moulds and sit on a baking tray lined with a sil-pat or baking parchment.

Melt the chocolate and butter in a double boiler over simmering water. Once it's almost completely melted, separate your eggs. Add all but 2 tablespoons of the sugar to the whites, the remainder to the yolks. Beat the whites to a soft meringue.

Whisk the yolks and sugar for 20 seconds, then mix in the melted chocolate. Stir one-third of the meringue into this, then gently fold in the remainder. Fill your ring moulds and bake for 9 minutes. Remove from the oven and leave to cool for at least 3 hours before serving.

Cranberry rosewater compote

Place the sugar, lemon juice and peel in a small pan and slowly bring to the boil. Once the sugar has dissolved add the cranberries and cook gently, stirring frequently, until they begin to bleed their juice into the syrup and burst. Stir in the vanilla then take off the heat. Gently stir in the rosewater, cover tightly and leave to cool. If upon tasting the compote the rosewater isn't pronounced enough, add some more to taste.

Almond cream

Lightly whip everything except the almonds to a soft peak. Mix in all but 1 teaspoon of the almonds and whip to a firm peak.

TO SERVE

Simply dollop the cream on to the cake and sprinkle the reserved crushed almonds on top, then spoon the compote around the cake.

JOHN
CAMPBELL

"My Obsession started at an early age, about four years old,
and I very quickly realised food made people happy and was
an emotive part of what we did every day. Later on in my
gastronomic infancy, perhaps pre-teens, I was very clear in what
I wanted to do for the rest of my life - I wanted to cook and
make people smile. Each plate of food is unique and can never be
recreated; although consistency plays a huge part in our focus
during a busy service, each dish is unique and a one-off.

The very foundation of life relies on food; creating beautiful
harmonies from nature's larder is one of the greatest gifts
mankind possesses. Food is about bringing people together, it is
about comfort and memories; nothing is more powerful or emotive
than food glorious food."

Tuesday 27th January

JOHN CAMPBELL
Vineyard at Stockcross, Berkshire

RISOTTO OF WILD MUSHROOMS,
TRUFFLE JELLY
Pinot Grigio, Venezia Giulia-Vinnaioli Jermann, 2000

BALLOTTINE OF ORGANIC CHICKEN
AND FOIE GRAS, PARSNIP PURÉE
Viognier, Eden Valley-Heggies, 2002

TURBOT
BRAISED OXTAIL
Sancerre Rouge, Pascal Jolivet, 2002

SLOW COOKED VEAL CHEEKS
SMOKED POTATO,
HORSERADISH EMULSION
Pinot Noir, Geelong and
Yarra Valley-Shadowfax, 2001

"MANDARIN"
PARFAIT, E'SPUMA, GRANITA
Essensia, Orange Muscat, Andrew Quady, 2000

INGREDIENTS

Malt swipe

100g	Liquid malt extract
50g	Water
1.5g	Agar

Mandarin e'spuma

400g	Reduced mandarin purée (1kg slowly reduced to 400g)
400g	Natural yoghurt
2	Leaves of gelatine

Mandarin granita

500g	Fresh mandarin juice
120g	Sugar
250g	Water
400g	Reduced mandarin purée (1kg slowly reduced to 400g)
3	Leaves of gelatine

Mandarin parfait

15	Egg yolks
250g	Caster sugar
5	Leaves of gelatine
300g	Double cream
250g	Mandarin reduction (1kg slowly reduced to 400g)
100g	Mandarin juice

Chocolate spray

300g	Dark chocolate
150g	Cocoa butter

Hobnob biscuit crumbs

300g	Plain flour
300g	Oats
395g	Demerara sugar
450g	Butter
15g	Baking powder
15g	Salt

Spiced jelly

50g	Light brown sugar
50g	Madeira
50g	Marsala
75g	Port
1/2	Vanilla pod
1	Clove
½	Star anise
2	Leaves of gelatine

METHOD

Malt swipe

Boil all the ingredients together and allow to cool to room temperature. The mixture will set firm. Blitz for 5 minutes in a Thermomix until smooth and reserve.

Mandarin e'spuma

Soak the gelatine in cold water. Warm the purée and add the softened gelatine. Mix well, whisk into the yoghurt and then pour into a 1 litre iSi cream whipper. Charge with two n20 gas canisters. Place in a fridge until required.

Mandarin granita

Soak the gelatine in cold water. Place all the other ingredients into a saucepan. Heat this syrup gently to dissolve the sugar, then add the gelatine. Mix well. Pour into a large tray and place in a freezer. Break up using a whisk every 20-30 minutes.

Mandarin parfait

Soak the gelatine in cold water. Whisk the egg yolks for 5 minutes. Boil the sugar to 120°C and pour onto the whisked yolks. Add the gelatine to the hot yolk/sugar mixture. Whisk until it cools to blood temperature. Semi whip the cream and fold half into the yolk/sugar mixture. Gently fold in the mandarin purée and fresh juice. Fold in the rest of the cream, place into cone-shaped moulds and freeze. Once frozen remove from the moulds and spray with chocolate.

Chocolate spray

Melt both ingredients together to just above blood temperature. Place in a small art paint sprayer.

When the parfaits are frozen place on a small tray with a little space around them to allow easy spraying. The mix will freeze immediately and form a shell. Return to the freezer until needed.

Hobnob biscuit crumbs

Cream the butter and sugar together for 5 minutes. Add the flour, oats, baking powder and salt. Mix gently to form a paste. Roll between greaseproof paper and bake in a pre-heated oven at 180°C/350°F/ gas mark 4 for 12-15 minutes until golden brown. Leave to cool and then break up into crumbs. Reserve in an air-tight container.

Spiced jelly

Soak the gelatine in cold water. Place the rest of the ingredients into a pan and reduce to 150g. Leave to cool for 10 minutes, then add the soaked gelatine. Pour into a small container and place in a fridge until set.

TO SERVE

Take a rectangular plate and place ½ tablespoon of the malt swipe in the bottom left corner. Using the back of a spoon and following the shape of an arc, drag the swipe mixture to the bottom right corner of the plate.

Place the parfait in the middle of the plate, towards the left. Add two spoons of hobnob biscuit crumbs to the right of the parfait. At the top of the plate, in the middle, place a large scoop of the spiced jelly at an angle.

Next, in the bottom of a tall shot glass, place a little hobnob biscuit crumb. On top of this fill the glass halfway up with the mandarin granita. Place the glass at the top of the plate towards the right-hand side. Fill the glass to the top with the mandarin e'spuma.

Serve immediately.

ROWLEY LEIGH

"My Obsession with food comes partly from the fact that I'm very greedy and I like food. I always grew up with good food and I always thought it rather mattered what you put in your mouth. I just love the business of transforming ingredients into something delicious."

Wednesday 28th January

ROWLEY LEIGH
Kensington Place, London

TUNA TARTAR WITH GOLDEN BEETS,
CHILLI AND CRÈME FRAÎCHE
Esporão Reserva, Alentejo-Herdade do Esporão, 2001

PIKE AND LOBSTER SAUSAGE
WITH CABBAGE
Montagny l'er Cru, Château de Saule-Alain Roy, 2002

PARTRIDGE WITH PIGS' TROTTERS,
CHESTNUTS AND LENTILS
Château Haut Pezat-St Emilion Grand Cru, 2000

TRUFFLED BRIE CHEESE
Champagne Vilmart and Cie, Grand Cellier d'Or,
Rilly-La-Montagne, 1997

BAKED QUINCES WITH AMARETTI CRUMBLE
AND VIN SANTO ZABAGLIONE
Vin Santo Villa di Vetrice, 1985

INGREDIENTS

2	Pigs' trotters
2	Onions, 1 sliced, 1 whole
1	Carrot, chopped
	Thyme sprigs
	Bay leaves
12	Peppercorns
100g	Green lentils
8	Cloves
1	Chilli
4	French (red-legged) partridges
	Salt & pepper
25g	Butter
1 tbsp	Cooking oil
1	Glass dry white wine
100ml	Chicken stock
16	Braised chestnuts

METHOD

Split the trotters (or ask your butcher to!) in half and rinse them in cold water. Put them in a pan with a sliced onion and carrot, thyme, bay leaves and the peppercorns. Bring to a boil, skim well and poach very gently for three hours. Leave to cool overnight.

Rinse the lentils and cover with cold water, adding an onion studded with 8 cloves, 2 bay leaves, a sprig of thyme and a chilli. Bring to a simmer and cook gently until the lentils begin to soften. Allow to cool.

Season the partridges very well with salt and pepper. Heat a heavy frying pan and melt a third of the butter together with the tablespoon of cooking oil. Brown the partridges in this fat on a steady heat, turning them three ways so that they are evenly coloured. Place the partridges, breast side up, on a deep roasting tray and place in a hot oven (230°C/450°F/gas mark 8) for 12 to 14 minutes. Remove the birds from the oven: they should still be slightly pink, but feel firm to the touch. Place the partridges on a plate in a warm place and leave to rest for 15 minutes.

With a small sharp knife, carefully remove the bones from the trotters and cut the meat into 2cm squares. Heat a knob of butter in a skillet and colour the trotter meat gently before adding the lentils, minus the onion and chilli.

Pour the
which the pa
and scrape u
adding the ch
these togeth
before whiski
Strain into a g
To dress,
centre of the
partridge, tr
around. Sauc

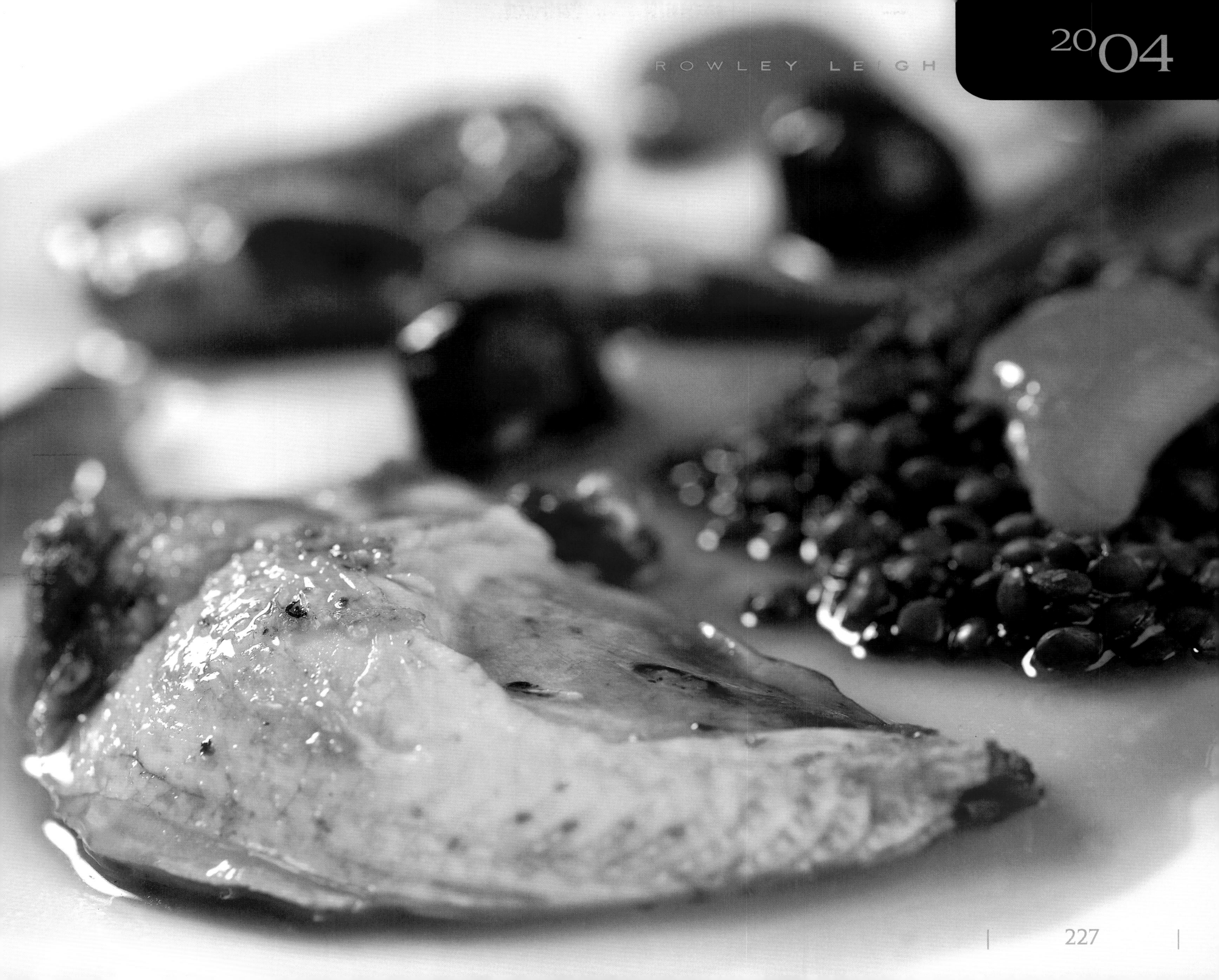

DARINA ALLEN

"I've been obsessed with cooking and using really good ingredients since I was a tiny child because I grew up with a kitchen garden, hens and a house cow. But now as a grandma my main Obsession is passing on the skills to my grandchildren to cook and sow seed and grow things so that they can grow their own ingredients. It's getting more difficult to source really good fresh produce – and that's what good health and good food are based on."

Thursday 29th January

DARINA ALLEN
Ballymaloe Cookery School, Co. Cork

POTATO, CHORIZO AND
FLAT PARSLEY SOUP
Marqués de Murrieta,
"Capellaina", Blanco Gran Reserva-Marques de
Murrieta, 1997

A PLATE OF SMOKED IRISH FISH WITH
HORSERADISH SAUCE, MUSTARD AND DILL
MAYO, CUCUMBER PICKLE, LEMON WEDGE
WHITE SODA BREAD, BALLYMALOE BROWN
YEAST BREAD
Chardonnay, "Wild Boy", Santa Barbara,
California-Au Bon Climat, 2000

ROAST FREE-RANGE ORGANIC PORK
WITH SPICED AUBERGINES AND
SCALLION CHAMP
SALAD OF ORGANIC LEAVES
Esporão Reserva, Alentejo-Herdade de Esporão, 2000

SELECTION OF IRISH AND ENGLISH
FARMHOUSE CHEESES
AND BALLYMALOE CHEESE BISCUITS
Vinhos Barbeito, Boal, Colheita Cask 81a, 1995

YOGHURT AND CARDAMOM CREAM WITH
POMEGRANATES AND ROSE
BLOSSOM WATER
Late Harvest Muscat-Brown Brothers, 2002

INGREDIENTS

50g	Butter
550g	Peeled diced potatoes, 1cm dice
110g	Diced onions, 1cm dice
Salt and freshly ground pepper	
1 litre or	Homemade chicken stock
	vegetable stock
100ml	Creamy milk
18	Slices of chorizo
Snipped flat parsley sprigs	

METHOD

Melt the butter in a heavy saucepan. When it foams, add the potatoes and onions and toss them in the butter until well coated. Sprinkle with salt and a few grinds of pepper. Cover with a butter wrapper or paper lid and the lid of the saucepan. Sweat on a gentle heat for approximately 10 minutes. Meanwhile bring the stock to the boil; when the vegetables are soft but not coloured add the stock and continue to cook until the vegetables are soft. Purée the soup in a blender or food processor. Taste and adjust seasoning. Thin with creamy milk to the required consistency.

Just before serving cook the slices of chorizo for a minute or two on each side in a non-stick pan – oil will render out of the chorizo.

Serve three slices of chorizo on top of each bowl, sprinkle a few flat parsley sprigs on top, drizzle a little chorizo oil haphazardly over the soup and serve immediately.

Most people have potatoes and onions in the house even if the cupboard is otherwise bare so you could make this simply delicious soup at a moment's notice. While the vegetables are sweating, pop a few white soda scones or cheddar cheese scones into the oven and wow, won't they be impressed.

DARINA ALLEN

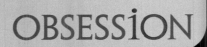

PHIL HOWARD

"I just remember meeting some great people this year. John Campbell, for one, has become a great friend over the years. I have dipped into Darina Allen's cookbook many times and I am reminded of how important this "cross pollination" of ideas that happens at The Festival is. The phenomenal local produce is showcased once again with the use of Lancashire venison."

Friday 30th January

PHIL HOWARD
The Square, London

SAUTÉ OF TIGER PRAWNS
WITH A TARTE FINE OF ONIONS
AND THYME
Pinot Gris, Boyzone Vineyard, Marlborough,
Kim Crawford, 2003

OXTAIL SOUP WITH CAULIFLOWER FOAM
Palo Cortado Regenta, Sánchez

LOIN OF MONKFISH,
SAVOY CABBAGE AND LENTILS
Menetou-Salon,
Clos des Blanchais, Domaine Henry Pellé, 2002

LOIN OF VENISON WITH PORT GLAZED
PEARS, POMMES SALARDAISE AND
CELERIAC PURÉE
Cartuxa de Évora Reserva-Fundação Eugénio de
Almeida, 1997

FONDANT OF BITTER CHOCOLATE
WITH MALTED MILK ICE CREAM
Banyuls, Vin Doux Naturel, M. Chapoutier, 1997

SAUTÉ OF TIGER PRAWNS WITH A TART FINE OF ONION AND THYME

Serves 8

INGREDIENTS

175g	Unsalted butter
8	Large white onions, sliced
Salt & pepper	
1 tsp	Thyme leaves
250g	Ceps
250ml	Whipping cream
300g	Puff pastry
40	Medium-sized, raw Tiger prawns
6	Garlic cloves, 5 finely sliced, 1 crushed

METHOD

Onions

In a large heavy based pan melt 75g of the butter and sweat the onions. This process is key. Start the onions over a high heat and without salt. If you add the salt too early it will turn to a mush. Let the onions start to soften and release their moisture. Cover with a lid, if it seems too dry, but stir every half a minute.

After about 5 minutes, by which time you should have a soft mix, add the salt and a twist or two of pepper, turn the heat down and continue to sweat until you have a pale golden, soft, sweet fondue of onions. Stir in half the thyme leaves, remove from the heat and drain in a colander. Chill.

Cep purée

Melt 50g of butter in a heavy based pan. Finely slice the ceps and add to the pan with a generous pinch of salt. Sweat until softened, add the cream, cover and cook for 10 minutes over a low heat. Blend to a smooth purée, pass through a fine sieve, transfer to a small pan, cover and reserve. This will make more than you need, but any excess can be thinned down with chicken stock and milk to make a delicious soup.

Tart fine

Roll out the puff pastry on a cold surface to a neat 30x12cm rectangle. Prick with a fork. Spread the onion mix evenly over the pastry, leaving a ½cm gap along the long sides. Bake in a hot oven at 200°C/400°F/gas mark 6 until the pastry is crisp and golden – about 20 minutes. Remove from the oven, place on a cooling rack and allow to rest for 5 minutes.

TO SERVE

Melt the remaining 50g butter in a large heavy based frying pan. Just at the point where it starts to smell nutty throw in the prawns and season. Sauté over a high heat for 2 minutes – turning the prawns half way. Add the garlic and remaining thyme leaves, toss once more and tip onto a serving dish.

Warm through the cep purée and place half a teaspoon in the centre of 8 plates. Cut the tart fine into 8 slices and sit one on each plate on the cep purée.

Now place a generous spoon of purée onto each plate and finish by placing 4 prawns on each piece of tart. Drizzle the pan juices around and serve immediately.

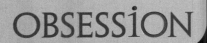

GIORGIO LOCATELLI

"Food for me is a way of life – the rhythm of the restaurant has dictated the rhythm of my life from when I was a young boy.

Creating the perfect sense of conviviality day in, day out, is the most gratifying thing in my career and is what is behind the passion I have for food."

Saturday 31st January

GIORGIO LOCATELLI
Locanda Locatelli, London

GRISSINI WITH PARMA HAM
CHICKPEA FOCACCIA
MIXED FOCACCIA, ONION, ROSEMARY
Taittinger Brut Réserve NV

CAPESANTE ALLO ZAFFERANO
[PAN-FRIED SCALLOPS WITH SAFFRON]
VINAIGRETTE
Taburno Greco, Cantine Del Taburno, 2002

RAVIOLI DI CODA DI MANZO
OXTAIL RAVIOLI
Vernaccia di San Gimignano, 2002

RISOTTO AL BAROLO E CASTELMAGNO
[BAROLO RISOTTO WITH CASTELMAGNO
CHEESE]
Barbera d'Alba "Ornati" Parussa, 2001

OCA ARROSTO CON VERZE E
FERGATO GRASSO
[ROAST GOOSE WITH SAVOY CABBAGE
AND FOIE GRAS]
Barolo, E. Pira, 1999

TIRAMISU
Targa Riserva 1840, Marsala Superiore Riserva, Florio

OXTAIL RAVIOLI

Serves 4

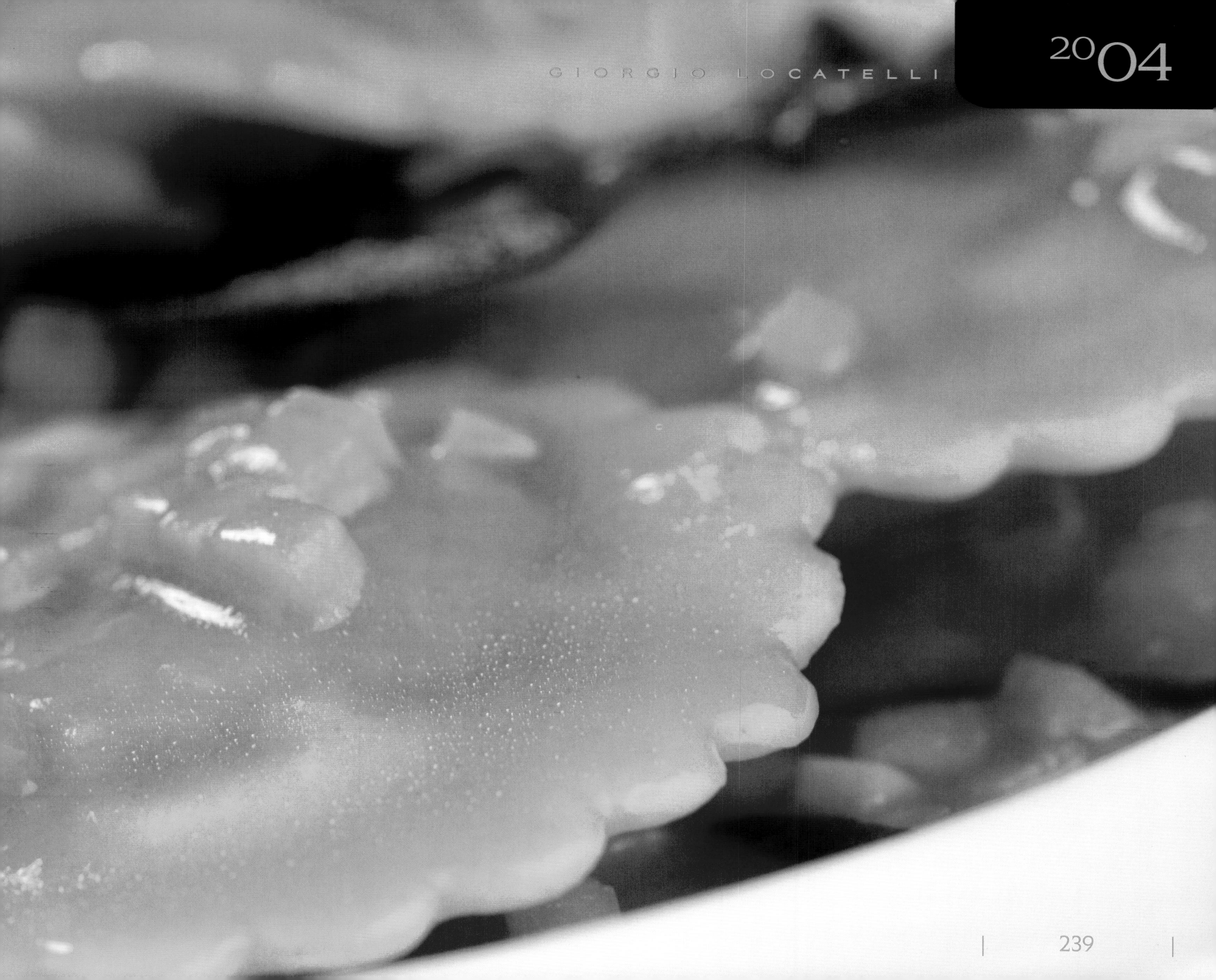

OXTAIL RAVIOLI

Serves 4

INGREDIENTS

3 tbsp	Extra-virgin olive oil
1	Oxtail
4	Chopped garlic cloves
2	Carrots cut into large dice
2	Banana shallots (or 4 small ones) cut into large dice
1	Bouquet garni, made with a sprig of rosemary and a small bunch of sage
70g	Pork belly
2 litres	Chicken stock
350ml	Dry white wine
50g	Tomato paste
40g	Grated parmesan cheese
1	Egg
20g	Unsalted butter
1	Carrot, finely diced

Pasta

500g	00 (doppio zero) flour, sieved
3	Large eggs plus 2 extra (large) egg yolks (all at room temperature)
Pinch of salt	

METHOD

Filling and sauce

To make the filling, cut the oxtail into 4 or 5 pieces, rinse, put in a large pot, cover with cold water and bring to the boil, then skim, drain and set aside. Put the extra-virgin olive oil in another pan big enough to hold the oxtail, with the chopped garlic cloves, the carrots and the banana shallots, and cook gently for about 10 minutes, then add the bouquet garni, the pork belly and the oxtail. Cook gently for 5-6 minutes, then add the white wine and continue to cook until the wine evaporates.

Next add the tomato paste and the chicken stock, bring to the boil, skim, then turn down the heat and simmer for 45-60 minutes, until the meat falls apart. Separate the meat and vegetables into two different bowls. Put the remaining cooking liquid through a fine sieve into a clean pan and put back on the heat and simmer until it thickens to a sauce-like consistency.

Flake the oxtail meat with your fingers, breaking the meat down as much as possible, discard the bones and any fatty parts (don't chop with the knife or you will lose the nice 'stringiness'). Mix in half of the reserved vegetables, put into a food processor and whizz to a rough paste. Add the grated parmesan cheese, taste and season, then add the egg and mix together – the mixture should come together easily in soft balls, but if it seems too dry, mix in a little of the sauce.

Pasta

Preferably make the pasta by hand – especially if you are making a relatively small quantity like this, which will be difficult for a food processor to mix well. Sieve the flour into a clean bowl, then turn it out into a mound on a clean surface and make a well in the middle (in Italy we call this the fontana di farina 'fountain of flour'). Sprinkle the salt into the well and then crack in the eggs.

Have a bowl of water on one side so you can dip your hands into it and wet them, to help bring the dough together if it is being stubborn towards the end of kneading. To begin, break the yolks with the fingertips of one hand, and then begin to move your fingers in a circular motion, gradually incorporating the flour, until you have worked in enough to start bringing it together in a ball. Then you can start to work the ball of dough by pushing it with the heel of your hand, then folding the top back on itself, turning it a little clockwise, and repeating, again and again, for about 10 minutes, wetting your hands if it helps, until the dough is springy, but still feels quite firm and difficult to work.

Don't worry that the dough feels hard; after it has relaxed for a while it will be perfect.

Divide the dough into 2 balls, wrap each in a damp cloth and rest for about an hour before using.

Roll the first ball of dough with a rolling pin (keep the rest covered in the damp cloth) – until it is about 1cm thick and will go through the pasta machine comfortably (if it is too thick, the pasta machine will have to use so much force to make it go through that it will damage the machine and squeeze out too much moisture in the process, so the pasta will be dry). There isn't an exact number of times you will need to feed the pasta through the machine – each time you make it might be slightly different (and not every pasta machine has the same number of settings), but use the next few steps as a guide, and after a while you will get the hang of rolling the pasta and feel your own way.

Put the machine on the first (thickest) setting to start with, then feed the piece of pasta through the machine turning the handle with one hand, and supporting the dough as it comes through with the other. Then change to the second setting, and put it through again. Repeat another 2-3 times, taking the setting down one each time. Don't worry if the pasta appears slightly streaky, this should disappear as you carry on rolling it.

Next, fold the strip of pasta back on itself, put the machine back onto the first setting and put the pasta through again. Repeat 3-4 more times, again taking the setting down one each time and you will see that the pasta begins to take on a sheen. As it begins to get longer, you will find that you have to pull it very gently, so that it doesn't begin to concertina. You shouldn't need to dust it with flour, unless you feel it is too soft and likely to stick and stretch too much.

Now you need to cut your strip in half. Keep one half covered in a damp cloth, then fold the length of the other strip into three, bringing one end in and the other over the top of that, so that the pasta is the same width as the machine. Roll it with the rolling pin, so it is no more than 0.5cm thick, then put the machine back onto the first setting and feed the pasta through – the opposite way this time, i.e. widthways, not lengthways. The idea of changing direction is to put equal elasticity and strength throughout the pasta. Keep feeding it through this way, taking it down two or three settings as you go.

Finally, fold the pasta back on itself, then put the machine back onto the first setting, and take it down again through the settings until it is about 1.5mm thick.

Repeat with the other half strip, then the other ball of dough.

Ravioli

To make the ravioli mark the halfway point of your first strip of pasta and brush one half with beaten egg, then place little mounds of filling (about a teaspoonful to make a round mound with a circumference of about 4cm) two abreast on the half that is brushed with egg, leaving a space of about 3-4cm between each mound. You should have enough to make around 30-32 so each person will get 7 to 8 ravioli each.

Fold the other half of the pasta over the top, carefully matching the long edges down one side and pressing them together, then doing the same the other side. Gently press down around each raviolo (don't worry if you compress the filling a little as you go).

Using a fluted ring cutter about 1cm bigger in circumference than the filling, cut out each raviolo and discard all the trimmings. Now you need to seal each one and press out any air trapped inside, so take

each raviolo and carefully, with your thumbs, pinch around the outside. If you hold each raviolo up to the light, you can see where the filling is, and whether or not you have smoothed out all the air pockets.

Bring a large pan of water to the boil for the pasta.

Melt the butter in a large sauté pan and, when the butter begins to foam, add the finely diced carrots and about 2-3 ladlefuls of the sauce.

Put the ravioli into the boiling water and cook for 3-4 minutes, then drain using a slotted spoon or a spider and transfer to the pan containing the sauce. Toss gently for a couple of minutes or so and serve.

NIGEL HAWORTH

"In detail there is an Obsession
to harmonise, to balance,
to perfect and not to overdo."

Sunday 1st February

NIGEL HAWORTH
Northcote, Lancashire

TREACLE SALMON, SCALLOPS,
PICKLED GINGER
Muscat "Collection" Series Kuentz Bas, 2000

BLACK PUDDING AND BUTTERED PINK
TROUT WITH MUSTARD AND
WATERCRESS SAUCE
Sauvignon Blanc Fairhall Downs, 2002

BOWLAND FOREST MILK-FED LAMB, LEEKS
AND BARLEY, YELLOW BEETS
Cabernet Merlot, Lark Hill, Canberra District, 1999

SIX MONTHS MATURE KIRKHAM'S,
RHUBARB JELLY
Palladius, Eben Sadie, 2002

MELTING GINGER PUDDING, ICED DOUBLE
CREAM CARAMEL CUSTARD
Pedro Ximénez, San Emilio Lustau

TREACLE SALMON, SCALLOPS, PICKLED GINGER

Serves 4

INGREDIENTS

1	Piece of treacle marinated salmon (see below)
4	King scallops
Salt	
1	Lemon
Few drops of sunflower oil	

Salmon marinade

350g	Middle cut salmon (skin on scale)
60g	Fine sea salt
60g	Caster sugar
6g	Chopped chili (hot, with seeds)
10g	Chopped lemongrass
15g	Coriander
40g	Root ginger, peeled and grated
125g	Treacle (at room temperature)
200ml	Dark soy sauce (at room temperature)

Salmon sauce

50ml	Rice vinegar
50ml	Soy sauce
50ml	Oyster sauce

Garnish for the salmon

12	Thin slices of pickled ginger
20g	Spring onions, sliced
40g	Beansprouts
1	Punnet mustard cress
16	Sprigs coriander
Maldon sea salt	

METHOD

Heat a medium-sized non-stick pan and add a small amount of oil. Lightly season the scallops with salt. Place the scallops into the pan, press slightly, cook for 1-2 minutes until golden on one side. Then turn the scallops over and cook for a further minute, add a squeeze of lemon juice. Then immediately remove from the pan onto a piece of absorbent paper. Season with Maldon salt and place on top of the treacle salmon.

Salmon marinade

Carefully score the skin side of the salmon with a sharp knife. In a Thermomix add the salt, sugar, chilli, lemongrass, coriander and root ginger, blitz to make a paste. Remove from the Thermomix and rub the paste evenly onto both sides of the salmon. Place the salmon into a vacuum pack bag, add the treacle and soy sauce, vac pac tight and leave to marinate for 12 hours. After 12 hours wash off the marinade and pat dry.

With a small amount of salmon sauce (see below) glaze the flesh side – this should be a nice dark colour.

Salmon sauce

Mix all the ingredients together and place into a small pan, reduce by half to make a syrup that holds when cold. Leave to cool, then place into a squeezy bottle.

TO SERVE

Cut the salmon into 3mm thick slices, remove the skin and the brown flesh – this gives 60g of salmon per portion. Place a number 80 cutter (round cutter 80mm in diameter) into the centre of the plate, line the cutter with 60g of treacle salmon, the glazed flesh to the outside. Put the pickled ginger, spring onions, beansprouts and an even layer of mustard cress on top. To finish put 10 dots of sauce evenly around the plate, 1 warm scallop on top, coriander and a few flakes of Maldon sea salt.

OBSESSiON

20O3

This was the first year of seven nights, and the year of many things. It was the year that Kaye got lost driving Christian Olsson back from Manchester airport, and ended up halfway to Wales before Christian noticed that they were heading in the opposite direction to Northcote. And it was the year of late nights with the Galvin brothers. One night we'd certainly had quite a bit to drink and Jeff and Chris were up for a really good night. Then they became hungry at about 4.30am, and the only thing we had which was convenient to cook in the fridges were the staff meat and potato pies left over from lunch, so Chris and Jeff quickly set about heating them up in the microwave, and tucking in. I couldn't keep my eyes open any longer so I had to leave them to it. The rest is history.

The Galvins did an incredible smoked quail consommé with a pithivier of quail which was absolutely stunning and great ravioli of sea scallops and langoustine. The milk-fed Pyrenean lamb they made was very interesting – they're very influenced by France, and they made a beautiful Sauternes soaked Forme d'Ambre with dried Muscat grapes, which was wonderful.

This was also the year of Heston's football match. Northcote played The Fat Duck in a game of football on what used to be the old tennis courts (which we won). He also fed Craig's children with his chocolate and caviar dish and snail porridge, which was greatly appreciated by the little Bancrofts. The funniest thing about Heston's night was getting the nitrogen from BOAC in Manchester. It was an absolute nightmare. They thought we were international terrorists or something – we had to get three tanks of this stuff for 50 people. At this point Heston was just on the cusp of greatness; The Fat Duck crew had to train Craig and the team to go around all the tables doing the famous nitro-poached green tea and lime mousses. Heston also made

an orange and beetroot reverse jelly, which had a wonderful quirky simplicity. One of the things that really hit home was the delice of chocolate with a cumin caramel – it was the first time anyone had touched cracking candy since childhood.

We then had probably the liveliest night of the festival, with Heston, Ashley and his pastry chef Jockey, who told many tales which were incredibly funny, but not for the pages of this cookbook.

Phil Howard's snails never arrived and he got lost on one of his famous runs. Phil used to go running every time he came up and this time he got lost between York Village and Rishton, and ended up by Blackburn Royal Hospital, which is about seven miles away. He had to get to a phone box to find out how to get home, and he ran back quite exhausted. Phil did an outstanding sweet and sour belly pork, but his pièce de résistance was a banana soufflé with chocolate ice cream, which was very dapper and a truly classy Howard dish.

Highlights of the food that year were Christian Olsson's seafood escabeche: scallop, lobster and octopus with garlic and parsley foam which was pretty special and a forward-looking dish for 2003. They use a lot of cloudberries in Scandinavia and he made a cloudberry granita with a little shot of lemonade, which was memorable.

Neil Wigglesworth flew in from Twin Farms in Vermont for our first chef visiting from America. Interestingly, Neil used to run a restaurant called Tiffany's in Great Harwood which at its height had eight in the Good Food Guide. It was in Tiffany's that I got to know Neil and where we had many a night with lashings of good food, wine and fun. I first discovered it after crashing my old Morris Ital (the worst designed car in the world) into a lamp-post nearby. He used to do a fabulous dish of sea bass on wilted lettuce with a julienne of vegetables and seafood veloute with chives, and it was always memorable. Then he married an American and moved to Vermont.

CHRIS AND JEFF GALVIN

"My passion for cooking was inspired by our childhood holidays driving through France. We would stop off at the most wonderful food markets brimming with locally grown produce, ingredients that I had not seen in the UK at that time (40 years ago!). I love to create food that makes people happy; even now cooking for family, friends and our diners at the restaurants is a pleasure that has never diminished.

Chris Galvin

My Obsession was partly due to seeing the passion and enthusiasm my brother Chris had for cooking and ingredients. I was lucky enough to have the best training possible under the tutelage of Anton Edelmann at the Savoy. This is an ever-evolving industry and it is impossible not to live and breathe cooking, you never have a chance to become bored and my enthusiasm for it never wanes."

Jeff Galvin

Monday 27th January

THE GALVIN BROTHERS

*Chris Galvin of Conran Restaurants and
Jeff Galvin of The Orrery, London*

PRESSED MULLET TERRINE,
BOUILLABAISSE DRESSING
Menetou-Salon, Clos des Blanchais-Domaine
Henry Pellé, 2000

SMOKED QUAIL CONSOMMÉ,
PITHIVIER OF QUAIL
Dry Oloroso, Don Nuño-Emilio Lustau

RAVIOLI OF SEA SCALLOPS AND
LANGOUSTINE, FENNEL BOUILLON
Pinot Grigio, Isonzo-Giovanni Puiatti, 2001

ASSIETTE OF PYRENEAN LAMB WITH
POMMES BOULANGER, BRAISED FENNEL
AND A DRIED FRUIT CONDIMENT
Château de Ferrand, Grand Cru Saint Emilion, 1994

SAUTERNES SOAKED FOURME D'AMBERT
AND DRIED MUSCAT GRAPE

ASSIETTE DE PATISSIER
Clos Labère, 2ème Vin de Château Rieussec -
Sauternes Bordeaux, 1990

ASSIETTE OF PYRENEAN LAMB WITH POMMES BOULANGER, BRAISED FENNEL AND A DRIED FRUIT CONDIMENT

Serves 4

INGREDIENTS

1	Rack of baby suckling lamb
1	Saddle of baby suckling lamb
1	Orange
200ml	Lamb juice

Dried fruit condiment

2	Fillets of salted anchovies
10	White raisins
8	Fresh almonds
2	Dried apricots
1	Branch rosemary
4	Garlic cloves
	Butter
1 tsp	Sugar
2 tbsp	Dried breadcrumbs
	Sherry vinegar

Lamb juice

1kg	Chopped lamb bones
200g	Lamb fat
2	Carrots
1	Onion
1	White leek
1	Head fennel
	Olive oil
	Half bottle dry white wine
2	Sprigs of thyme
2	Sprigs of rosemary
1	Garlic bulb
200g	Deseeded tomatoes
3 litres	Water

Pommes boulanger

1	Baby lamb shoulder
2	White onions, very finely sliced
1	Garlic bulb, halved
5	Large desiree potatoes
1 litre	Lamb juice (see above)

Braised fennel

2	Large bulbs of fennel
	Olive oil
400ml	Water
2	Garlic cloves
	Pinch fennel seeds
	Salt & pepper

To serve

4	Whole fresh ceps
	Olive oil
	1 dstspn Butter

METHOD

Trim the rack and saddle leaving a little fat on the back of the meat. Wash the orange, peel off a little peel and keep; juice the orange through a strainer into a pan, add the lamb juice and reduce over a medium heat until syrupy, add the peel and cool. Brush all over the lamb and set in the fridge to marinate.

Dried fruit condiment

Rinse the anchovies and let them soak for 2 hours, drain and dry, then crush with the back of a fork and set aside. Soak the raisins in hot water for 1 hour, then drain, open the fresh almonds, peel and cut in two. Slice the dried apricots into strips, chop the rosemary very finely and set aside in a bowl. Peel and quarter the cloves of garlic, take out the centre germ, sauté in some hot butter until golden, sprinkle with the sugar and let them caramelise, then set aside. Toast the breadcrumbs in some more hot butter and drain.

In a pan heat a dash of olive oil, add the raisins, almonds, apricots, garlic and rosemary, add a few drops of sherry vinegar, sprinkle on the toasted breadcrumbs and mix to dry out, spoon in the anchovies and season.

Lamb juice

Roast the bones in a hot oven at 150°C/300°F/gas mark 2 until brown. Chop all the vegetables roughly and caramelise in a deep pan in a little olive oil. Place in the lamb bones, wine, herbs and tomatoes, cover with the water and place the pan with no lid into the oven at 150°C/300°F/gas mark 2 with the fat for around 4 hours, remove and let it cool and settle for 1 hour. Then pour through a cheese cloth and set aside for later use.

Pommes boulanger

Place the lamb shoulder in a deep ovenproof dish, peel and slice the onion very fine, cut the garlic in half and cover the lamb. Put a lid on the dish and place in a medium oven for 4 hours, 150°C/300°F/gas mark 2.

Cool the lamb for 1 hour; pick all the meat off the bone, shred into smaller pieces with your fingers, being careful not to have too much fat incorporated, then set aside. Peel the potatoes and slice very finely on a Japanese mandolin, layer the potatoes up in a shallow ovenproof dish; when half-way up place the meat in a thin layer, finish with layers of potato to the top. Heat the lamb juice and pour over, place into a medium oven 150°C/300°F/gas mark 2 for approximately 1½ hours, press down half way through with a palette knife to help colour on top. When done the potato should be dry, well coloured and a knife should pass through easily. Leave to cool.

Braised fennel

Trim and peel the fennel, cut in half, heat a pan with a dash of olive oil, colour the fennel all around until golden and place in a deep pan. Heat the water, add the garlic and fennel seed, season and poach very lightly until tender.

TO SERVE

Heat a large sauté pan and cook the cuts of lamb in a little olive oil for 12 minutes, turning frequently. When done place on a warm grill to rest for 10 minutes.

While the lamb is resting, cut your potato into a shape to suit, place in a hot oven at 200°C/400°F/gas mark 6 to warm.

Slice the fennel into equal wedges and keep warm.

Take 4 whole fresh ceps, trim and clean then sauté in a little hot olive oil, finish with butter to glaze, keep warm.

Take 4 serving plates, place the potato in the centre, cut the lamb into portions and arrange with the fennel and ceps around the potato, sprinkle over some fruit condiment and serve the rest on the side.

Pour around a little more reduced lamb juice.

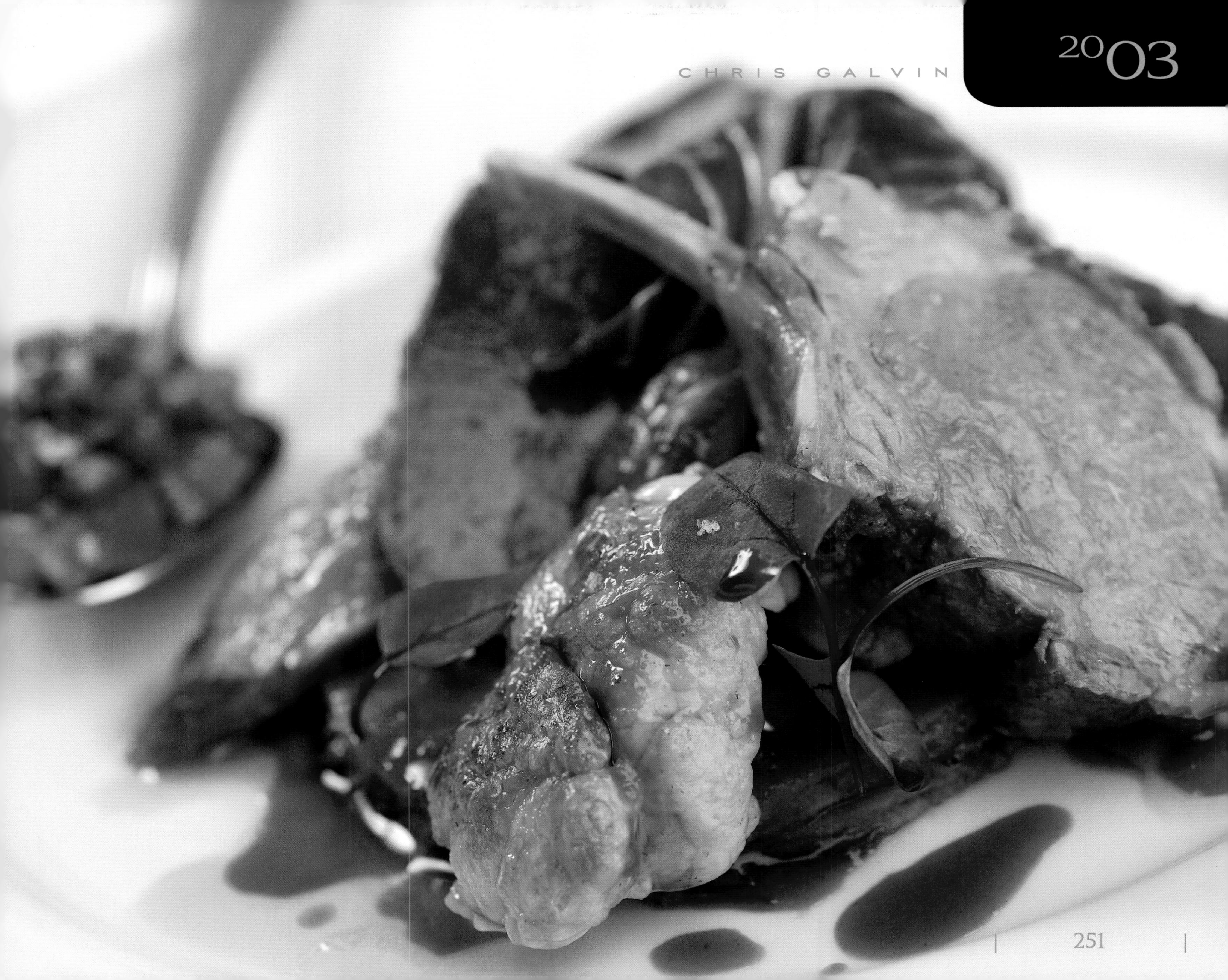

SMOKED QUAIL CONSOMMÉ, PITHIVER OF QUAIL

Serves 4

INGREDIENTS

5	Jumbo quails
10	Quail carcasses (to be smoked then used in clarification)
200g	Cherry wood chips for smoking

Clarification

100g	Chicken breast
4	Smoked quail breasts
10	Smoked quail carcasses
50g	Onion, peeled
80g	Carrot, peeled
50g	Leek, washed
50g	Celery, washed
2	Egg whites
Sprig of tarragon	
2 litres	Brown chicken stock

Pithiver

2	Quail breasts
6	Quail legs, boned
4	Quail legs, slow cooked
50g	Italian lardo (pork fat)
50g	Chicken breasts
20g	Fresh white breadcrumbs
1	Egg yolk
1 tsp	Chopped parsley
Salt & pepper	
200g	All butter puff pastry (rolled 3mm thick)
Egg yolk for egg wash	
Garnish	
4	Quail breasts
4	Soft poached quail eggs
1	Plum tomato, diced
4	Blades of truffle cut into julienne (straw like)
Chervil, to garnish	
Few drops of black truffle oil	

METHOD

Clean the quails and remove the wish bone and legs. Reserve 6 legs for the pithiver and bone them for mincing; the other 4 should be slow cooked in duck fat (see pithiver recipe).

The breasts should all be smoked on the crown, along with the carcasses. 4 breasts are for the garnish, two are for the pithiver and the rest go into the clarification.

To hot smoke

In a small roasting tray heat the cherry wood chips until they are smoking, place a wire rack over the chips and place both the quails and the quail carcasses on top. Smoke constantly for 10 minutes then remove the quail and allow to cool. Remove all the breasts off the bone and reserve. The breasts should be nice and pink at this stage.

Clarification

Place all the clarification ingredients, except the chicken stock, into a Robot Coupe (food processor) and blitz for a minute or two. Whisk on to the cold chicken stock and bring to the boil, stirring every few minutes to form a pad (a pad is what forms when the proteins rise to the top and the liquid clarifies) then simmer gently for 20 minutes. Pass through a muslin cloth.

Pithiver

Mince the quail breasts, meat from the boned quail legs, chicken breast and pork fat together. Add the breadcrumbs, egg yolk and parsley. Check the seasoning, mould in to a 2cm cutter. Remove the thigh bone and skin from the slow-cooked quail legs and put them on top of the mince fillings. Cut the puff pastry into 8 discs and use them to make the pithiver, leaving the bone sticking out of the top. Egg wash twice then score the pattern on the top. Rest for at least an hour then bake for 8 minutes at 180°C/350°F/ gas mark 4.

Consommé and garnish

Warm the quail breasts and quail eggs and place in the consommé cups. Add the tomato dice, truffle and chervil then pour in the boiling consommé, drizzle on a few drops of truffle oil and serve with the warm pithiver.

JEFF GALVIN

CHRISTIAN OLSSON

"I'm obsessed with food because I have an ongoing craving to make today's food better tomorrow. What drives that passion is my imagination and also that I constantly surround myself with interesting and professional people in my kitchen."

Tuesday 28th January

CHRISTIAN OLSSON
Vassa Eggen, Stockholm

CAULIFLOWER TARTE, OSCIETRE CAVIAR,
LANGOUSTINE
La Gitana, Manzanilla-Vinicola Hidalgo

FOIE GRAS TERRINE, POMMES GRATIN
APPLE JELLY, BRIOCHE
Gewürztraminer, Grand Cru Hengst-Josmeyer, 1996

SEAFOOD ESCABECHE, SCALLOP, LOBSTER,
OCTOPUS, GARLIC PARSLEY FOAM
Muscadet de Sevre et Maine, Sur lie, Château de
Chasseloir-Chéreau-Carré, 1994

SOLE, TRUFFLE, OYSTER, LEEK PURÉE
Sauvignon Blanc, Adelaide Hills-Shaw and Shaw, 2001

CLOUDBERRY GRANITÉ AND LEMONADE

VENISON "FIVE SPICES", BLACKCURRANT
Valduero Reserva-E Valduero, Ribera del Duero, 1997

LIQUORICE, RASPBERRY, LEMON
Elysium Black Muscat-Andrew Quady California, 2000

INGREDIENTS

10	Ripe (preferably Sicilian) tomatoes
3	Garlic cloves
5	Sprigs of thyme
1 tbsp	Sugar
1 tbsp	Coarse sea salt
1 tbsp	Olive oil
½	Cucumber
½ tbsp	Spanish pimento powder
1 pinch	Spanish saffron
	Juice from 1 lime
1	Red chilli pepper, chopped
	Garlic oil
	Salt & pepper
1	Bunch coriander, chopped (including the stems)

Parsley and garlic foam

50ml	Parsley and garlic infused oil (put 200ml oil, 1 garlic clove and a bunch of fresh Italian parsley in a blender until the oil is hot then strain through a filter)
50ml	Whipping cream
1 tbsp	Champagne vinegar
	Salt

Seafood

1	Scottish lobster, cooked and separated
4	Scallops
1	Baby octopus, cooked and char grilled

Vegetables and fruit

4	Baby artichokes cooked 'au barigoule' (parboiled in salted water, cooled and leaves removed)
100g	Sweet watermelon, cubed
1	Grilled red bell pepper, sliced
1cm	Square avocado terrine (made with avocado, agar agar, chilli, salt and lemon)

Spring onions, thinly sliced to garnish
Nori, finely chopped to garnish

METHOD

Cut the tomatoes in half and place in a baking pan. Crush some garlic cloves and put in the pan along with the thyme, salt, sugar and olive oil. Place in the oven at 200°C/400°F/gas mark 6 for about 10 minutes. Remove from the oven, cover with cling film and leave to rest for 15 minutes. Strain slowly and carefully through a chinoise (sieve) – don't push it through.

Roast the pimento powder in a small pot, add a little water to make a paste and then add saffron and mix.

Peel and blend the cucumber; let it strain by itself slowly through a chinoise.

Mix a little of the tomato water with the paste so there are no lumps. Then season with the cucumber juice, lime juice, sherry vinegar, garlic oil, chopped red chilli, salt and pepper, sugar and chopped coriander.

Let it sit for an hour before serving then strain.

Parsley and garlic foam

Put the oil, cream and vinegar in a bowl, season with salt and blend carefully before pouring it into a siphon. Charge with two cream chargers and shake the siphon very carefully, continually testing the mixture until it is the consistency of shaving foam.

Keep cool but not too cold.

TO SERVE

Place a little of the strained tomato liquid in a dish. Assemble the lobster, scallops and baby octopus on top with the baby artichoke, sweet watermelon, baby tomatoes, red pepper and avocado terrine. Scatter with a little puffed wild rice, spring onions and nori.

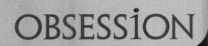

PHIL HOWARD

"I remember Neil Wigglesworth impressing me with a cooking technique involving a toilet roll – it was clever but that has long since been forgotten. Heston was here to work his magic and certainly didn't disappoint. My third year and I've still not learnt to avoid the bloody soufflés! It is beginning to become evident that modern cooking techniques are spreading far and wide."

20O3

Wednesday 29th January

PHIL HOWARD
The Square, London

RILLETTE OF SMOKED MACKEREL
WITH CUCUMBER JELLY AND
OSCIETRA CAVIAR
Muscadet de Sèvre et Maine, Sur Lie Château de
Chasseloir Vinifié en Futs de Chêne Neufs
Château-Carré, 1994

SWEET AND SOUR PORK BELLY,
CARAMELISED ENDIVE AND STAR ANISE
Gewürztraminer, les Folastries, Josmeyer, 2000

ROAST TURBOT,
CREAMED POTATO AND TRUFFLE BUTTER
Montagny l'er Cru Château de la Saule-Alain Roy, 2000

A SLICE OF ROAST SIRLOIN BEEF
WITH A PERSILLADE OF SNAILS
AND RED WINE
Cartuxa de Évora Reserva-Fundação Eugénio de
Almeida, 1997

BANANA SOUFFLÉ WITH CHOCOLATE
ICE CREAM
Mâcon Clessé Selection de Grains Sendrés
Quintaine-Guillemot-Michel, 1992

BANANA SOUFFLÉ WITH CHOCOLATE ICE CREAM
Serves 8

INGREDIENTS

10	Large bananas
500ml	Milk
6	Egg yolks
280g	Sugar
25g	Cocoa powder
100g	Valrhona 70% chocolate
125g	Mascarpone
20g	Cornflour
100ml	Banana liqueur
100g	Softened butter
100g	Dried banana bread, blended into a fine crumb
360ml	Egg whites
Icing sugar, to serve	

METHOD

Bake 8 of the bananas in their skins in an oven at 160°C/325°F/gas mark 3 for 20 minutes – they will turn black.

Meanwhile, bring the milk to the boil in a heavy based pan. Whisk the egg yolks with 100g sugar and the cocoa powder. Pour on the milk, whisk briefly to incorporate the yolks, return to the heat and cook, stirring continuously, until the custard coats the back of a wooden spoon (84°C). Remove from the heat, add the chocolate and mascarpone and whisk until homogeneous. Chill and churn in an ice cream machine until set. Store in a freezer.

Remove the bananas from the oven, allow to rest for 10 minutes. Remove the pulp and transfer to a large bowl. Discard the skins. Fork through the banana to create a rough purée.

Mix the cornflour with 40ml of the banana liqueur, add to the banana and transfer to a heavy based pan. Bring this mix to the boil and cook out, beating vigorously, for 3 minutes. Transfer to a blender and purée until smooth. Reserve at room temperature.

TO SERVE

Carefully brush the soufflé moulds (10x5cm) with butter, using vertical brush strokes. Coat each mould with banana breadcrumbs by pouring the crumbs into a buttered mould and tipping into the next while rotating.

Transfer the ice cream from the freezer to the fridge 20 minutes prior to serving.

Peel the two remaining bananas and mash with a fork. Add the banana mix equally then add the 30ml of banana liqueur to each. You will need to make the soufflés in two batches if using a standard-sized electric mixer.

Place 180g egg whites into the mixer and turn onto the lightest setting. Once lightly aerated, gradually add 90g sugar and beat until stiff. Add a large spoon of mix to one of the bowls and whisk briefly. Then incorporate the rest of the mix for that batch carefully with a rubber spatula. Repeat the same process with the second batch of whites.

Spoon the finished mix into the soufflé moulds, gently tapping on the work surface. Using a large palette knife, smooth off the surface of each soufflé. Run the tip of your thumb round the inside of the rim by pinching with your thumb and forefinger and rotating the mould. This will prevent them from sticking.

Place the soufflés in an oven, preheated to 170°C/340°F/gas mark 3½. Make sure there is at least an 8cm clearance! They will take 8-10 minutes. Turn the tray after 5 minutes. If they have risen at least 3-4cm after 8 minutes, remove the soufflés carefully, dust with icing sugar and serve immediately. Drop a ball of ice cream into the middle of each soufflé.

PHIL HOWARD

HESTON BLUMENTHAL

"I love the fact that food and cooking have the ability to stimulate social interaction and produce emotions in people. And eating is the only thing that we do that uses all of the five senses at the same time: the way that sound, sight, touch, taste and smell all interact during such a simple everyday process is fascinating to me."

Thursday 30th January

HESTON BLUMENTHAL OBE
The Fat Duck, Bray

NITROGEN POACHED GREEN TEA
AND LIME SOUR

ORANGE AND BEETROOT JELLY

SNAIL PORRIDGE,
JABUGO HAM
Bourgogne Blanc-Vallet Frères, 2000

POMMERY MUSTARD ICE CREAM
RED CABBAGE GASPACHO

CRAB BISCUIT
ROAST FOIE GRAS, MARINATED SALMON,
CRYSTALLISED SEAWEED,
OYSTER VINAIGRETTE
Vouvray, Cuvée des Fondraux-Champalou, 1997

POACHED ANJOU PIGEON BREAST
A PASTILLA OF ITS LEG WITH CHERRIES,
PISTACHIOS, COCOA AND QUATRE ÉPICE
Esporão Reserva, Alentejo-Herdade de Esporão, 1999

POMMES PURÉE
WHITE CHOCOLATE AND CAVIAR BUTTON
PARSNIP CEREAL
SHERBET DIB DAB

MANGO AND DOUGLAS FIR PURÉE
BAVAROIS OF LYCHEE AND MANGO,
BEETROOT AND GREEN PEPPERCORN JELLY
Sauvignon Blanc, Late Harvest,
Semi-Dulce, Bornos, 2000

BASIL TARTLET
RED PEPPER CARAMEL
BEETROOT JELLY

DÉLICE OF CHOCOLATE
CHOCOLATE SORBET, CUMIN CARAMEL
Recioto di Soave, Capitelli-Anselmi, 2000

SNAIL PORRIDGE, JABUGO HAM

Serves 2

SNAIL PORRIDGE, JABUGO HAM
Serves 2

INGREDIENTS

Duck ham

1	Bay leaf
15g	Black peppercorns
15g	Coriander seeds
50g	Sel gris (grey salt)
5g	Sprigs of thyme
5	Gressingham duck breasts, fat scored

Parsley butter

550g	Unsalted butter
85g	Garlic, minced
10g	Lemon juice
50g	Dijon mustard
40g	Ground almonds
15g	Table salt
240g	Curly leaf parsley
	Clarified butter
40g	Ceps, cut into 1cm dice
60g	Shallots, cut into brunoise (2mm squares)
80g	Reserved duck ham, cut into brunoise (2mm squares)

Chicken bouillon

3kg	Chicken (2 good-sized chickens)
250g	Carrots, peeled and finely sliced
250g	Onions, finely sliced
100g	Celery, finely sliced
75g	Leeks, white and pale green parts only, finely sliced
10g	Garlic, crushed
3	Cloves
10g	Black peppercorns
50g	Sprigs of thyme
20g	Parsley leaves and stems
3g	Bay leaves

Braised snails

100g	Helix pomatia snails (shelled weight)
2	Cloves
120g	Onion, cut in half
40g	Carrot, cut in half
90g	Leeks, cut in half
2	Sticks of celery
30g	Garlic bulb, cut in half
2	Bay leaves
50g	Sprigs of rosemary
50g	Sprigs of thyme
120g	Water
250g	Dry white wine
50g	Parsley leaves and stems

Walnut vinaigrette

75g	Walnut vinegar
145g	Grapeseed oil
5g	Dijon mustard

Snail porridge

10g	Fennel, shaved paper-thin
	Reserved walnut vinaigrette
	Table salt
	Black pepper
	Fleur de sel
30g	Unsalted butter
12	Reserved braised snails
30g	Reserved chicken bouillon
10g	Porridge oats, sieved to remove the powdery bits
30g	Reserved parsley butter, at room temperature
20g	Jabugo ham, cut into chiffonade (long, thin strips)

Pinch of micro parsley and micro coriander to garnish.

METHOD

Duck ham

Snip the bay leaf into 8 pieces. Grind the peppercorns and coriander, combine with the sel gris, thyme and bay leaf. Spread a layer of this mixture over the bottom of a roasting tray and place the duck breasts on top. Cover completely with the remaining salt mixture, then refrigerate for 24 hours.

Brush the salt cure from the breasts, wrap them in muslin and tie securely with string. Hang in a cellar or other cool place for at least 20 days. Remove the duck from the muslin and refrigerate until needed.

Parsley butter

Melt 50g of the unsalted butter in a pan, add the garlic and sauté until pale gold and fragrant. Add the lemon juice to the pan, then transfer the mixture to a Pacojet beaker along with the mustard, ground almonds, salt and the remaining 500g unsalted butter.

Chop the parsley, sprinkle on top of the butter mixture and run the beaker through the Pacojet machine. Remove the beaker and freeze the mixture until completely solid. Run the frozen mixture through the Pacojet, then freeze solid again. Repeat this process until all trace of the parsley has disappeared. After the final use of the Pacojet, at which point the mixture will have an ice cream consistency, set aside the butter at room temperature until needed.

Heat some clarified butter in a pan, add the ceps and sauté until caramelised.

Strain and set aside.

Wipe the pan clean, then heat some more clarified butter in it. Add the shallots and cook over a very low heat for 30–40 minutes, until very soft and translucent.

Fold the caramelised ceps, the cooked shallots and the duck brunoise into the reserved parsley butter. Refrigerate or freeze until needed.

Chicken bouillon

Place the chickens in a large pan and cover with cold water. Bring to the boil, then carefully remove them and discard the water. Rinse the chickens under cold running water to remove any scum.

Put the chickens in a pressure cooker and add just enough cold water to cover them. Bring to a simmer, skimming off any scum on the surface. Add the vegetables, cloves and freshly crushed peppercorns to the pan. Put the lid on, bring to full pressure and cook for 30 minutes.

Remove the pan from the heat, allow to depressurise, then remove the lid. Add the thyme, parsley and bay leaves and leave to infuse for 30 minutes.

Strain the bouillon through a fine sieve lined with several layers of damp muslin. Refrigerate or freeze until needed.

Braised snails

Rinse the snails in several changes of water to remove any grit. Preheat the oven to 120°C/250°F/gas mark ½.

Press a clove into each half of the onion, then place in an ovenproof casserole with all the other ingredients, apart from the snails and parsley, and bring to a simmer on the hob.

Add the snails, cover with a cartouche (circle of paper to stop a skin forming) and place in the oven for 3–4 hours. Remove the casserole from the oven, add the parsley and set aside to cool.

Drain the snails from the liquid and trim away their intestines and white sac.

Refrigerate until needed.

Walnut vinaigrette

Combine all the ingredients, mix thoroughly and set aside until needed.

Snail porridge

Dress the fennel with the vinaigrette, season with table salt, freshly ground pepper and fleur de sel and set aside.

Heat 20g of the butter until foaming, then sauté the snails and season with table salt and freshly ground pepper. Add the remaining butter to the snails, then remove from the heat and keep warm.

Heat the chicken bouillon in a small saucepan. When hot, stir in the oats. Once they have absorbed the liquid, add the parsley butter and season to taste with table salt and freshly ground pepper. Adjust the consistency of the porridge with chicken bouillon if necessary until it resembles wet rice pudding. (It is important not to overcook the oats or else they will become starchy and lose their texture.)

TO SERVE

Divide the porridge between 2 warm plates and cover with the Jabugo ham. Place the warm snails on top, add the dressed fennel and micro salads to serve.

NEIL
WIGGLESWORTH

"You would have to have an Obsession to open a high
quality restaurant in Great Harwood on the site of the
Old Launderette, which is exactly what I did. Tiffany's
was certainly my Obsession all those years ago - it had
passion, it had flair and fun which was a success but maybe
not the huge success I would have wanted it to be. So we
went overseas sto follow our Obsession where food was a
principal part of a fantastic journey, to come back from
the USA to cook with an old friend alongside great names
and show my talents was a great honour and of course much
fun, thanks Nigel. "

Saturday 1st February

NEIL WIGGLESWORTH
Twin Farms, Vermont

TOSTADA CARNITAS WITH ANCHO CHILI
AND CILANTRO ESSENCE
PICO DE GALLO
CUMIN CRÈME FRAÎCHE
Fino Marismeno, Reservas Especiales-Sánchez Romate

ARMAGNAC-ROASTED CHICKEN LIVERS
ON SOFT WHIPPED FOIE GRAS TARRAGON
SCENTED BRANDADE
CARAMELISED WHITE PEARL ONIONS
IN CIDER SYRUP
Viognier-Chardonnay, Bien Nacido Cuvée-Qupé, 2000

SEARED BLACK BEAN ENCRUSTED AHI
TUNA ON SEA VEGETABLES
WITH A GINGERED SUSHI RICE PYRAMID,
YUZU LEMONGRASS PONZU SAUCE, SEA
URCHIN FOAM, WASABI TOBIKO
Tokay Pinot-Gris, Le Fromentau Josmeyer, 1999

WARM LANCASHIRE CHEESE SOUFFLÉ
WITH WINTER TRUFFLES AND A GRILLED
RADICCHIO CORN SALAD,
MUSCAT GRAPE VINAIGRETTE,
ROASTED PISTACHIO OIL
Late Picked Muscat-Brown Brothers

HEATHER-FED BOWLAND LAMB,
MORECAMBE BAY SHRIMP, DRY-CURED HAM
AND HERB POLENTA, TOMATO LAMB JUS
Zinfandel, Les Vieilles Vignes,
Napa Valley-Fife Vineyards, 1998

BUBBLE SUGAR CAMPFIRE S'MORES
KNOB CREEK KENTUCKY BOURBON CREAM,
CHOCOLATE MALT
Essensia, Orange Muscat - Andrew Quady, 1999

HEATHER-FED BOWLAND LAMB, MORECAMBE BAY SHRIMP, DRY-CURED HAM AND HERB POLENTA, TOMATO LAMB JUS

Serves 4

INGREDIENTS

2	Short loins of heather-fed Bowland lamb (silverskin removed and trimmed)
Salt	
Butter	
Herb polenta (see below)	
80g	Morecambe Bay shrimps (warmed and seasoned)
Tomato lamb jus (see below)	
Paprika, to dust	

Dry-cured ham and herb polenta

30g	Butter
100g	Fine polenta
Salt, to taste	
300g	Chicken stock
40g	Double cream
40g	Dry-cured ham, cut into small dice
2g	Chopped chives
2g	Chopped parsley
2g	Chopped tarragon
20g	Grated parmesan

Tomato lamb jus

150g	Chopped onion
40g	Butter
100g	Sliced tomatoes
150ml	Madeira
500ml	Lamb stock
500ml	Chicken stock
1 tsp	Fecule (potato flour) mixed with a few drops of water before adding to sauce to thicken (or cornflour)

METHOD

Roll the loin of lamb in cling film, put in a vacuum pack bag and seal tight. Cook the lamb in a water bath at 68°C for 14 minutes. Allow to rest for 5 minutes. Remove from the vacuum pack bag and season with salt.

In a non-stick hot frying pan, seal the lamb for 2-3 minutes, basting in butter. Remove from the pan and carve into 8 slices.

Dry-cured ham and herb polenta

Bring the chicken stock to the boil. Meanwhile, in a medium pan, melt the butter then add the polenta with a pinch of salt. Add the boiling chicken stock and bring back to the boil. Cover and simmer for 5-10 minutes. Once cooked add the cream, dry-cured ham and chopped herbs, check the seasoning.

Tomato lamb jus

Sweat off the onions in the butter until they caramelise, add the tomatoes and cook for a further 3-4 minutes. Add the Madeira and reduce by two-thirds. Add the lamb and chicken stocks and reduce to approximately 300ml then lightly thicken with fecule or cornflour. Blitz the sauce with a stick liquidiser for a few seconds and check the seasoning.

TO SERVE

Take a rectangular plate and put 2 dessertspoons of the ham and herb polenta down the centre. Place 4 slices of the lamb on the top, scatter around the shrimps and finish with the jus and paprika.

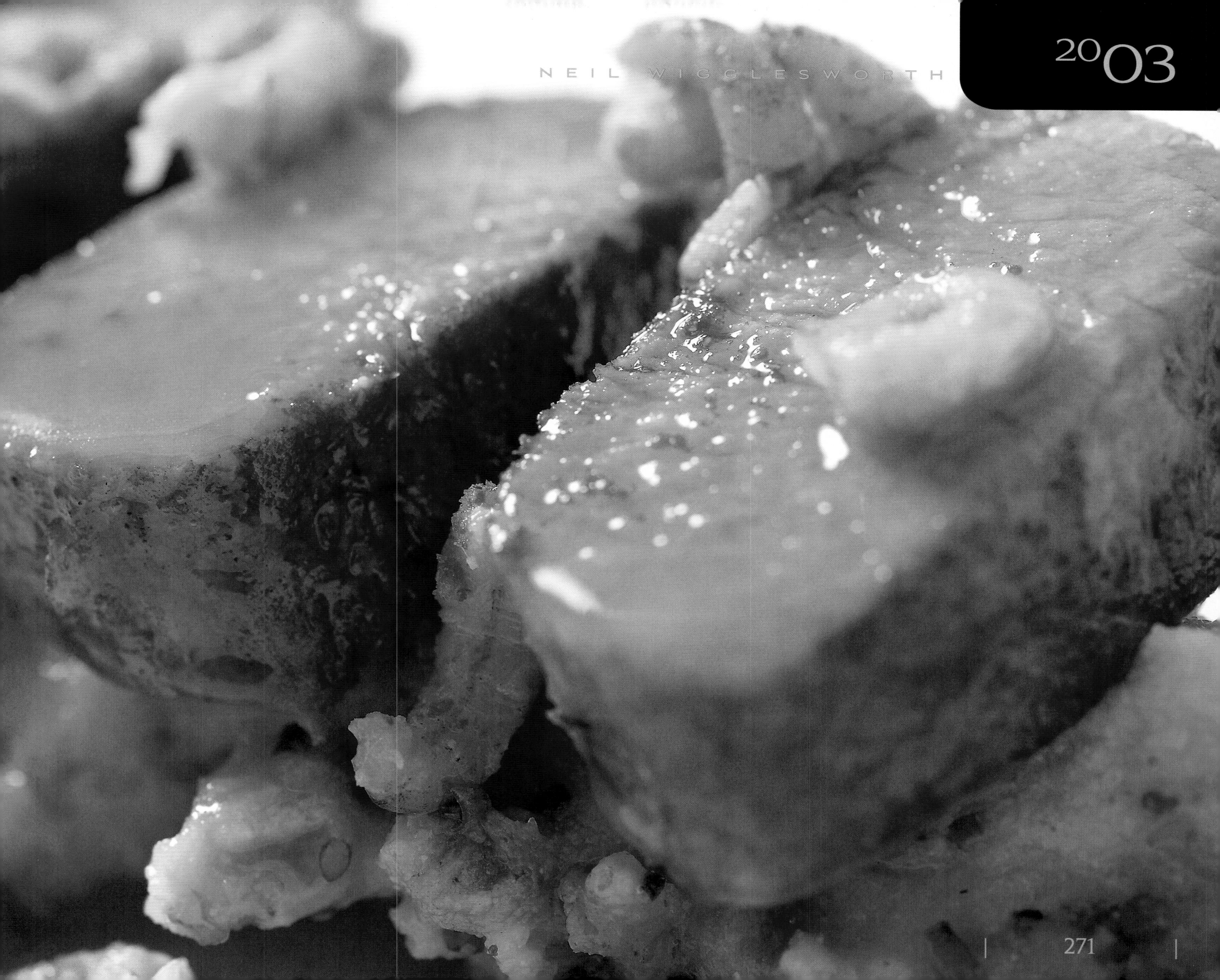

NIGEL HAWORTH AND CHARLES METCALFE

"To be obsessed with the theatre of kitchen is comforting, almost womb-like."

Sunday 2nd February
NIGEL HAWORTH
CHARLES METCALFE
Northcote, Lancashire

SLOW BRAISED CHIPPING HAM,
PEA CREAM
Cava, Rosado, Brut-Juvé y Camps

POTTED MORECAMBE BAY SHRIMPS, TINY
HERB SALAD, MALTED BREAD, TABASCO
Esporão Reserva, Alentejo-Herdade do Esporão, 2000

"HINDLE WAKES" BROTH
GOOSNARGH CHICKEN BROTH FLAVOURED
WITH DRIED PLUMS,
BROWN RICE, STREAKY BACON AND BASIL
Dry Oloroso, Don Nuño, Emilio Lustau

LANCASHIRE HOT POT
BOWLAND HEATHER FED LAMB SLOWLY
BRAISED IN THE AGA, PICKLED RED
CABBAGE, OYSTER FRITTER,
BABY CARROTS
Reserva-Marques de Murrieta, 1997

APPLE CRUMBLE SOUFFLÉ,
LANCASHIRE CHEESE ICE CREAM
Sauvignon Blanc, Late Harvest,
Semi-Dulce, Bornos, 2000

"HINDLE WAKES" GOOSNARGH CHICKEN BROTH FLAVOURED WITH DRIED PLUMS, BROWN RICE, STREAKY BACON AND BASIL

Serves 4

INGREDIENTS

4	Slow-cooked chicken wings (see below)
	Chicken mousse (see below)
4	Dried plums (see below)
	Brown rice and bacon (see below)
4	Crispy chicken skins – (see below)
4	Chiffonade of basil leaves (long thin strips)

Chicken broth
(makes 10 portions)

500g	Ground Goosnargh chicken mince
250g	Finely chopped vegetables (onions, carrots, celery and leeks)
2	Parsley stalks/chervil
1	Sprig of thyme
1	Bay leaf
80g	Egg whites
5g	Chicken bouillon
	Salt
6	Crushed black peppercorns
2 litres	Good white chicken stock

Chicken mousse

200g	Chicken breasts, diced
250ml	Cream
1	Egg yolk
10g	Chives, chopped
5g	Chervil, finely chopped
4g	Salt

Slow cooked chicken wings

4 x 300g	Chicken wings
2g	Thyme, chopped
40g	Rock salt
1	Garlic clove, crushed

Dried plums

2	Victoria plums
	Salt
	Icing sugar, to dust

Brown rice and bacon

| 40g | Brown rice, washed |
| 10g | Diced streaky bacon |

Crispy skin

| | Chicken skin from 2 large chicken breasts |
| | Salt |

METHOD

Chicken broth
(makes 10 portions)

Combine the ground chicken, chopped vegetables, herbs, egg whites, bouillon and seasoning in a mixing bowl. Mix well.

Put the chicken stock into a large heavy bottomed pan. Carefully mix in the ground chicken mince. Mix well and check the seasoning. Place the pan on to the stove and bring to a simmer over a medium heat, stir the contents of the pan frequently until the pad starts to set on the surface of the stock. Once the pad has risen give it a final stir and then allow the pad to set, make a small opening to the side and allow the broth to boil. Gently simmer for 1½ hours.

Once the broth is cooked remove from the heat and carefully strain through a tammy cloth, being careful not to disturb the pad too much. Check the seasoning.

Chicken mousse

Place the diced chicken, 100ml of cream, egg yolk and salt into a Pacojet beaker. Freeze to -20°C. Once frozen, Pacojet three times.

Place into a metal bowl over ice and beat in the remaining 150ml of cream until smooth and shiny. Mix in the chives and chervil, check the seasoning and put into a piping bag.

Slow cooked chicken wings

Cut the knuckle and the tip of each wing off. Place the wings on a stainless steel tray and sprinkle with thyme, rock salt and crushed garlic. Marinate for 4 hours.

Wash off the marinade under cold running water and then dry. Place the wings in a vacuum pack bag and seal, place into a water bath at 75°C for 10 hours.

Remove the wings from the bag, leave to just cool then remove the two bones in the wing, being careful not to tear the wing. Once you have removed the bones pipe chicken mousse into each wing then cover with cling film, sealing the ends tight. Put the wings into a steamer for 10 minutes, then keep warm.

Dried plums

Cut the plums in half and remove the stone, being careful not to cause damage. Lightly season the halves with salt and a dust of icing sugar. Put the plum halves skin down, flesh up on to a tray and place in a dehydrator at 57°C for 10 hours.

Brown rice and bacon

Place the washed rice into a pan, season with salt and cover with 2.5cm of water above the rice. Bring to the boil on a high heat. Once the water has nearly evaporated, turn the heat down low, cover with a lid and allow the rice to cook completely in the steam for 13 minutes.

In a non-stick frying pan, fry the bacon until just crispy. Drain off the excess fat and mix into the steamed rice, check seasoning and reserve.

Crispy skin

Cut the skin in half to make 4 pieces. Lightly season with salt. Place the skin flat between 2 metal plates and put into a fryer at 160°C for 6-8 minutes until the skin is crispy and golden. Remove from the fryer and leave to cool.

TO SERVE

Cut the ends off each steamed chicken wing, place into a bowl, add the dried plum and a small spoon of the bacon and brown rice. Pour in the broth, stand the chicken side up and finish with a chiffonade of basil.

20O2

This year we'd grown the line-up to six chefs. I'd been chatting to Accrington College senior lecturer and old friend Neil Hogg about an educational link with a Swedish Cookery School, Matpedagogerna. He asked me to cook a six-course regional menu for 60 people at their Hotel School in Stockholm. When I was in Stockholm the senior lecturer, Stefan Brandhoffer, took me to a restaurant called Fredsgatan 12, and there I met the head chef Danyel Couet, who was a key player in the Swedish cookery team that won gold in the "Culinary Olympics" in 2000. I approached Danyel to cook at the 2002 Food Festival; he agreed and became the first of our many starred overseas chefs. That's how I recruited the first of the chefs for 2002.

I had known Brian for several years and cooked with him in Mauritius after winning the Wedgwood Chef and Potter competition in 2000 that led to him joining the bill that year – great to have a Yorkshireman of such note in the Red Rose county, an incredible character who we all have learnt to respect over the years. Everyone loved him red wine and all! Then Phil Howard said he'd do it again and my very good friend Robbie Millar came on board. I met Robbie at the 1996 Michelin awards, which was the year we got our star. I was sitting with Robbie, Terry Laybourne, Tom Aikens and Eric Chavot and we all got merrily drunk. Robbie and I clicked and he became a very good friend of mine. Tragically, Robbie was killed in a car crash on 13th August 2005.

Germain Schwab opened the food festival; one of his courses being his famous tri-coloured cannelloni with a langoustine and chicken mousse, and sweetcorn sauce,

and a beautiful chocolate pavlova with gold leaf to finish. Winteringham Fields was a truly great restaurant and one of only several two stars ever to be awarded in the north; having a two Michelin-starred Swiss chef to cook at Northcote was another great milestone.

Phil Howard got the first of many speeding offences on his way up here in his old Aston Martin. Phil was getting into his stride at that time. He did a roast turbot with hand-rolled macaroni, chanterelles and thyme, an inspirational dish. One of the memorable incidents that happened that year was a Michelin inspection. It was at lunch service on the Tuesday prior to Phil's evening. We were open as normal for lunch in those days. The pastry chef had forgotten to make any ice cream on that day and, of course, this particular inspector ordered ice cream. So we had to rush around making the ice cream base, and getting it churned in what was a very old Robot Coupe in an incredibly busy kitchen. Funnily enough, after we'd finished the festival and Phil had gone back down to The Square, he phoned to say he'd been inspected on that day too – at dinner time. Sods law.

Robbie Millar did the best dish I think I've ever had with pheasant. It was a fricassée of pheasant with chestnuts and it was really imaginative, and a totally different way of cooking the bird. Instead of roasting it or cooking it whole, he cut the breast into goujons and quickly pan-roasted it off and put them into a chestnutty cream sauce – and it worked really well and went down tremendously. At that time his signature dish was a salad of pancetta and chicken liver with lentils and he did that wonderfully too.

Brian bounced in with classic British food coinciding with the release of his book on his life story *A Yorkshire Lad 'My Life with Recipes* – a tremendous rack of English veal finishing off with a classic English trifle, proving the point that simple things often can be the best.

Danyel did some wonderful dishes including a marinade of scallops with green chilli which went down fantastically well in the restaurant apart from Reg Johnson (The Chicken Man) and the Goosnargh gang. Danyel for his brushetta gourmand required a specific Rougie bloc foie gras which had been overlooked as a specific – we had only got normal foie gras – so we had to send someone all the way down to London to get it for him, which was rather expensive.

I wrapped up the festival for the first time on a Saturday, again matching wines with Charles Metcalfe, and it was the first time we used the ice cream (that later became infamous on The Great British Menu with Oliver Payton's dislike of cheese with desserts) in one of my favourite dishes, apple crumble soufflé with Lancashire cheese ice cream. There's a favourite saying of my business partner Craig that can be applied to this dish. It's an old Lancashire saying that goes "a kiss without a squeeze is like apple pie without the cheese".

We had a couple of late nights this year, particularly with Robbie Millar who was the life and soul of the party. He just wouldn't go to bed, especially when he had a good bottle of wine in his hands. He was the wild man of 2002 and the other guys were comparatively sedate in his wake.

GERMAIN SCHWAB

"Some people are born with a talent: artists, poets, writers etc. I believe it is the same with cooking. You create; discover and satisfy an inner need to please others. From the age of seven I knew I wanted to cook. My grandparents ran a mountain restaurant in the Jura, Switzerland, raising their own livestock for the table; making cheese and cooking to please all who sat at their tables, and this was all I wanted to do. There is no greater joy for a chef than to watch his food being enjoyed and appreciated. If, at the end of the day, the 'great and the good' also like what you do then you can consider it a job well done and grab your five minutes of fame."

Monday 21st January

GERMAIN SCHWAB
Winteringham Fields, North Lincolnshire

AMUSE BOUCHE OF PROVENCALE TERRINE,
SAFFRON VINAIGRETTE
Viognier-Chardonnay, Bien Nacido Cuvée,
California Qupé, 1998

CONSOMMÉ OF MILK-FED PIGEON WITH
PAN-FRIED BREAST
Dry Oloroso, Don Nuño, Emilio Lustau

TRI-COLOURED CANNELLONI,
FRESH LANGOUSTINE AND CHICKEN
MOUSSE, SWEET CORN SAUCE
Albariño, Martin Codax, 2000

QUASIS OF VENISON WITH CHESTNUT,
MUSHROOMS AND RED CABBAGE
COMPOTE, GNOCCHIS AND SAUCE
GRAND VENEUR
Reserva, Monte Real, Bodegas Riojanas, Rioja, 1996

PAVÉ OF CHOCOLATE AND HAZELNUT,
CLEAR MANDARIN AND VANILLA SAUCE
Essensia Orange Muscat-Andrew Quady, 1999

QUASIS (RUMP) OF VENISON WITH CHESTNUT, MUSHROOMS AND RED CABBAGE COMPOTE, GNOCCHIS AND SAUCE GRAND VENEUR

Serves 6

INGREDIENTS

Quasis of venison

1kg (approx 180g pp)	Rump of venison
4 soup spoons Dijon mustard	
3	Garlic cloves
2	Garlic cloves, finely chopped
2	Sprigs of thyme
400g	Sliced, fresh cep mushrooms
4 tbsp Duck fat	
15ml	Hare's blood
4g	Green peppercorns
200ml	Red burgundy wine
50ml	Cognac
4 tbsp Redcurrant jelly	
Freshly milled salt & pepper	

Red cabbage compote

1kg	Red cabbage, thinly sliced
2	Large shallots, thinly sliced
2	Cloves garlic, crushed
20	Cooked chestnuts
25ml	Malt vinegar
20g	Demerara sugar
20g	Raisins
100ml	Red burgundy wine
1 litre	Chicken stock
Zest and juice of one orange	
1 soup spoon Duck fat	
1	Bay leaf
1	Cinnamon stick
Pinch grated nutmeg	
2	Cloves
4	Juniper berries
Salt & pepper	

Potato gnocchi

1kg	King Edward potatoes
1	Egg
300g	Pasta flour
Salt & pepper	
Grated nutmeg	
50g	Grated parmesan
Double cream	
Olive oil	

METHOD

Quasis of venison

Season the venison with freshly milled salt and pepper and roll in the Dijon mustard, cover and keep in the fridge overnight.

Preheat the oven to 220°C/425°F/gas mark 7. In a roasting tray heat the duck fat, place the already seasoned quasis in the hot duck fat, seal and brown. Place into the oven with the sprigs of thyme and 3 whole cloves of garlic, and roast for 20 minutes. Remove from the roasting dish, cover with foil and leave to rest for 10 minutes. Remove all fat from the roasting dish and deglaze with a little water, keeping the juices to one side to finish the sauce later.

Pan fry the sliced ceps in duck fat until golden brown, add the finely chopped garlic cloves, cook for a few more seconds, place in a serving dish and deglaze the pan with half of the Cognac, once again keeping this for the sauce.

To finish the sauce, mix together all the deglazed juices in the pan. Add the red wine, the rest of the Cognac, the green peppercorns and redcurrant jelly. Bring to the boil and reduce slightly. Take off the heat and leave to cool a little; add to this the hare's blood a little at a time – it may not be necessary to use all the blood depending on the reduction already achieved.

Red cabbage compote

Into a heavy-based casserole dish place the duck fat, thinly sliced shallots and crushed cloves of garlic, cook gently until soft but not coloured. To this add the juice of the orange, red wine, vinegar and the chicken stock, keep simmering gently. Then add the raisins, bay leaf, cinnamon stick, nutmeg, cloves, juniper berries, the zest of orange and the sugar. Bring to the boil and cook for 5 minutes, season to taste. Add the thinly sliced red cabbage, cook for 25 minutes. In the last 10 minutes of cooking time add the chestnuts. Remove the cinnamon stick before serving. The cabbage will keep for several days in the fridge (without the added chestnuts).

Potato gnocchi

Preheat the oven to 220°C/425°F/gas mark 7. Wash and bake the potatoes until soft, remove the insides and pass through a fine sieve. Place in a bowl. Season then beat in the egg quickly. Add two handfuls of the pasta flour and bind together until a silky smooth dough is achieved. Place the rest of the flour on to a pastry table, tip out the dough and knead until all the flour is incorporated. Do not overwork the dough. Divide the dough into 4 and roll into long sausage shapes the thickness of your finger, cut at an angle into 2cm long pieces.

Bring a large pan of salted water to the boil and add the gnocchi, reduce to a simmer for 2 to 3 minutes – the gnocchi will rise to the top when cooked. Remove from the pan with a sieve, drain and place in a tray, sprinkle with olive oil. The cooked gnocchi will keep in the fridge for 2 to 3 days.

Place the gnocchi into an ovenproof dish, pour over a little double cream and sprinkle with parmesan, grate over a little nutmeg, cook for 10 minutes until starting to colour.

TO SERVE

Sauce the plates, add a little of the red cabbage, slice the rump and place on top, add the ceps and gnocchi.

PHIL HOWARD

"I guess this was the year of Robbie Millar – such a great lad and a fantastic cook. He is sadly missed but I had one of the longest, rambling and enjoyable food conversations I can recall with him. Hand rolled macaroni for 100? Second year, second mistake! My second trip to Northcote also enlightened me to the bond and relationship between supplier and chef. In London, it is business, here it appears to be a wholesome partnership. Impressive."

Tuesday 22nd January
PHIL HOWARD
The Square, London

AMUSE BOUCHE – GAME CONSOMMÉ
Dry Oloroso, Don Nuño, Emilio Lustau

**MILLE-FEUILLE OF RED MULLET AND
AUBERGINES WITH A VINAIGRETTE OF
SARDINES AND WILD ROCKET**
Esporão Reserva, Alentejo Herdade de Esporão, 2000

**SEARED LOIN OF VENISON WITH A TRUFFLE
CREAM, SALAD OF BEETROOT AND APPLE**
Rubicon, Stellenbosch, Meerlust, 1997

**ROAST TURBOT WITH HAND ROLLED
MACARONI, CHANTERELLES AND THYME**
Montagny l'er Cru, Chateau de la Saule,
Alain Roy, 1999

**SOUFFLÉ OF RAISINS AND
PEDRO XIMÉNEZ SHERRY**
Ratafia de Champagne, Vilmart et Cie,
Rilly-La-Montagne

MILLE-FEUILLE OF RED MULLET AND AUBERGINES WITH A VINAIGRETTE OF SARDINES AND WILD ROCKET

Serves 8

INGREDIENTS

Sardine vinaigrette

1	Red onion, finely sliced
Salt	
200ml	Olive oil
12	Sardine fillets
100g	Plain flour
6	Garlic cloves, crushed
6	Plum tomatoes, roughly chopped
1	Sprig of basil
Pinch of sugar	
250ml	Tinned, peeled tomato pulp or passata
Zests of ¼ lemon and 1/8 orange	

Aubergine

4	Round Italian aubergines
Salt & pepper	
10ml	Extra virgin olive oil
8	Leaves of basil, finely sliced

Mille-feuille

16	Sheets feuille de bric
Olive oil	
1 tsp	Ground cumin

Mullet

16	Fillets of red mullet from 340g fish
Olive oil	
Flour	
8	Leaves of basil, finely sliced

Garnish

2	Bunches wild rocket

METHOD

Sardine vinaigrette

In a heavy based ovenproof pan, sweat the red onion with a pinch of salt, in half the olive oil. Dip the sardine fillet, skin side down, into the flour to lightly coat the skin and pan fry, skin side down, in the remaining olive oil. When they are nearly cooked, turn over, add the garlic and swirl the pan for 30 seconds. Tip into the pan with the onions. You may need to do this in two batches. Add the tomatoes, basil, sugar and tomato pulp. Stir briefly, cover with a lid and cook in a slow oven at 110°C/225°F/ gas mark ¼ for half an hour.

Remove from the oven and push, carefully, through a fine sieve. This should give rise to a rich, oily, sardine vinaigrette. Add the zests, stir and reserve at room temperature.

Aubergine

Cut the aubergines in half, season with salt and pepper, brush with some of the extra virgin olive oil, wrap in foil and bake until completely tender at 170°C/335°F/ gas mark 3½. This will take about 45 minutes. Carefully scrape out the flesh and drain in a colander for half an hour. Transfer to a bowl, add the remaining extra virgin olive oil, and break down the aubergine with the back of a fork. Adjust the seasoning if necessary and finish with basil leaves. Reserve at room temperature.

Mille-feuille

Lay 8 sheets of feuille de bric out in front of you. Brush sparingly with olive oil, season with the cumin and cover each with a second sheet and press. Out of these, cut 16 ovals measuring 10x5cm and bake until golden between parchment paper, pressed between two baking sheets at 160°C/325°F/gas mark 3. Reserve at room temperature.

TO SERVE

Pan fry the red mullet fillets in olive oil until just cooked. Start them, lightly floured, skin side down and after 1½ minutes turn them for half a minute to finish. Place the fillets on a tray and brush liberally with sardine vinaigrette.

Place a tiny bit of aubergine in the centre of each of 8 plates. Cover with a sheet of feuille de bric. Spoon a small layer of aubergine over this and top with a fillet of red mullet. Repeat for a second layer. Spoon a little bit of sardine vinaigrette around the plate and garnish with a few rocket leaves dressed in olive oil.

ROBBIE MILLAR

"Robbie was obsessed with food, wine and restaurants. Shanks in Bangor County Down, which he ran with Shirley from 2004, reflected their eclectic yet contemporary style. He used the best of local ingredients, blended with Mediterranean and Asian influences. Robbie was awarded a Michelin Star in 1996 . He cooked every day and under his leadership Shanks was undoubtedly one of Ireland's finest restaurants. Robbie the man was warm, caring and exciting to be around, he lit up a room whenever he entered, and with Robbie we always had fun. As a chef with food he was intelligent, articulate and precise — he was an exceptional cook. A loving husband, a great family man and a true friend sadly missed."

Wednesday 23rd January

ROBBIE MILLAR
Shanks Restaurant, Bangor

SPICED TUNA TARTAR WITH BASIL SCENTED
COUSCOUS, QUAIL EGG AND OVEN
DRIED TOMATO
Tokay Pinot-Gris, Le Fromentau, Josmeyer, 1997

SALAD OF CHICKEN LIVER AND PANCETTA
WITH CREAMED LENTILS,
BALSAMIC VINEGAR AND TRUFFLE AIOLI
Juliénas, Domaine Gérard Descombes, 1999

SEARED SCALLOPS WITH A PURÉE OF
CARROT AND GINGER,
CRISPY CARROTS AND CHINESE FIVE SPICE
Pouilly-Fumé Cuvee d'Eve, Vieilles Vignes,
Jean Claude Dagueneau, 1999

A FRICASSÉE OF PHEASANT WITH
CHESTNUTS, POTATOES, SAVOY CABBAGE,
MORELS AND MADEIRA
Rioja Gran Reserva, Bodegas Sierra Cantabria, 1994

AMARETTI STUFFED PEAR WITH HONEY
ANGLAISE AND MASCARPONE
Muscat de Frontignan, Midi, Château de la Peyrade

SEARED SCALLOPS WITH A PURÉE OF CARROT AND GINGER, CRISPY CARROTS, CHINESE FIVE SPICE

Serves 4

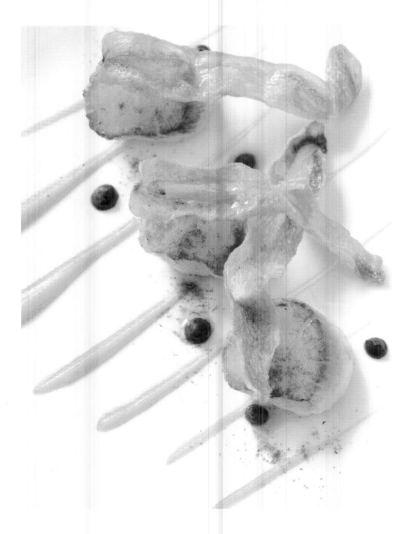

INGREDIENTS

12	Medium king scallops
	Lemon juice
	Carrot and ginger purée (see below)
	Carrot crisps (see below)
	Watercress purée (see below)
	Chinese five spice

Carrot and ginger purée

100g	Carrots, sliced thinly
10g	Grated root ginger
10g	Butter
100g	Cream

Watercress purée

40g	Parsley
240g	Watercress leaves
50ml	Cream
2g	Roast garlic
3g	Salt

Carrot crisps

2	Peeled carrots

METHOD

Place the scallops into a hot non-stick frying pan, press slightly, cook for 2-3 minutes until golden on one side turn the scallops over, add a squeeze of lemon juice and cook for a further minute. Remove from the pan and place onto absorbent paper.

Carrot and ginger purée

Sweat the sliced carrots and ginger with the butter for 3-4 minutes, without colouring them. Season, add the cream and cook for 10-12 minutes until the carrots are soft. Place into a blender and blend until smooth, pass though a fine sieve and check the seasoning.

Watercress purée

Blanch the parsley in boiling water for 2 minutes and the watercress for 1 minute, refresh in iced water. Squeeze the watercress and parsley, removing all the excess water. Place in a Pacojet, add the cream, garlic and seasoning then freeze to -20°C.

Remove from the Pacojet, process, then place in a small pan and gently reheat.

Check seasoning and put into a squeezy bottle.

Carrot crisps

Slice the carrot lengthways, as thinly as possible, ideally on a mandolin. Deep fry at 160°C until golden and crispy. Remove from the fryer and season with salt.

TO SERVE

Put 7 lines of carrot and ginger purée across the plate. Place the 3 scallops in the middle, 6 dots of watercress purée around and finish with the carrot crisps and a dusting of Chinese five spice.

BRIAN TURNER

"I love sitting round a table with friends, so to be able to provide food and drink that tastes good is what drives my passion; and a good old roast is my favourite."

Thursday 24th January
BRIAN TURNER CBE

TERRINE OF SMOKED CHICKEN AND SLOW
COOKED DUCK
WITH A CHUNKY TOMATO DRESSING
Chardonnay, Eden Valley, Heggies, 1998

SEARED WEST COAST SCALLOPS AND
WHITE PUDDING
ON A BED OF SPICY AUBERGINE
Gewürztraminer, Domaine Albert Mann, 1998/99

ROAST RACK OF ENGLISH VEAL,
BUTTER BRAISED CARROTS AND
PARSLEY POTATOES
Bergerac Rosé, Château Tour des Gendres, 2000

WENSLEYDALE AND APPLE CHUTNEY
Côteaux du Layon, Saint-Aubin de Luigné,
Domaine des Forges, 1996

WHITE CHOCOLATE AND
RASPBERRY TRIFLE
Saumur Cardinal, Noir de Noirs,
Gratien and Meyer

ROAST RACK OF ENGLISH VEAL, BUTTER BRAISED CARROTS AND PARSLEY POTATOES

Serves 6

INGREDIENTS

Small rack of veal (1.3kg with bones)
1 tsp   Turmeric
1 tsp   Cumin
1 tsp   Paprika
1 tsp   Oil
57g   Butter
24   Even-sized new potatoes
57g   Butter
Salt & pepper
1 tbsp   Chopped parsley
450g   Carrots
Pinch sugar
57g   Butter
113g   Butter
1 glass   Dry white wine
½ glass   Madeira
3   Shallots, finely chopped
236ml   Chicken stock
1 tbsp   Chopped parsley

METHOD

Trim the veal leaving the eye of the meat and the rib bones.

Mix the turmeric, cumin and paprika.

Colour the veal meat side in a hot roasting tray or frying pan then leave to cool.

Rub with the mix and leave to rest for 24 hours.

Heat the oil and 57g butter. Add the veal and roast in a hot oven 200°C/400°F/gas mark 6 for 10 minutes, turn down to 180°C/350°F/gas mark 4 and roast pink to medium, for approximately 30 minutes, take out and leave to rest.

Meanwhile cook the new potatoes in salted water, drain, season, add 57g of butter and the parsley, keep warm.

While the potatoes are cooking cut the carrots and cook in boiling salted water with a pinch of sugar; when cooked drain and add 57g butter, season and keep warm.

Remove the veal from the tray and keep it warm. Pour away any excess fat. Put one-third of the chopped shallots into a roasting tray. Add the white wine and Madeira and reduce by two-thirds.

In a clean pan, sweat off the rest of the shallots in 57g butter. Then add the stock and reduce by half. Strain the wine mixture into this sauce and reduce to desired taste.

TO SERVE

Stir in cold butter to the sauce as desired, re-season, add parsley and serve with the veal, potatoes and carrots.

BRIAN TURNER

D A N Y E L
C O U E T

"My upbringing with a French father gave me a free path
into genuine food culture. I have always loved the endless
potential that comes with creating innovative courses with
unexpected combinations based on the best of traditional
cooking. I love the mixture of direct physical action
together with an Obsession for the aesthetic output.
There is always a new goal to achieve!"

Friday 25th January

DANYEL COUET
Fredsgatan 12, Stockholm

MARINATED SCALLOPS WITH GREEN CHILLI
Chablis l'er Cru, Montmain, Denis Race, 2000

BRUSCHETTA "GOURMANDE",
BLACK TRUFFLE AND FIGS
Gewürztraminer, Domaine Albert Mann, 1999

SAKE BAKED DOVER SOLE WITH CRISP
VEGETABLES AND SOY
Sauvignon Blanc, Ponder Estate, Marlborough, 2001

SQUAB ROASTED ON THE BONE,
CAULIFLOWER AND FRESH PLUMS
Pedroncelli Zinfandel, Sonoma County, 1999

LIME "KEY WEST", MANDARIN SORBET
Noble Riesling, Brown Brothers, Victoria, 1996

BRUSCHETTA "GOURMANDE", BLACK TRUFFLE AND FIG

Serves 4

INGREDIENTS

240g	Fillet of beef
4	Slices of brioche
200g	Terrine of duck liver (foie gras)
2	Figs, peeled and cut into
8	wedges
1	Small black truffle
1 tbsp	Mayonnaise
Salt & black pepper	
Salad leaves or watercress for garnish	
400ml	Red port
2 tsp	Sherry vinegar
2 tbsp	Olive oil

Port vinaigrette

400ml	Red port
2 tsp	Sherry vinegar
2 tbsp	Olive oil

METHOD

Roll the fillet in cling film and freeze lightly. Slice thinly and put on cling film. Grate half of the truffle finely and mix with the mayonnaise. Slice the rest of the truffle and keep for a garnish.

Toast the brioche and allow to cool. Put the terrine of duck liver on top. Place the 4 quarters of fig on the duck liver. Then put the thin slices of the fillet above the terrine and top with the truffle mayonnaise and slices of truffle. Garnish with salad leaves or watercress and serve with the port vinaigrette.

Port vinaigrette

Pour the port into a heated pan and reduce to 100ml. Add the sherry vinegar, salt, black pepper and olive oil. Take the figs and place in a small bowl and macerate for 30 minutes in half of the port reduction.

NIGEL HAWORTH AND CHARLES METCALFE

"To be obsessed with the quality of the ingredient is to be obsessed with the very essence of flavours."

Saturday 26th January
NIGEL HAWORTH
CHARLES METCALFE
Northcote, Lancashire

TEMPURA KING PRAWN, SCALLOP,
JALAPEÑO TARTAR
Champagne Boizel Brut Réserve N/V

WARM SALAD OF RED LEG PARTRIDGE,
ROAST FOIE GRAS AND BEETROOT
Chassagne Montrachet l'er Cru 'Clos St Jean',
Domaine Ramonet, 1997

SOUP OF FLOOKBOROUGH SHRIMPS,
RAVIOLI OF POTTED SHRIMPS
Chablis l'er Cru 'Beauroy' Domaine, L. Tribut, 1999

WHOLE ROAST SCOTCH FILLET OF BEEF,
CREAMED CELERIAC AND
SPRING CABBAGE, OYSTERS AND PARSLEY
PESTO, MULLED SHALLOTS, RED WINE JUS
Nuits St George l'er Cru 'Les Pruliers',
Domaine D Durban, 1996

APPLE CRUMBLE SOUFFLÉ, LANCASHIRE
CHEESE ICE CREAM
Tokaji Furmint Vendage Tardine, 2000

APPLE CRUMBLE SOUFFLÉ, LANCASHIRE CHEESE ICE CREAM

Serves 4

INGREDIENTS

Apple soufflé

150g	Egg whites
75g	Caster sugar
300g	Apple purée (see below)
	Crumble topping (see below)

Apple purée

500g	Bramley apples, cored and thinly sliced
200g	Caster sugar

Crumble topping

90g	Plain flour
55g	Unsalted butter
55g	Granulated sugar

Lancashire cheese ice cream

210ml	Double cream
210ml	Milk
5	Egg yolks
90g	Caster sugar
150g	Philadelphia cheese
75g	Medium Lancashire cheese, grated

Apple compote

Granny Smith apple

Apple baskets

2	Cox's apples, medium size
	Caster sugar

METHOD

Apple soufflé

You will need 4 ramekins, twice buttered and lined with sugar.

Whisk the egg whites to soft peaks, then slowly add the sugar until fully incorporated.

Put the apple purée into a clean bowl. Mix in one-third of the egg whites and then carefully fold in the remainder. Place in a piping bag.

Half fill the ramekins with the soufflé mix, put 1 teaspoon of apple purée in the middle, pipe the rest of the mix on top, put 1 more teaspoon of apple purée on top and spread evenly. Tap the bottom of the ramekin then, with the point of a small knife, clean the lip of the ramekin (this stops the soufflé from possibly sticking). Finish with a generous amount of crumble on top and bake at 180°C/350°F/gas mark 4 for 7-8 minutes.

Apple purée

Place the finely sliced apples and sugar in a vacuum pack bag and seal tightly. Cook at 70°C for 15 minutes until the apples are soft. Remove from the vacuum pack bag into the Thermomix and blitz until smooth. Pass through a fine sieve and reserve.

Crumble topping

Rub together the flour and butter to resemble breadcrumbs. Stir in the sugar. Place on a metal tray and bake for 15 minutes at 180°C/350°F/gas mark 4.

Lancashire cheese ice cream

Boil the cream and milk together. Mix together the egg yolks and caster sugar. Add one-third of the cream/milk mixture to the egg yolks and caster sugar. Add the remainder of the milk and cream. Pass through a fine sieve. Allow to cool until the mixture is just warm then blitz in the grated Lancashire cheese and Philadelphia. Churn in an ice cream machine and reserve.

Apple compote

Cut the apple into small diced pieces. Blanch for 10 seconds in sweetened acidulated (with lemon juice added) water. Drain and reserve.

Apple baskets

Slice the apples thinly on a mandolin. Place on a silpat on a flat tray. Sprinkle with caster sugar. Bake at 150°C/300°F/gas mark 2 for approximately 10-15 minutes until golden. Remove from the oven. Place the apple rings in a non-stick dariole mould, overlapping as you go – the mould will take approximately 5 rings. Allow to set and simply remove.

TO SERVE

Put a small amount of apple purée and 4 pieces of diced apple compote onto the plate, followed by an apple basket with a large scoop of Lancashire cheese ice cream and the hot soufflé.

NIGEL HAWORTH AND CHARLES METCALFE

20O1

This was the first ever Festival of Food and Wine (Obsession); it was a daunting prospect and understandably there were a lot of nerves flying about. We produced a really low-key brochure on a very tight budget. I remember talking to all the chefs about the essence of the festival, which was to cook in an environment that was relaxing, professional and above all friendly, trying to bring people together as a gathering of friends actually cooking and relaxing, exchanging views and experiences. In that sort of environment you get to see the real chef, the real person and their families more intimately. Over the years many strong and lasting relationships have been forged, many of the festival chefs have since become great friends.

The festival began its infancy with Terry Laybourne on the Tuesday night, cooking some typically great 21 Queen Street food. Terry is a legend in Newcastle and he started the festival with a warm, set potato terrine with caviar which was outstanding, it was simply wonderful. He also did a tempura lobster with fennel; stunningly crisp and with great flavours.

At the beginning I didn't know whether we'd fill any of the nights and I certainly didn't know if we'd fill mine, which is why we asked Charles Metcalfe, the respected wine critic and great friend to come and join us – we did it as a wine and food night, so that we didn't fall flat on our faces. We were basically dead in January in those days, so it was very much a suck-it-and-see scenario; that evening I cooked a selection of Spanish tapas as we were doing an evening of Spanish food and wine matching with Charles. I remember I had to bring two extra fryers into the kitchen to cook the king prawn and squid for the Spanish tapas. I also prepared figs in Pedro Ximénez sherry, which was well received.

Then the Thursday was the start of Phil Howard's ten-year pilgrimage to the North, a Two-Star Chef cooking in Lancashire was a real coup. He did his legendary dish of tortellini of crab with herb – which will live with me forever – among many other exciting things that he did on that night. The evening went down an absolute storm to much acclaim from our most discerning guests who now visit The Square in London on a regular basis.

Nick Nairn closed the festival on the Friday and cooked a great array of dishes – one which I'll always remember is the truffled honey with the Cashel Blue and toasted walnut bread, which was just simplicity itself. Of course, one of his signature dishes is the salad of wood pigeon with black pudding, which was wonderful. That wrapped up the first year, and we hadn't a clue whether it had been successful, but we'd managed to fill the nights and laid the foundation stones of success, and it was onwards and upwards to 2002.

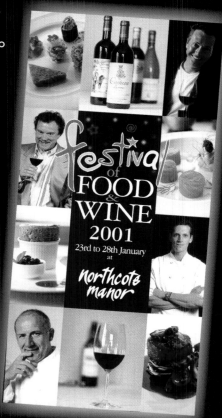

festival of FOOD & WINE 2001
23rd to 28th January at northcote manor

Sunday 27th January

JAZZ BRUNCH
FEATURING KENNY DAVERN
Northcote, Lancashire

MISSISSIPPI RICE BALLS

SHRIMP RISOTTO WITH CUCUMBER
AND JALAPÉNO
Sauvignon Blanc, Marlborough, South Island,
Ponder Estate, 2001

ROAST LEMON PEPPER DUCK,
RED WINE VINEGAR SAUCE
Gigondas, Domaine Bernard Cassan, 1998

PUMPKIN BREAD PUDDING,
CALIFORNIA GRAPEFRUITS
Sauvignon Blanc, Late harvest, Semi-Dulcee,
Bornos, 2000

THE FRENCH LAUNDRY

CHEF'S TASTING MENU
FEBRUARY 28, 1999

CAULIFLOWER "PANNA COTTA"
WITH MALPEQUE OYSTER GLAZE AND SEVRUGA CAVIAR

HAWAIIAN HEARTS OF PALM SALAD
WITH MEDJOOL DATE VINAIGRETTE, GRATED COCONUT
AND CILANTRO-INFUSED OIL

PAN ROASTED FILET OF RED MULLET
WITH ITALIAN PARSLEY PUREE AND "LOZANGE D' AIL"

"MACARONI AND CHEESE"
SWEET BUTTER POACHED MAINE LOBSTER WITH CREAMY LOBSTER BROTH
AND ORZO ENRICHED WITH MASCARPONE CHEESE

SAUTÉED HOFFMAN FARMS WHITE QUAIL
WITH MELTED SAVOY CABBAGE, GRANNY SMITH APPLE COMPOTE
AND APPLEWOOD SMOKE BACON "MOUSSE"

SADDLE OF ELYSIAN FIELDS FARM LAMB
WITH A "CASSOULET" OF WINTER POLE BEANS,
"LANGUE ET RIS D'AGNEAU" AND "CONFIT" OF VINE RIPE TOMATO

"ROQUEFORT"
WITH ROSEMARY POACHED WINTER FRUITS AND ROSEMARY-INFUSED OIL

PASSION FRUIT SORBET
WITH ROASTED MAUI PINEAPPLE AND SWEET BLACK RICE

BITTERSWEET VALRHONA CHOCOLATE "FONDANT"
WITH COFFEE CUSTARD SAUCE AND A CHOCOLATE "DENTELLE"

MIGNARDISE

PRIX FIXE 95.00

6640 WASHINGTON STREET, YOUNTVILLE CA. 94599 707.944.2380

Wednesday
24th January

Charles Metcalfe
presents
A Truly Spanish Wine Evening
with genuine Spanish cabaret from the
London-based
Montuno Trio

MENU

Tapas –
A selection of Spanish delicacies

✲ ✲ ✲

St. Shoulder of Lamb studded with
Fry and Garlic, Poached Plum Tomatoes,
French Beans, Puree Potatoes

✲ ✲ ✲

Poached Figs in Pedro Ximenez Sherry,
Caramelised Saffron Bread

✲ ✲ ✲

Freshly Ground Coffee and Petit Fours

Friday
26th January

Nick Nairn

MENU

Gateau of Hot Smoked Salmon, Avocado and Mango
Salsa, Langoustine Vinaigrette

✲ ✲ ✲

Warm Salad Wood Pigeon, Stornoway Black Pudding,
Fileshire Bacon and Cumberland Sauce topped with
Crispy Parsnips

✲ ✲ ✲

Fillet of John Dory,
Cabbage and Bacon, Mini Fondant Potato,
Caviar Butter Sauce, Balsamic Roast Cherry Tomatoes

✲ ✲ ✲

Toasted Walnut Bread, Cashel Blue, Truffled Honey

✲ ✲ ✲

Hot Raspberry Souffle, Raspberry Sorbet

Thursday
25th January

Philip Howard

MENU

Tortellini of Crab with Herbs

Ballotine of Foie Gras, Poulet De Bresse
and Artichokes

Papillotte of Red Mullet with Cri

Herb Crusted Saddle
with Shallot Puree and

Date and Honey
Crème Fraiche

✲ ✲ ✲

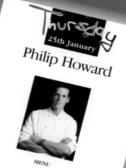

Tuesday
23rd January

Terry Laybourne MBE

MENU

Potato Terrine with Caviar

✲ ✲ ✲

Celeriac Soup with Black Truffle

✲ ✲ ✲

Tempura of Lobster and Fennel
Asian Cream

✲ ✲ ✲

Rug's Duck - Cooked 5 Ways

✲ ✲ ✲

Coconut Pannacotta

TERRY
LAYBOURNE

"My Obsession with food comes from the fact that what
we do is effectively in a permanent state of flux. The
product today is different from the product tomorrow — food
is alive and is constantly changing, which means I have
to continually adapt and shift in order to move forward.
I like to think I put myself at the service of the food
rather than view the food as a medium I then need to
manipulate in order to work with — I try to work hard to
do as little as possible to the ingredients and let them
speak for themselves. "

Tuesday 23rd January

TERRY LAYBOURNE MBE
21 Queen Street, Newcastle

POTATO TERRINE WITH CAVIAR

CELERIAC SOUP WITH BLACK TRUFFLE

TEMPURA OF LOBSTER AND FENNEL,
ASIAN CREAM

REG'S DUCK – COOKED 5 WAYS!

COCONUT PANNA COTTA WITH
TROPICAL FRUITS

INGREDIENTS

Panna cotta

300g	Tinned, sweet coconut cream
335ml	Whipping cream
4	Gelatine leaves
1 tbsp	Malibu

Syrup

1	Clove
¼tsp	Chinese 5 spice
Zest from 1 lime	
Zest from 1 orange	
Zest from ¼ lemon	
1	Vanilla pod, split
1	Bulb lemon grass
½ tsp	Grated ginger
2	Coriander seeds
75g	Sugar
500ml	Water

Tropical fruits

1	Small ripe mango
3	Passion fruits
1	Kiwi fruit
1	Slice pineapple (20mm thick)
1	Orange
2	Mint leaves (finely shredded)

Mango sorbet (to serve)

METHOD

Panna cotta

Soak the gelatine in cold water. Bring the whipping cream to a boil, add the soaked gelatine and pour on to the coconut cream. Pass through a fine chinoise (sieve) and stir in the Malibu. Divide between 4 dariole moulds. Place in a refrigerator for 3-4 hours to set.

Syrup

Mix everything together, bring to a full boil and allow to cool.

Tropical fruits

Peel the mango and cut into neat dice. Scoop out the pulp from the passion fruits, peel the kiwi and pineapple and cut into neat dice. Segment the orange and cut into chunks. Strain the cold syrup over the fruit and chill for 2 hours.

TO SERVE

Turn out the panna cotta into the centre of a chilled dessert plate. Spoon a little of the fruit salad and its syrup around the edge of the plate. Add a spoonful of mango sorbet. Decorate with mint leaves.

NIGEL HAWORTH AND CHARLES METCALFE

"To evolve this Obsession is a journey and an achievement that has no end."

Wednesday 24th January

NIGEL HAWORTH IS JOINED BY CHARLES METCALFE
Northcote, Lancashire

TAPAS – A SELECTION OF
SPANISH DELICACIES

CONFIT SHOULDER OF LAMB STUDDED
WITH ROSEMARY AND GARLIC, POACHED
PLUM TOMATOES, FRENCH BEANS,
PURÉE POTATOES

POACHED FIGS IN PEDRO XIMÉNEZ
SHERRY, CARAMELISED SAFFRON BREAD

CONFIT SHOULDER OF LAMB STUDDED WITH ROSEMARY AND GARLIC, POACHED PLUM TOMATOES, FRENCH BEANS, PURÉE POTATOES

Serves 10

INGREDIENTS

2.4kg	Boneless shoulder of lamb
110g	Coarse sea salt
10g	Picked rosemary (small plushes/sprigs)
25g	Sliced peeled garlic (cut the cloves into 3, lengthways)
110g	Coarse sea salt
	Duck fat
	Mash potatoes (see below)
500g	French beans (see below)
10	Plum tomatoes (see below)
	Roast gravy (see below)

Roast gravy

250g	Banana shallots, sliced
350ml	Madeira
1 litre	Lamb stock
750ml	Chicken stock
50g	Butter

Mash potatoes

1.6kg	Peeled and chopped Maris Piper or desiree potatoes
300ml	Milk
100g	Butter
	Salt

Poached plum tomatoes

10	Medium-size plum tomatoes
100ml	White wine
200ml	Olive oil
30	Slices of garlic clove
	Good handful of rosemary
	Good pinch of salt
	Few turns of the peppermill

French beans

500g	Extra fine French beans (top and tail)
50g	Butter
	Sea salt
	Black pepper

METHOD

Take the shoulder of lamb and salt overnight (approximately 12 hours), wash off the excess salt under cold running water then dry the shoulder thoroughly with a kitchen cloth. Make small incisions on both sides of the shoulder and stud with the rosemary and garlic. Slow cook the shoulder in duck fat for 3-3½ hours at 140°C/275°F/gas mark 1, make sure the lamb is completely covered in the duck fat, then cover with silicon paper and tin foil.

When the lamb is ready remove from the oven and allow to cool a little before removing it from the pan and placing it on to a tray to cool. Allow the shoulder to set, then place onto a carving board and, with a very sharp knife, cut the shoulder into 10 pieces.

When ready to serve the lamb place the shoulder pieces under the bottom of a salamander or in a hot oven 200°C/400°F/gas mark 6 until crispy on the outside.

Roast gravy

Sweat off the shallots lightly to caramelise, add Madeira, reduce by three-quarters, add the lamb and chicken stock. Reduce down to the desired consistency and pass through a tammy cloth, blend in the butter and reserve.

Mash potatoes

Place the potatoes into a pan of water and boil until cooked. Then strain away the water, add the milk, butter and salt and beat until smooth. Put the mash into a piping bag and keep warm.

Poached plum tomatoes

Gently poach the tomatoes in the white wine, olive oil, garlic and rosemary. Season with salt and pepper, reserve when ready.

French beans

Take the French beans and boil in lightly salted water until al dente, take the beans out and refresh in iced water. When the beans are cold pour off the ice and water and keep them on a small tray ready for use. The beans are reheated in a little butter, a few drops of water and seasoned with salt and pepper.

TO SERVE

Take a large white pasta bowl and place a quenelle of hot mash to one side. Put the shoulder of lamb at the side of the mash then add the poached tomato, garlic and rosemary. Put the French beans on top, pour over the gravy and serve.

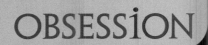

PHIL HOWARD

"I felt I was only there in order to demonstrate that Northcote is an equal opportunity employer – the token southerner! Date soufflé in an unfamiliar kitchen – first year, first mistake. I had never really met Craig and Nigel before but their mark was made. What impressed me most was their display of Lancastrian hospitality."

Thursday 25th January

PHIL HOWARD
The Square, London

TORTELLINI OF CRAB WITH HERBS

BALLOTINE OF FOIE GRAS, POULET DE
BRESSE AND ARTICHOKES

PAPILLOTTE OF RED MULLET WITH
CREAMED FENNEL

HERB CRUSTED SADDLE OF LAMB
WITH SHALLOT PURÉE AND ROSEMARY

DATE AND HONEY SOUFFLÉ,
CRÈME FRAÎCHE ICE CREAM

TORTELLINI OF CRAB WITH HERBS

Serves 8

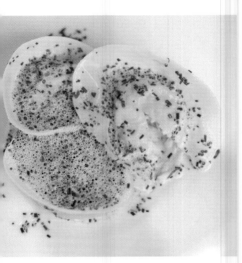

INGREDIENTS

325g	'00' pasta flour
12	Eggs
4	Yolks
Salt	
1 tbsp	Olive oil
200g	Scallops, out of the shell, skirts reserved
200ml	Double cream
Juice of ½ lemon	
400g	White crab meat
4	Basil leaves, finely sliced
2	Shallots, finely sliced
½	Head of fennel, finely sliced
1 tbsp	Olive oil
1	Star anise
10	Fennel seeds
10	Coriander seeds
250ml	Champagne
300ml	Water
100g	Crème fraîche
20	Tarragon leaves, finely chopped
1	Bunch of chives, finely chopped
½	Bunch chervil, finely chopped

METHOD

To make the pasta dough place the flour, the eggs and 3 yolks in a food processor with a pinch of salt and a tablespoon of olive oil. Blend until the mix turns to a crumb. If it tries to clump into a dough, add a bit more flour. The pasta dough must be firm or making the tortellini will be trying to say the least. Turn the mix onto a work surface, press together firmly and briefly knead into a dough. Wrap tightly and chill.

Crab mix

First of all make the mousse. Blend the scallops in a chilled food processor bowl with a generous pinch of salt. Scrape down the sides of the bowl during this process. Add the remaining egg yolk and blend for 30 seconds. Re-chill in the fridge.

Now place this scallop purée into a decent sized bowl set over ice. With the use of a wooden spoon incorporate the double cream, bit by bit, while beating vigorously. Once all the cream is added season with lemon juice and chill. To confirm you have made a good mousse place half a teaspoon of this mix in a pan of simmering water. Remove from the heat. The mousse should cook – becoming light and springy in texture. If it 'splits' and disperses across the surface you have probably added the cream too fast or not incorporated it with enough vigour. Taste the mousse to check for seasoning. Now mix the mousse with the crab and add the basil. Mix and reserve in the fridge.

Sauce

This is a simple, fresh sauce and should be made quickly. Rub the scallop skirts (the frill running around the shell) with plenty of salt to clean. Rinse under running water. In a shallow heavy based pan sweat the shallots and fennel together in olive oil until soft. Add a pinch of salt, the star anise, fennel seeds and coriander seeds. Cook over a high heat for one minute – do not colour.

Add the scallop skirts. These will release liquid. Reduce until this has all gone. Add the Champagne and similarly reduce. Add 300ml water, bring to the boil and cook gently for 5 minutes. Pass through a fine sieve into a small pan, add the crème fraîche and whisk. Taste and adjust the seasoning if necessary. Reserve in the fridge.

To make the raviolis

Roll out the pasta dough and cut into discs 5cm in diameter and no more than 2mm thick. You will need 24 discs but roll out a few extra! Cover a plate with cling film, place the discs on top, covering immediately so they do not dry out. Place a large pan of water on to boil. Have a large bowl of iced water to refresh the ravioli and a bag of flour to hand and dust the work surface lightly. Divide the crab mix into 24 little spoonfuls on another plate and keep chilled.

Take the first disc, put it through the pasta machine to take it to 1mm thick. Turn the machine now to the penultimate setting to roll the disc once more. You should end up with an oval approximately 12x10cm. Put the crab mix in the centre, fold the disc over and press to seal. Do not have excess flour or the pasta will not stick. Now pick up the half made raviolis in your left hand with the curve of the pasta running above your fingertips. Gently holding one side of this inbetween your thumb and index finger wrap the other end around your thumb and pinch firmly to secure. Keep your hands dusted with flour. Once all 24 are made, blanch them for 2 minutes in the salted water, refresh in the iced water, drain and reserve chilled until required.

TO SERVE

Reheat the tortellini in a large pan of preheated, salted water for 3 minutes. Drain and divide among 8 bowls. Heat up the sauce. Blend with a hand blender to aerate, add the herbs, briefly blend and spoon over the ravioli.

NICK NAIRN

"Cooking gives me a means of expression, in fact, it's the medium through which I communicate the best. And it continues to challenge me. There's always something new to discover and that's why I enjoy it as much now as I did 25 years ago."

Friday 26th January

NICK NAIRN
Nairn's Glasgow, Glasgow

GATEAUX OF HOT SMOKED SALMON,
AVOCADO AND MANGO SALSA,
LANGOUSTINE VINAIGRETTE

WARM SALAD OF WOOD PIGEON,
STORNOWAY BLACK PUDDING,
FIFESHIRE BACON AND
CUMBERLAND SAUCE
TOPPED WITH CRISPY PARSNIPS

FILLET OF JOHN DORY,
CABBAGE AND BACON, MINI FONDANT
POTATO, CAVIAR BUTTER SAUCE,
BALSAMIC ROAST CHERRY TOMATOES

TOASTED WALNUT BREAD, CASHEL BLUE,
TRUFFLED HONEY

HOT RASPBERRY SOUFFLÉ,
RASPBERRY SORBET

WARM SALAD OF WOOD PIGEON, STORNOWAY BLACK PUDDING, FIFESHIRE BACON AND CUMBERLAND SAUCE, TOPPED WITH CRISPY PARSNIPS

Serves 6

Cooked properly – nicely rosy pink – pigeon (without the rubbery skin) is one of my favourite game birds and available all year round. There are certain flavours that are just made for each other, and the pigeon and black pudding combo is one of them. Although my natural preference is for the fantastic black pudding from Stornoway (comes in a thick log and has no great gobbits of fat in it!), other local black puddings can be used instead. The parsnip crisps can be cut two ways – long and ribbon-like so that they curl around each other, or into rounds like normal crisps. This was something of a signature dish in my Braeval days.

INGREDIENTS

Cumberland Sauce

500g	Redcurrant jelly
250ml	Ruby port
	Juice and grated zest of 2 lemons
	Juice and grated zest of 2 oranges
1 tsp	Ground cinnamon
2 tsp	English mustard

Salad

50g	Puy lentils, soaked overnight
8	Slices Fifeshire streaky bacon
3	Slices Stornoway black pudding
4	Skinned wood pigeon breasts
	Sea salt and freshly ground black pepper
	Sunflower oil for deep-frying, plus 1 tbsp
150g	Parsnips, thinly sliced lengthways or rounds
150g	Mixed washed salad leaves
½	Red onion, sliced paper thin
3 tbsp	Extra virgin olive oil
1 tsp	Aged sherry vinegar (or more to taste)
2 tbsp	Water
1	Shallot, finely diced
	Sea salt and freshly ground black pepper

METHOD

Preheat the oven to 220°C/425°F/ gas mark 7.

Cumberland sauce

Place all the ingredients into a saucepan and bring to the boil. Skim away the froth and reduce over a medium heat for approximately 30 minutes. Strain through a fine sieve and cool. When cold, it should have the consistency of runny honey. This zingy, fruity sauce keeps sfor up to eight weeks in the fridge. I store mine in a squeezy bottle so that I can easy drizzle it around the plate.

Salad

Drain the lentils and put them in a saucepan with just enough water to cover and cook them very slowly for eight to ten minutes until tender. Drain the lentils again and put them in a bowl.

Lay the sliced bacon and black pudding on a tray lined with baking parchment and pop them into the oven to cook for 3-4 minutes. When the bacon is crisp and the black pudding cooked, remove from the oven, drain the bacon on kitchen paper then crumble to break it up. Cut each slice of black pudding into quarters. Keep warm.

Season the pigeon breasts with salt and pepper. Heat a frying pan until it's very hot, add 1 tbsp sunflower oil and lay the breasts skinned side down. Sear the pigeon

breasts for about two minutes on each side. Remove from the pan to a warm tray and allow to rest in a warm place for at least 10 minutes. Keep hold of the frying pan and do not wash.

While the pigeon is resting, heat the oil to 190°C/375°F/gas mark 5 or until a bread cube turns golden in 20 seconds. Deep-fry the parsnips until golden. Drain and leave them on a sheet of kitchen paper until required. Sprinkle with salt.

Slice the pigeon breasts thinly – about a dozen slices per breast (they should still be very pink inside) – and put in a bowl with the black pudding and bacon. Have the salad leaves mixed with the onion ready in a separate bowl.

TO SERVE

At the very last moment, mix the oil, vinegar, water, chopped shallot and lentils together, season well and use to deglaze the pigeon pan, heating it through at the same time. Once reduced by half, pour over the leaves and toss gently with your hands to coat. Finally, carefully mix the leaves with the pigeon, black pudding and bacon. Divide between four shallow bowls or plates, drizzle with Cumberland sauce and top each pile with some crispy parsnips. Serve immediately before it all goes soggy!

COOKING AT HOME

All the chefs involved in Obsession kindly agreed to contribute a recipe that is their favourite to cook at home, not as challenging in most cases, although musk thistle might be! Enjoy.

Nigel

Michael Caines and Eric Chavot cooking at home

MUSK THISTLE AND MILK SKIN SALAD WITH GARLIC OIL AND TIGER NUT JUICE
Serves 4

ANDONI LUIS ADURIZ

Musk thistle is sweeter and tenderer than the more common thistle. This is because it is sheltered from the outdoor elements during cultivation, as it is almost completely covered with blocks of soil. This technique is very uncommon and is basically limited to family run farms. Due to the amount of care required and the disappearance of traditional practices, this product will most likely cease to exist in the near future.

INGREDIENTS

Thistle

1	Heart of musk thistle
2	Musk thistle stalks
Water	
Parsley with stems	

Vinaigrette

75ml	Extra virgin olive oil
25ml	Garnacha wine vinegar

Mille-feuille

1 litre	Milk
100g	Lactose

Tiger nut juice

1 litre	Mineral water
250g	Tiger nuts
50g	Extra virgin olive oil
3g	Garlic
Salt	

METHOD

Thistle

Prepare a bowl full of very cold water with chopped parsley. This will partially prevent the oxidation of the thistle chunks.

Use the tip of a knife to break up the heart of the thistle. Break it into medium walnut-size chunks. Place the thistle pieces into the cold water infusion that you have previously prepared with the parsley.

Next, cut the thistle stalks into 5-6 cm pieces. Carefully remove the inner and outer peeling from them. Cut the sectioned stalks into sticks, approximately 1cm wide.

Vinaigrette

Mix the two ingredients together, without emulsifying them.

Mille-feuille

Set up a double boiler with the temperature at 75°C, and place a tray measuring 30x20x5cm over it, so that it is partially submerged. Try to keep this tray slightly submerged in the water, taking care not to allow water to get inside it. Pour the milk into the tray, and wait for it to form a fine dry film or 'skin'. Use a narrow rod to detach the film from the sides and bottom of the tray, carefully moving the rod from one side to the other so as not to break the film. Place the film, or 'skin' on another tray, sprinkle with lactose and allow to dry for 1 hour at room temperature.

Tiger nut juice

Soak the tiger nuts in water for 24 hours, then drain.

Place the tiger nuts and the water in a blender and blend at the highest setting until the tiger nuts are completely blended into the water.

Strain and pour the liquid back into the blender, adding the oil, salt and garlic, and blend again.

Pour into small tubes.

TO SERVE

Toss the thistle with the vinaigrette in a wide serving dish and stack the thistle randomly. Place the milk skin over it in an arbitrary fashion, allowing it to droop over the thistle. Drizzle the tiger nut juice over the milk skin.

POTATO GNOCCHI WITH BUTTERNUT SQUASH AND MUSHROOMS

Serves 5

INGREDIENTS

Gnocchi

600g	Mashed rooster potatoes
100g	Plain flour
75g	Fine polenta
25g	Grated parmesan
	Salt & pepper
	Grated nutmeg
½	Whole egg
2	Egg yolks

Garnish

2 tbsp	Olive oil
150g	Small dice of butternut squash
50g	Butter
125g	Sliced mushrooms
2 tbsp	Double cream
25g	Grated parmesan

ANDREW FAIRLIE

METHOD

Gnocchi

Bake the potatoes in their jackets in a hot oven (220°C/425°F/gas mark 7) until tender. Cut in half, scoop out the flesh and pass through a sieve. Weigh out 500g.

Gently mix the flour, polenta and parmesan with the warm potato, season with salt, pepper and grated nutmeg.

Mix the egg and yolks together, add to the potato and gently knead together, being careful not to over mix.

Lightly dust the table with flour, divide the gnocchi mix into four. Using the palms of your hands roll each piece into a rope 2.5cm thick, then cut each rope into 5cm pieces. Roll each piece into neat balls and shape using the prongs of a fork into grooved cylinders.

Bring a large pot of boiling salted water to the boil, add the gnocchi, bring the water back to the boil – as the gnocchi cook they will float to the surface. Scoop them out using a slotted spoon and drain on clean kitchen towel.

TO SERVE

Heat a frying pan with the olive oil, add the diced butternut squash and cook for 4 to 5 minutes until just tender. Add the cooked gnocchi to the pan, raise the heat slightly, add the butter and cook until the gnocchi are golden brown. Add the sliced mushrooms and continue to cook for another two minutes. Add the cream, bring to a simmer, and season. Tip out onto serving plates and sprinkle grated parmesan over the top.

FRICASSÉE OF LOCAL PHEASANT WITH AMPLEFORTH APPLES, YOUNG LEEKS, PRUNES AND CIDER CREAM, CELERIAC PURÉE

Serves 2

INGREDIENTS

A splash of olive oil
50g   Diced onion
2   Breasts of pheasant, skin on and cut into 2cm dice
2   Rashers smoked bacon or pancetta, cut into lardons
200ml   Cider
200ml   Whipping cream
50ml   Game stock, reduced by two-thirds
2   Eating apples, diced or balls
10   Pitted Agen prunes
8   Young leeks
Seasoning

Celeriac purée

½   Celeriac, peeled and cut into 1cm dice
200ml   Whipping cream
200ml   Milk
Seasoning (use ground white pepper)
20g   Unsalted butter

A N D R E W
P E R N

'Faisan à la Normande' was one of the first dishes I cooked as a child – we always had pheasant in abundance on the farm. They were raised from day-old chicks in circular, floodlit, plywood pens, then released for the rough shoots in later life.

The creamy cider sauce, along with a can of Woodpecker from the village shop, was as far as I got as a youngster. Now, with the addition of tender young leeks from the garden, pitted Agen prunes and silky celeriac purée, it has become a lot more suave, yet still within the boundaries of comfort food in the depths of winter.

METHOD

In a little olive oil, sweat off the onion, pheasant and bacon, colour until golden brown. Add the cider, cream and game stock, reduce by half – cook for approximately 10 minutes. Add the apples, prunes and leeks, and warm through gently for 1 to 2 minutes; check seasoning. Serve immediately with the celeriac purée.

Celeriac purée

Cover the celeriac in the cream and milk in a pan, and bring to the boil. Simmer until cooked, such that the liquid is absorbed into the vegetable. When soft, place in a blender and purée until smooth, season and add butter. Serve hot, as required.

T-BONE STEAK WITH SALSA VERDE
Serves 1

INGREDIENTS

Salsa verde

1	Garlic clove
4	Fresh anchovies in vinegar
2 tbsp	Capers
2 tbsp	Cornichons
	Olive oil
½	Bunch large parsley
	Red wine vinegar

Steak

450g	T-Bone steak
	Salt
	Pepper
	Olive oil
	Butter
½	Garlic head
	Thyme

Salad

Cherry tomatoes
Shallot
Chives
Olive oil
Balsamic vinegar
Salt
Pepper
1 bulb of roast garlic

ANGELA HARTNETT

METHOD

Salsa verde

Blend the garlic, anchovies, capers and cornichons in a Robot Coupe. Add enough oil to form a paste. Add the picked parsley and blend until smooth, adding more oil as needed. Add a few tablespoons of red wine vinegar as needed and season to taste.

Steak

Season the T-Bone on both sides with salt and pepper. Coat with olive oil and grill on a high heat for 2 minutes, then cross for another 2 minutes turn over and repeat the crossing.

Put the steak in a skillet, add a cube of butter on top, add the garlic and thyme and cook in the oven at 180°C/350°F/gas mark 4 for 5-6 minutes for medium.

Make a quick salad by cutting the cherry tomatoes in half, finely slicing the shallots, chopped chives, season with olive oil, balsamic vinegar, salt and fresh pepper.

Once the T-Bone is cooked, take out of the oven and leave to rest for a few minutes (keep all the juices that are left on the skillet and then also the juices when it rests).

TO SERVE

Add the steak to the salad, pour over the cooking juices (quickly heat up the juices from cold) and add a big spoonful of salsa verde. Serve with the roast garlic.

ANTHONY FLINN

BRAISED LAMB SHANK
Serves 4

INGREDIENTS

Lamb shanks

4	Lamb shanks (trimmed)
1 litre	Good meat stock
Oil	

Lentils

100g	Lentils
1	Garlic clove
250ml	Light meat stock
1	Sprig of thyme

Silver skinned onions

16	Silver skinned onions
1	Garlic clove
Knob of butter	
Olive oil	
1	Sprig of thyme

Mash potato

500g	Peeled, chopped potatoes
Salted water	
300g	Cream
Garlic clove	

Other ingredients

Thyme leaves
Sliced olives
Diced tomato
Reduced meat sauce
Olive oil

METHOD

Lamb shanks

Preheat the oven to 120°C/250°F/gas mark ½. Brown the lamb shanks in a pan with a little oil. When fully coloured place in the stock and bring to the boil. Once boiling, place in the oven for around 3 hours or until the meat is soft but not falling from the bone. When cooked, pass through a chinoise (sieve) the excess stock into a separate pan, reduce until a sticky sauce consistency and reserve for the finished lamb shank. Place the lamb shank into the reduced meat sauce and bring to the boil.

Lentils

Place all the ingredient into a pan. Slowly simmer the lentils until cooked. Once fully cooked, drain off the stock and remove the garlic and thyme.

Silver skinned onions

Peel the onions. Place them in a foil bag with the garlic, butter, oil and the thyme. Roast in the oven until soft.

Mash potato

Boil the potatoes in the water until cooked. Strain off the water and leave to steam off and drain fully. Do not let the potato go cold. Place the cream and garlic in a pan and reduce by half. Once the potatoes look dry pass them through a mouli or ricer until lump free. Pass the cream through a sieve and pour over the potatoes Beat together until fully incorporated. Finish with salt to taste.

TO SERVE

Once the shank is hot and glazed with the sauce remove the shank and add the lentils, thyme leaves, olives, tomatoes and the onions to the sauce. Pipe the creamy hot mash into a bowl and sit the lamb shank on top. Spoon the sauce and all the garnish over the shanks and finish with a drizzle of good olive oil. Serve.

PIGEON WITH VANILLA BEETROOT
Serves 4

INGREDIENTS

8	Pigeon supremes
10g	Ginger garlic paste
5g	Garam masala powder
30ml	Oil
Salt, to taste	

Vanilla beetroot

Oil	
500g	Beetroot slivers
20g	Panch poran spice
50ml	White vinegar
100g	Caster sugar
2	Vanilla pods
Salad leaves, to serve	

METHOD

Clean the pigeon supremes and trim off any excess fat. Marinate the pigeon with the ginger garlic paste, garam masala, powder, oil and salt. Leave in this marinade for 2 hours. Cook in a moderately hot tandoor oven until done (or conventional oven at 180°C/350°F/gas mark 4 for 15-20 minutes.

Heat the oil and temper (crackle in hot oil) the panch poran spices. Add the remaining ingredients and cook until the beetroot is soft and the moisture has evaporated.

TO SERVE

Assemble the pigeon on a plate with salad leaves and the vanilla beetroot.

ATUL KOCHHAR

ROAST COD WITH BOILED POTATOES, PURPLE SPROUTING BROCCOLI AND SEAWEED BUTTER

BRETT GRAHAM

Serves 4

INGREDIENTS

100ml	Water
1 tsp	Cornflour mixed with 2 tbsp water
1	Small baked potato, scooped out while hot and passed through a sieve
200g	Butter
500g	Small new potatoes
Salt	
4 x 150g	Pieces of cod
Juice of ½ lemon	
2	Bunches of purple sprouting broccoli
Chopped seaweed including 1 tsp of dried nori powder	

METHOD

Boil 100ml of water and thicken with the paste made from the cornflour and water, add the baked potato and whisk until smooth, then slowly add butter until a nice smooth shiny sauce is achieved. Keep warm.

Boil the new potatoes in salted water until tender.

Roast the cod in a hot pan in the oven and finish with some butter and lemon juice.

Place the purple sprouting broccoli in some boiling water and cook until tender, drain well.

TO SERVE

Place a few new potatoes in a large bowl followed by a piece of cod then some purple sprouting broccoli. Add the chopped seaweed to the potato butter and pour over the cod.

CREAMY VANILLA RICE PUDDING WITH SPICED BLACKBERRY JAM

Serves 4

INGREDIENTS

Creamy vanilla rice pudding

118ml	Milk
354ml	Double cream
57g	Unrefined caster sugar
1	Vanilla pod, split
113g	Arborio rice
118ml	Double cream, whipped

Spiced blackberry jam

57g	Butter
340g	Blackberries
113g	Unrefined caster sugar
118ml	Water
1	Vanilla pod, split
2.5cm	Cinnamon stick
1	Star anise
1	Pinch nutmeg

B R I A N T U R N E R

METHOD

Creamy vanilla rice pudding

Heat the milk and cream. Add the sugar and split vanilla pod. Shower in the rice, stir and cook on the stove top with lid on for approximately 45 minutes. Take off the heat and leave to rest for 5 minutes. Fold in the whipped cream.

Spiced blackberry jam

While the rice pudding is resting, heat the butter in a pan, add 113g blackberries. Add sugar and allow to caramelise. Put to one side and add the water. Bring back to the boil. Add the split vanilla pod, cinnamon, star anise and nutmeg. Cook for 5 minutes then take out the vanilla pod and star anise. Purée in a machine/blender, then strain into a clean pan. Bring to the boil and reduce until it looks jam like. Take off the heat and add the rest of the blackberries. Stir in and leave to cook for 10 minutes. Serve in the centre of the rice and with some on the side.

HOT CROUSTADE OF PRUNE AND ARMAGNAC, PRUNE AND ARMAGNAC ICE CREAM

Serves 4

BRUCE POOLE

INGREDIENTS

4	Sheets feuille de bric (from North African or Middle Eastern speciality shops) or filo pastry, although the recipe doesn't work quite as well with this
1	Egg yolk, lightly beaten
20	Agen prunes marinated in Armagnac with sugar (bring 150g caster sugar and 250ml of Armagnac to the boil, take off heat and add prunes. Once cooled and stored in an air-tight container such as a kilner jar, these prunes will keep almost indefinitely)

Frangipane

100g	Butter
100g	Caster sugar
100g	Whole egg (about 3 large or 4 small eggs)
100g	Ground almonds

Ice cream

500ml	Milk
500ml	Double cream
50g	Sugar
15	Egg yolks

Glazing the croustade

100g	Melted butter – ideally clarified – for glazing the croustades
	Icing sugar

METHOD

Ice cream

To make the ice cream, bring the milk and cream up to the boil. In a roomy bowl, beat the sugar into the egg yolks well and combine with the scalded milk and cream. Return back to the pan and to the heat to cook, stirring constantly until the mixture thickens perceptibly – the old coating on the back of a wooden spoon test works well here. Avoid over cooking or the mixture will scramble, probably irretrievably. When the mixture has cooled, churn in an ice cream machine. Take 12 of the prunes and chop each prune into about 6 pieces. Pour some of the Armagnac syrup into the ice cream as it churns – stopping the machine to taste. How much booze you add is up to you – I like quite a lot. And in the ice cream! Towards the end of the churning process, add the chopped prunes and continue churning just long enough to combine ice cream and fruit.

This will produce more ice cream than you need for the croustades, but it cannot really be made in smaller quantities easily and keeps well. It is in fact a great dessert just on its own. This can, of course, be made the day before.

Frangipane

Make the frangipane by creaming the butter (not the melted butter) and the sugar, either by hand or in a mixer. Add gradually and alternately the beaten egg and

ground almonds. This will yield more frangipane than you need for this recipe but it is difficult to make in smaller quantities and it is always useful in other desserts. This can be made beforehand and refrigerated, but needs to be at a cool room temperature when assembling the croustades. Heat the oven to 180°C/350°F/gas mark 4.

Cut each sheet of bric into large, neat, even-sided triangles, discarding the trim. Using a pastry brush, carefully paint a 1cm border with beaten egg yolk – this will act as glue. Working fairly quickly, place a small spoonful of frangipane in the middle of the pastry, arrange two prunes on top of the frangipane and gather up the sides of the triangle to

form a slightly crumpled tent shape – not dissimilar to the Hogwarts sorting hat featured in one of the early Harry Potter movies. Seal the edges well with your fingers to make the parcel airtight.

Carefully paint the croustades with the melted – ideally clarified – butter (using a water sprayer filled with the melted butter is best for this – or use a fine pastry brush) and dust generously with icing sugar. Bake in the preheated oven until pleasingly golden and crisp – somewhere between 15 and 20 minutes.

Rest the croustades for five minutes out of the oven before serving on warmed plates, Serve with a scoop of the ice cream and a little more Armagnac syrup, if you like.

DUCK CONFIT WITH SAVOY CABBAGE, HARICOT BLANC AND BLACK PUDDING

Serves 4

INGREDIENTS

4	Confit duck legs
1 tsp	Duck fat
1	Garlic clove, crushed
½	Spanish onion, finely sliced
12	Slices black pudding
50ml	Olive oil
2	Rashers of streaky bacon, cut into matchsticks
¼	Head of Savoy cabbage, washed and shredded
4 tbsp	Water
100g	Haricot blanc (beans) cooked with whole carrots (if you can, cut grooves into the edges of the carrots with a cannelle cutter. After cooking the carrots are removed and sliced into coin-shaped pieces)
Salt & pepper	
1 tsp	Very roughly chopped parsley
60ml	Duck jus, to serve

CHRIS GALVIN

METHOD

Heat a thick bottomed pan and place the duck legs skin side down to crisp the skin and heat through in the oven at 180°C/350°F/gas mark 4 for about 10 minutes.

In another heavy pan heat the duck fat, add the garlic and cook without colour for a minute then add the onion and sauté for a further minute.

Brush the black pudding with a little olive oil and grill for 1½ minutes.

Turn up the heat, add the bacon and stir until it begins to crisp, then quickly add the cabbage with the 4 tablespoons of water. Place a lid on top and shake the pan, stirring frequently until the cabbage is softened but still brilliant in colour. Pull the pan to the side of the heat.

Stir haricot blanc and carrots into the cabbage, season to taste with salt and a few twists of the peppermill, pour in a little of the juice and duck fat from the confit pan, stir in half the parsley and set aside.

TO SERVE

Divide the cabbage between four plates, add the black pudding and carrots, place a crispy duck leg on top of each, pour a little duck jus around, sprinkle the remaining parsley on top of the duck and serve.

CHRISTIAN'S HOME-STYLE PIZZA
Serves 4

CHRISTIAN OLSSON

Quite often on Sundays when I'm off I let my boys Jack and Sam (six and eight years old) decide what's going to be on the menu for the evening and this pizza is a favourite. They love making pizza and I love cooking together with them. To be able to deal with the mess in the kitchen afterwards I need a good glass of red wine, help from my wife and great music.

INGREDIENTS

Dough

50g	Fresh yeast
300ml	Cold water
2 tbsp	Olive oil
500-600g	Plain flour
1 pinch of salt	
1 pinch of sugar	

Tomato sauce

2	Jars of Sicilian whole and peeled tomatoes
2	Shallots
1	Garlic clove
½	Dutch chilli
3 tbsp	Olive oil
1 dash of white wine	
1 tbsp	Red wine vinegar
Salt & pepper	

Topping

75g	Mozzarella cheese
75g	Brie de maux
100g Italian	Fresh salciccia (thin pork sausage), sliced
2 tbsp	Capers (the bigger kind that come in salt water), deep fried
2 tbsp	Calamata olives
1	Red onion
6	Cocktail tomatoes
6	Sardines in olive oil
3	Quail or hen eggs, hard boiled to leave a soft centre, shelled and halved
1	Bunch of rocket
Basil for garnish	
A few rounds with the peppermill	

METHOD

Stir the yeast into the water, add the olive oil, salt and sugar. Add the flour and work to a smooth dough. Cut into individual-sized pizzas.

To make the tomato sauce, chop the shallots, garlic and chilli, sauté in the olive oil. Add the tomatoes, white wine and red wine vinegar and let it boil until it becomes a thick and chunky sauce. Season.

Spread a thin layer of tomato sauce on each pizza then spread with the cheeses, tomatoes and red onion. Bake in the oven at 250°C/475°F/gas mark 9 for about 15 minutes (keep checking that it does not burn). Top with the remaining ingredients, season and serve.

CARPACCIO OF CORNISH POLLOCK
Serves 2

INGREDIENTS

250g   Pollock
Salt
Almond oil
Truffle oil
Half a black radish
1   Lemon, zest only
Mixed herbs
Black truffle

METHOD

Sprinkle the pollock with salt and leave for 6 minutes. Wash, drain and pat dry. Slice as thinly as possible and set aside.

Slice half a black radish as thinly as possible and set aside.

Take a round medium-sized plate. Shake one drop of almond oil onto it and smear around to create a film. Arrange with 2 slices of pollock followed by 1 slice of radish, 2 slices of pollock, 1 slice of radish continuously until all the ingredients have been used. Sprinkle with almond oil, lemon zest and mixed herbs.

Finish with dots of truffle oil around the plate and shavings of black truffle.

CLAUDE BOSI

DANIEL CLIFFORD

PANCAKES

Serves 8

INGREDIENTS

473ml   Semi-skimmed milk
453g   Plain flour
10 eggs
Vegetable oil

METHOD

Mix the flour and eggs and add the milk a little at a time to make a batter.

Heat a non-stick frying pan with a little oil.

Using one ladleful per pancake, spread the mixture around the pan, leave to cook for 30 seconds and toss, repeat then serve with your favourite filling.

LAMB MEATBALLS WITH FETA
Serves 6

INGREDIENTS

1.5kg	Minced lamb
1	Egg yolk
2 tbsp	Cold water
59ml	Feta, crumbled plus extra for garnish
1 tsp	Marjoram, chopped plus extra sprigs for garnish
1	Garlic clove, crushed
1 tsp	Oregano, chopped
1 tsp	Cumin
56g	Butter, for frying
2 tbsp	Olive oil, for frying
4	Plum tomatoes, grated
Grated peel from 1 lemon	
59ml	Olive oil
2 tbsp	Sherry vinegar
Salt & black pepper	

INGREDIENTS

Mix the minced lamb, egg yolk and a little salt to a paste. Add the cold water, the feta, marjoram, garlic, oregano and cumin. Roll into small meatballs and fry in butter and oil until they have a good colour.

Mix together the tomatoes, with 59ml olive oil, the grated lemon peel and the sherry vinegar. Season with salt and pepper. Serve with the meatballs. Top with crumbled feta and oregano.

DANYEL COUET

DARINA ALLEN

This delectable tart is an adaptation of a traditional recipe which was originally cooked in a bastable over the open fire – everyone adores it. You could also add a couple of teaspoons of freshly grated ginger to the rhubarb, but try it unadorned at first, it's seriously good.

ROSCOMMON RHUBARB PIE
Serves 6-8

INGREDIENTS

900g	Red rhubarb
255-285g	Granulated sugar

Topping

310g	Plain flour
20g	Caster sugar
1 heaped teaspoon baking powder	
Pinch of salt	
50g	Butter
1	Egg
175ml	Full cream milk, approx
Egg wash (1 egg yolk beaten with 2 tsp milk)	
Granulated sugar	

METHOD

You will need a 23x5cm round tin. We use a heavy stainless steel sauté pan which works very well, if you don't have a suitable pan, par-cook the rhubarb slightly first.

Preheat the oven to 230°C/450°F/gas mark 8.

Trim the rhubarb, wipe with a damp cloth and cut into pieces about 2.5 cm in length. Put into the base of a tin or sauté pan and sprinkle with the sugar. We put the stainless steel sauté pan on a low heat at this point while we make the dough.

Sieve all the dry ingredients into a bowl. Cut the butter into cubes and rub into the flour until the mixture resembles coarse breadcrumbs. Whisk the egg with the milk. Make a well in the centre of the dry ingredients, pour in the liquid all at once and mix to a soft dough. Turn out onto a floured board and roll into a 23 cm round about 2.5 cm thick. Place this round on top of the rhubarb and tuck in the edges neatly. Brush with a little egg wash and sprinkle with granulated sugar.

Bake in the fully preheated oven for 5 minutes then reduce the temperature to 180°C/350°F/gas mark 4 for a further 35 minutes approximately or until the top is crusty and golden and the rhubarb soft and juicy.

Remove from the oven and allow to sit for a few minutes. Put a warm plate over the top of the sauté pan, turn upside down onto the plate but be careful of the hot juices.

Serve warm with soft brown sugar and cream.

SQUID STIR FRIED WITH SPRING ONIONS

Serves 2 with rice, more if with other dishes

INGREDIENTS

½ tbsp   Peeled Thai garlic
Sea salt
1   Orange chilli
200g   Scored cleaned squid
2 tbsp   Organic sesame oil
Cleaned spring onion, cut into 2 cm
lengths on a slight bias
A little light chicken stock or water
1-2 tbsp   Light soy sauce
Pinch white sugar
Pinch ground white pepper

METHOD

Make a coarse garlic paste with the peeled Thai garlic and salt then add the chilli and bruise.

Prepare and heat a well seasoned wok. Add the oil then almost immediately the squid and stir fry for several moments before adding the garlic paste. Be careful not to let the garlic burn. Add the spring onions (and perhaps a drizzle of additional oil, sesame or perfumed) and continue to stir fry for a moment or two as it becomes quite dry and increases in fragrance before moistening with the stock. Season with the soy, sugar and white pepper.

DAVID THOMPSON

KOSCHINA'S SCRAMBLED EGG TOASTED SANDWICH WITH WHITE ALBA TRUFFLES

Serves 4

INGREDIENTS

3	Slices of white bread
3	Medium eggs
15ml	Cream
3 tsp	Caviar (of your choice)
20g	White alba truffle

METHOD

Cut the bread out with a cutter 6cm wide and toast on each side. Crack the egg into a mixing bowl and add the cream and whisk. Place into a pan and cook until just combined, but not liquid. Butter the toast on one side then put a good spoon of scrambled egg onto each piece. Place a teaspoon of caviar on top and finish with grated alba truffle.

DIETER KOSCHINA

CURED SALMON WITH WASABI
Serves 4

Cured salmon

500g	Salmon side, trimmed
200g	Salt marinade (brine)

Wasabi dressing

20g	Egg yolks
40g	Egg white
25g	English mustard
25g	Wasabi paste
35ml	White balsamic vinegar
15g	Pickling syrup
50g	Olive oil
50g	Grapeseed oil
Salt & pepper to taste	

Dill oil

100g	Dill chopped and frozen
55ml	Vegetable oil
55ml	Olive oil
Salt & pepper	

Lemon oil split dressing

250ml	Olive oil
150ml	Lemon olive oil
8g	Lemon thyme
5g	Sage
5g	Lime leaves
50ml	White wine vinegar
50ml	White balsamic vinegar
300ml	Water
6g	Salt
6g	Sugar
3g	Ground pepper

To garnish (for each person)

Olive oil
Sparkling water
Salt & pepper
Lemon juice
Lemon zest

Cucumber balls, peeled
Cucumber jelly (made with a little pickling syrup)
Focaccia croutons (squares of focaccia cooked in oil until a light golden colour)
Pickled ginger
Fresh bulb of fennel, passed through a mandolin and kept in iced water
Wasabi fish roes
Shisu cress
Tahoon cress
Dill
Split lemon dressing
Fresh dill stalks
Charlotte potatoes, cooked and cubed

METHOD

Split the salmon side into four, trim away the blood line and score the skin. Vacuum with the brine and press between two trays. Leave to cure turning twice a day, for a day to two days. When ready, rinse, pat dry, roll in cling film with a little lemon oil and vacuum.

Wasabi dressing

Proceed like a mayonnaise and mix all the ingredients together; taste for the balance of sweetness and heat.

Lemon oil split dressing

Mix together the olive and lemon oils, lemon thyme, sage and lime leaves. Vacuum and cook at 55°C for one hour. Leave to infuse for at least 24 hours – longer is better. Dissolve sugar and salt into the vinegar; add pepper and water. Pass this mixture through a sieve onto the vacuumed mixture.

Dill oil

Blend all the ingredients in a Thermomix to break them up. Take care not to let the oil become too warm. Place in a Pacojet and freeze; blend until more or less smooth.

TO SERVE

Place the salmon in the centre of an oblong plate. Microwave the cucumber with olive oil, sparkling water, salt and pepper. Remove excess liquid, add the potatoes and dress with the split lemon dressing.

When making the cucumber jelly, add a little pickle syrup. Roll the croutons in a golden caramel; add a little lemon juice and zest, and a little olive oil.

Brush the plate with wasabi dressing, topped with pickled ginger and fennel salad (dressed with a little lemon dressing). Arrange the potatoes, cucumber balls, jelly, salmon and croutons attractively on the plate. Top with the herbs and cress, and drizzle with a little dill oil.

Bon apétit.

ERIC
CHAVOT

FERGUS
HENDERSON

MINCE AND TATTIES
Serves 6

INGREDIENTS

1	Onion, peeled and thinly sliced
1	Leek, cleaned, sliced lengthways in half, then thinly sliced across
1	Carrot, peeled, sliced lengthways in half, then thinly sliced across
4	Garlic cloves, peeled and chopped

Splash of olive oil

1kg	Minced beef
2	Tinned tomatoes

Handful of oatmeal

1	Shot glass of Worcestershire sauce
1/3	Bottle of red wine

Chicken stock, if needed
Sea salt & black pepper

12	Potatoes for boiling

METHOD

In a large pan sweat the onion, leek, carrot and garlic in the splash of olive oil until softened. Add the mince, giving it a healthy stir to break it up. Add the tinned tomatoes, keep stirring and add the oatmeal, but not too much as you don't want to end up with porridge. Stir, add the Worcestershire sauce and red wine, then stir again. Take a view on the liquid content – if it seems a bit dry add some stock. You are looking for a loose lava consistency. Check the seasoning.

Allow the mince to simmer gently for 1 ½ to 2 hours – if it starts drying out add more stock.

While the mince cooks, peel the potatoes and simply boil them in salty water. When cooked serve them with the mince.

After a long journey there is no dish more welcoming. Also, a dram doesn't go amiss!

TARTINE OF PAN FRIED LAMBS' KIDNEYS
Serves 4

INGREDIENTS

4	Fresh lambs' kidneys
4	Slices wholemeal bread
2	Garlic cloves, crushed
1	Garlic clove
2	Shallots, finely diced
1 tbsp	Dijon mustard
1/2	Small bunch flat-leafed parsley
1/2	Small bunch chives
Knob butter	
1/2	Lemon
2 tbsp	Cognac
25ml	Dry white wine
Drizzle of olive oil	
1/2 tbsp	Plain flour
Salt & pepper	

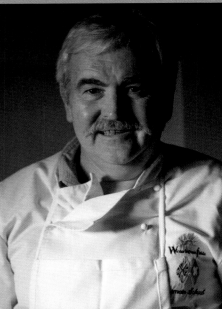

**GERMAIN
SCHWAB**

METHOD

Remove skin and denerve the fresh lambs' kidneys, slice thinly, season with salt and pepper then roll in the mustard. Sprinkle with the flour.

Take a frying pan drizzled with olive oil and heat; into the hot oil place the kidneys for a few seconds, add the garlic, shallots, chopped parsley and chives. Sauté for a few more seconds, remove everything from the pan and keep warm in a covered dish. Keep the pan on the heat and deglaze with the white wine and Cognac, add the knob of butter and remove from the heat. Toast the bread and rub with a clove of garlic, pile the kidneys on to this, pour the sauce on top and squeeze over a few drops of lemon juice over to finish.

BANANA AND CHESTNUT MILLE-FEUILLE WITH BANANA AND CARAMELISED WALNUTS ICE CREAM

Serves 4-6

INGREDIENTS

400g	Puff pastry
60g	Icing sugar

Bubbly decoration

150g	Icing sugar
50g	Full fat milk
50g	Plain flour

Chocolate sauce

10g	Cacao powder
40g	Chocolate (64% cocoa), broken into pieces
30g	Whipping cream
10g	Glucose
100g	Syrup made from 50g water and 50g sugar

Diced banana

1	Banana
Juice of 1	lemon
200ml	Water
30g	Sugar
5g	Pectin

Marron glacé (chestnut) cream (or buy ready made)

100g	Marron glacé paste (chestnut purée)
300g	Milk
100g	Whipping cream 35%
70g	Sugar
35g	Cornflour
125g	Egg yolks

Marron glacé

4	Marron glacé (chestnuts candied in sugar syrup and glazed)

Caramelised walnuts

125g	Water
300g	Caster sugar
500g	Walnuts

Ice cream

648g	Milk
160g	Cream
152g	Milk powder
284g	Dextrose
40g	Caster sugar
8g	Stabiliser
700g	Fresh bananas
240g	Caramelised walnuts

Frangipan crisp

18g	Melted butter
20g	Icing sugar
15g	Egg whites
10g	Almond flour
8g	Plain flour
2g	Amaretto
1	Vanilla pod

METHOD

Puff pastry

Roll the puff pastry as thin as possible, cut rectangles of 3.5x9cm and cook them at 180°C /350°F/ gas mark 4 for 6 minutes between two oven trays to prevent it from rising. Cool to room temperature, dust some icing sugar on top and caramelise with a blow torch. Rest in a container with silica gel to keep dry.

Bubbly decoration

Mix the icing sugar and flour together then add the milk, mix with a whisk until it all comes together; rest in the fridge for two hours. Shape into long thins and cook at 165°C/335°F/gas mark 3 for 4 minutes. Allow to cool.

Chocolate sauce

Put the syrup and the glucose in a pan, bring to the boil, add the cacao powder slowly and bring back to the boil. Remove from the heat and put on the top of the chocolate, emulsify (mix) and add the cream, mix again and rest in the fridge.

Diced banana

Boil the water, add the sugar and pectin, cook for a minute and cool down in the fridge. Dice the banana into 0.5cm pieces, dip in the lemon juice and add to the pectin sauce. Reserve until required.

Marron glacé (chestnut) cream

Make an infusion with the milk, cream and marron glacé paste, rest for half an hour, mix in the yolks, cornflour and sugar, sieve the liquid, mix with yolks and cook until 85°C. Leave to rest in the fridge.

Marron glacé

Break the marron glacé into small pieces.

Caramelised walnuts

Toast the walnuts at 180°C/350°F/ gas mark 4 for 5 minutes. Meanwhile heat the water and sugar in a large sauté pan (big enough to hold the walnuts) and bring the temperature up to 117°C. Add the walnuts and cook until caramelised.

Ice cream

Hand blend the milk, cream, milk powder and dextrose and bring to 40°C in a pan.

Combine the caster sugar and stabiliser, add to the mix and bring to 85°C/173°F and rest in the fridge for 6-12 hours.

Add the bananas to the mix and hand blend. Place in an ice cream machine, rest at -25°C and serve at -18°C.

Break the walnuts into pieces and add to the ice cream just before serving.

Frangipan crisp

Mix all the dry ingredients in a food processor, then add the amaretto, mix, add the egg whites, mix again and add the melted butter. Mix for 1 minute then rest in the fridge. Make into the shape that you need (here it is a rectangle) and cook at 165°C/335°F/gas mark 3 for 4-6 minutes.

TO SERVE

Spread 4 rectangles of puff pastry with the chestnut cream, banana and marron glacé pieces, put one on top of the other, making a mille-feuille, put an empty layer of puff pastry on top and add it to the plate. Dot some chocolate sauce up the centre of the plate, place a scoop of ice cream on top of a frangipan crisp rectangle and put a bubble decoration on top of the ice cream.

ROYALE OF GOATS' CHEESE AND PINEAPPLE ON STICKS, WATERCRESS PURÉE

Serves 6

INGREDIENTS

Royale

300ml	Double cream
115g	Goats' cheese, crumbled
	Salt & freshly ground black pepper
3	Free-range eggs, beaten
	Small handful parmesan or cheddar cheese, finely grated (for the top)

Jelly

200ml	Fresh pineapple juice
1	Leaf of gelatine

Pineapple

½	Large pineapple, peeled
250g	Unsalted butter, melted

Syrup

500ml	Fresh pineapple juice

Garnish

300ml	Vegetable oil, for deep frying
	Small handful fresh watercress

METHOD

Preheat the oven to 220°C/425°F/gas mark 7.

Royale

Pour the cream into a small pan and bring to the boil over a high heat. Add the goats' cheese and season with salt and freshly ground black pepper. Pour into a bowl, add the beaten eggs, whisk and pass through a sieve into an ovenware dish. Sprinkle the top with parmesan cheese.

Place the dish in a baking tray, fill with boiling water to half-way up the sides of the dish (this is called a bain-marie) and cook for 25-30 minutes.

Jelly

Heat the pineapple juice in a small saucepan over a medium heat. Place the gelatine leaf into a small bowl, cover with cold water and leave until softened. Drain off the water, squeeze out the excess and add the soaked gelatine leaf to the hot pineapple juice. Remove from the heat and leave to dissolve for 1-2 minutes. Stir well and then pour the jelly into a square tub to set. Once set cut into 2.5cm squares.

Pineapple

Reduce the oven temperature to 130°C/250°F/gas mark 1.

Submerge the pineapple in melted butter in a small baking tray and gently cook in the oven, turning frequently, for 10 minutes or until tender and then cut into 2.5cm squares.

Syrup

Pour the pineapple juice into a non-reactive pan and simmer over a medium heat for 5 minutes or until reduced to a syrup. This should make around 200ml of syrup.

Garnish

Pour the vegetable oil into a large saucepan or deep fat fryer and heat to 180°C or until a small cube of bread turns golden in 30 seconds. (CAUTION: hot oil can be dangerous. Do not leave unattended.)

Carefully drop the watercress into the hot oil and fry for one minute or until crisp. Remove with a slotted spoon and drain on kitchen paper.

TO SERVE

Cut the goats' cheese 'royale' into pieces the same size as the pineapple squares and place on top of the pineapple squares. Place the jelly squares on top and stick a cocktail stick through the middle to secure. Place two goats' cheese 'royales' onto each of four to six plates, pour over the pineapple syrup and garnish with deep-fried watercress.

GLYNN PURNELL

HESTON BLUMENTHAL

Eccles cakes have been made and sold in the town of Eccles near Manchester since 1793 and possibly long before that. Traditionally served with Lancashire cheese, they go extremely well with Stilton too. This recipe makes 16 mini Eccles cakes and plenty of potted stilton to slather on top of them.

ECCLES CAKES AND POTTED STILTON

Makes 16 mini Eccles cakes

INGREDIENTS

Eccles cakes

100g	Unsalted butter
150g	Caster sugar
200g	Currants
25g	Red wine vinegar
5g	Mixed spice
500g	Puff pastry
	Egg wash (1 egg yolk beaten with 2 tsp milk)

Potted stilton

100g	Stilton cheese
35g	Mascarpone
90g	Butter
3.5g	Salt
55g	Water
3.5g	Sherry vinegar
30g	Pedro Ximenez sherry

METHOD

Eccles cakes

Melt the butter in a saucepan, add the sugar and heat until the mixture begins to bubble. Remove the pan from the heat and stir in the currants, vinegar and mixed spice. Allow to cool slightly.

Roll out the pastry on a cold surface to 3mm thick. Cut out circles using a 9cm pastry ring and brush the circles with egg wash. Place a little filling in the centre of the circles and fold in the pastry to cover the filling. Press together to seal then turn each cake over and slash the top with a knife 3 times. Rest for at least 30 minutes in the fridge then brush the surface with egg wash again and bake at 200°C for 20–25 minutes.

Potted Stilton

Put the Stilton, mascarpone, butter and salt into a bowl and blitz with a hand-held blender until it becomes a smooth and homogenous mixture.

Gently warm the water and sherry vinegar together then slowly add this mixture to the cheese. Pour in the PX sherry and mix carefully. Decant into small ramekins and put in the fridge to set. Take the ramekins out of the fridge 10 minutes before serving with the Eccles cakes.

TROPICAL FRUIT SALAD
Serves 4

INGREDIENTS

1	Pitahaya (dragon fruit)
1	Mango
½	Pineapple
3	Kiwis
1	Papaya

Rose water jelly

500ml	Water
90g	Sugar
80g	Rose water
3g	Agar agar
1.7g	Gelling agent

Apple yuzu sorbet

500ml	Sugared water (575g sugar, 1 litre water)
500ml	Juice of Granny Smith apples
3 tsp	Glycerine
30g	Pro sorbet
105ml	Yuzu juice

Vanilla ice cream

500ml	Milk
500ml	Cream
240g	Sugar
4	Egg yolks
20g	Pro crema
30g	Glucose
5	Pieces vanilla
Peel of ¼ lemon	
2g	Glycerine

Garnish

Matcha powder (green tea powder)
Violets
Orchidee
Apple blossom
Flowers of pineapple sage

METHOD

Rose water jelly

Place all the ingredients into a pan, bring to the boil until the liquid thickens. Pour into a stainless steel bowl and refrigerate.

Apple yuzu sorbet

Put all the ingredients together and place in an ice cream machine.

Vanilla ice cream

Put all the ingredients together, cook then put in an ice cream machine.

Tropical fruit salad

Cut all the fruits into 1cm cubes, arrange mosaic-like in a mould to make a square (about 5x5cm). Then put some rose water jelly over the squares and refrigerate.

TO SERVE

Place the jelly in the middle of a dish and top with flowers. Add a quenelle of yuzu sorbet and a quenelle of vanilla ice cream. Put a small amount of matcha powder on top of the ice cream.

JACOB JAN BOERMA

JASON ATHERTON

CRAB TOASTIES

Serves 3–4 as a snack or light lunch

INGREDIENTS

80–100g	White crabmeat
100g	Cream cheese (at room temperature)
2 tbsp	Mayonnaise
15g	Dried white breadcrumbs
1 tsp	Soy sauce

Pinch of cayenne pepper
Sea salt & black pepper

1	Small ciabatta or baguette, thinly sliced on the diagonal

Mesclun and herb salad, dressed with a little vinaigrette, to serve

METHOD

Preheat the oven to 170°C/325°F/ gas mark 3.

Pick over the crabmeat and remove any tiny pieces of shell. Soften the cream cheese in a bowl, then mix in the mayonnaise and crabmeat. Add the breadcrumbs and soy sauce, season with the cayenne and salt and pepper to taste.

Spread the crab mix evenly on the bread slices and place on a baking sheet. Bake in the oven for 10 minutes. Serve with the mesclun and herb salad.

TAGINE OF LAMB WITH COUSCOUS
Serves 4

INGREDIENTS

Tagine of lamb

1	Lamb shoulder
Oil	
2kg	Carrots
2	Sticks of celery
1	Leek
1kg	Onion
3	Garlic cloves
1 tsp	Cinnamon powder
1	Small piece of fresh ginger
½ tsp	Whole cumin
¼	Cinnamon stick
1 tsp	Pimento all spice
1 tsp	Cardamoms
1 tsp	Coriander seeds
1 tsp	4 spice
250 ml	White wine
4 litres	Brown lamb stock
1 tsp	Harissa paste

Couscous

160ml	Hot chicken stock
Drop of olive oil	
Salt & pepper	
170g	Couscous
30g	Butter
½	Onion, finely chopped
1	Small red pepper, finely diced
1 tbsp	Sherry vinegar
2 tbsp	Golden raisins
2 tsp	Fresh parsley, finely chopped
½	Bunch fresh coriander, finely chopped
2 tsp	Fresh mint, finely chopped
Courgettes, carrots and wild rocket drizzled with olive oil, to serve	

METHOD

Tagine of lamb

Brown the lamb in a heavy bottom saucepan in a little oil, remove the lamb, then brown the roughly chopped vegetables and garlic in the same pan. Add the spices to the pan and cook gently for a few minutes, being careful not to burn them. Add the lamb and all other ingredients except for the harissa paste and bring to the boil, skim and cover with a lid. Cook in the oven for 2 ½ hours at 110°C/225°F/ gas mark ¼. Allow to cool in the cooking liquor.

Remove the lamb carefully, then pass the liquid through a fine sieve or muslin cloth.

Reduce the liquid by half and finish with a little harrissa to taste – this makes the sauce.

Couscous

Bring the stock, oil, salt and pepper to the boil in a saucepan. Remove from the heat.

Add the couscous to the hot liquid. Cover with a lid. Leave to swell for 5-10 minutes. Incorporate all of the remaining ingredients. Season to taste and stir briefly, so that the butter melts.

TO SERVE

Remove the lamb from the bone. Reheat the lamb in a little of the cooking liquor, reducing until the lamb is nicely glazed and shiny. Mix the lamb through the hot couscous, serve with some courgettes, carrots and wild rocket and drizzled with olive oil.

JEFF GALVIN

JOHN CAMPBELL

COTTAGE PIE
Serves 4

INGREDIENTS

Oil	
1	Large onion, chopped
1	Garlic clove, crushed
2	Medium carrots, chopped
550g	Lean beef mince
200g	Pancetta diced into 1cm cubes
150g	Chestnut mushrooms, chopped
400g	Vine cherry tomatoes, quartered
600g	Beef stock
1	Bay leaf
Fresh thyme leaves from 1 sprig	
2 tbsp	Tomato purée
3 tbsp	Worcestershire sauce
Salt and freshly ground black pepper	

For the topping

750g	Potatoes, peeled and chopped
225g	Parsnips, peeled and chopped
2 tsp	Horseradish sauce
75g	Butter
50g	Milk
Salt and freshly ground black pepper	
50g	Extra mature cheddar cheese, grated

METHOD

Heat a little oil in a large pan. Fry the pancetta until golden, then add the onion, garlic and carrot and cook over a medium heat for 5 minutes until soft, do not allow to colour, add the mushrooms and cook for a further 3 minutes.

Add the minced beef and cook for 3-5 minutes to brown.

Add the tomatoes, purée, beef stock, Worcestershire sauce, bay leaf and thyme. Cover and simmer for 30 minutes. Season.

The mash

Boil the potatoes and parsnips in water until soft. Drain and mash with the butter and milk. Stir in the horseradish and season with salt and pepper.

Spoon the meat into an ovenproof dish. Top with the mash and then with the cheese. Bake for 30 minutes in a preheated oven at 190°C/375°/gas mark 5 until golden brown.

STEAMED CANTONESE STYLE FISH
Serves 4

INGREDIENTS

450g	Firm white fish fillets, such as cod or sole, or a whole fish such as sole or turbot
1 tsp	Coarse sea salt or plain salt
1½ tbsp	Fresh ginger, finely shredded
3 tbsp	Spring onions, finely shredded
2 tbsp	Light soy sauce
2 tsp	Dark soy sauce
1 tbsp	Peanut or groundnut oil
2 tsp	Sesame oil

Handful of fresh coriander sprigs, to garnish

METHOD

Pat the fish or fish fillets dry with kitchen paper. Rub evenly with the salt on the outside as well as the inside of the fish.

Set up a steamer or put a rack into a wok or deep pan and fill it with 5cm of water. Bring the water to the boil over a high heat. Put the fish on a heatproof plate and scatter the ginger evenly over the top.

Put the plate of fish into the steamer or onto the rack. Cover the pan tightly and gently steam the fish until it is just cooked. Flat fish will take about 5 minutes to cook. Whole fish or fillets such as sea bass will take 12-14 minutes. You will see the fish turning opaque and flaking slightly but still remaining moist.

Remove the plate of cooked fish, pour off excess liquid that may have accumulated on the plate, and scatter the spring onions on the fish together with the light and dark soy sauces.

Heat the peanut and sesame oils together in a small saucepan until they are smoking and hot, then pour on top of the fish.

TO SERVE

Scatter with a handful of coriander and serve at once.

KEN HOM

LISA ALLEN

SHORROCK'S TASTY LANCASHIRE CHEESE ON TOAST, GOTT'S BACON, WORCESTERSHIRE SAUCE

Serves 2

INGREDIENTS

2 Slices	Peter Gott's streaky bacon
2	Slices of organic white bread
Knob of butter	
200g	Creamy Lancashire cheese (Shorrocks Bomber)
1 bottle	Worcestershire sauce
50ml	Apple juice

METHOD

Put the bacon on to a tray and under the grill until crispy. Toast the bread on each side. Butter the toast on one side, cover with the Shorrocks Bomber Lancashire cheese, place on a baking tray, then grill until the cheese has melted.

Boil the Worcestershire sauce and the apple juice together and reduce by half until a syrupy-like texture.

TO SERVE

Put the 2 slices of cheese on toast onto a slate, put the crispy bacon on top and serve with the Worcestershire sauce dressing.

WOODCOCK WITH WASABI SALSA
Serves 4

INGREDIENTS

4	Woodcock plucked and breasts removed
2	Handfuls of pea shoots or watercress plus lemon and olive oil to dress

Olive oil
Butter

For the salsa

4 tsp	Wasabi pickle (wasabi zuke)
2 tbsp	Finely chopped onion
1 tsp	garlic
2 tbsp	Grapeseed oil

Mix all ingredients together

For the mushrooms

200g	Golden enoki mushrooms (you can substitute with any mushrooms of your choice)
2 tbsp	Olive oil
2	Garlic cloves sliced
2 tbsp	Sake
1 tbsp	Light soy sauce

Sea salt
Black pepper

1 tbsp	Yuzu juice (or lemon juice)

MARK EDWARDS

I do a lot of game shooting in my spare time and really enjoy cooking what I have shot at home; woodcock is my favourite to shoot and to eat.

METHOD

Preheat an oven to 450°F/230°C/ gas mark 8. Wipe and clean the mushrooms, try to keep the mushrooms whole if possible.

Place the mushrooms, olive oil, garlic, sake and light soy sauce into an earthenware pot or casserole dish with a tight fitting lid. Season with sea salt and pepper and mix well to ensure all the mushrooms are coated.

Bake in the oven with the lid on for 8 minutes, remove the lid and add the yuzu juice and mix.

While the mushrooms are cooking season the woodcock breasts and sauté in a pan with olive oil and butter skin side down. Cook for 3-4 minutes then turn over and cook for 1-2 minutes making sure that the breasts remain slightly pink

TO SERVE

Serve 2 breasts per person with the mushrooms and cooking liquor, wasabi salsa and pea shoot salad

Note: You can vary the variety of mushrooms that are used in this dish to suit your taste

MARK HIX

You can create the same dish with wild duck, or pheasant etc and vary it throughout the game season.

PARTRIDGE ON TOAST WITH WILD MUSHROOMS
Serves 4

INGREDIENTS

2	Oven-ready partridges, preferably with their livers (or if not, buy 120g chicken or duck livers)
A couple of good knobs of butter	
2	Shallots, peeled and finely chopped
1	Garlic clove, peeled and crushed
A couple of good knobs of butter	
Salt and freshly ground black pepper	
2 tbsp	Sherry
120-150g	Wild mushrooms
A handful of dandelion leaves or small salad leaves, prepared and washed	
4	Slices of white or brown bread cut 1cm thick from a small bloomer-style loaf
A handful of dandelion leaves or small salad leaves, prepared and washed	

Dressing

1 tbsp	Cider vinegar mixed with 3 tbsp rapeseed oil

METHOD

Clean the livers, cut them into even-sized pieces and dry them on some kitchen paper. Heat a good knob of butter in a frying pan and briefly fry the shallots and garlic for a minute or so without colouring. Season the livers and add to the pan and continue to fry on a medium heat for 2-3 minutes, stirring every so often. Stir in the sherry, then remove from the heat.

Preheat the oven to 220°C/425°F/gas mark 7.

Rub the breasts of the partridges with all but one knob of the remaining butter, season and cook them in the oven for 10-15 minutes, keeping them nice and pink.

Meanwhile, chop the liver mixture by hand or in a food processor as finely or as coarsely as you wish, tasting and seasoning again if necessary.

Heat a knob of butter in a frying pan and gently cook the mushrooms, seasoning them and turning them with a spoon during cooking.

Toast the bread on both sides, then spread with the liver mixture.

Remove the breasts from the partridge, slice and arrange on top of the liver mixture. Shred any leg meat from the birds and mix with the salad leaves and dressing, season and arrange on plates. Place the toasts in the centre of each plate and scatter the mushrooms over.

LENTILS WITH POACHED EGG
Serves 4

INGREDIENTS

4	Eggs
250g	Puy, Casteluccio or similar small slate green lentils (red and brown ones will not do)
1	Carrot
1	Onion
1	Stick celery
1	Leek
115ml	Olive oil
750ml	Stock (chicken or vegetable)
1 tsp	Nam pla (Vietnamese fish sauce), optional
1 dstspn	Red wine vinegar, optional
1 tsp	Dijon mustard, optional
Salt & pepper	

MATTHEW FORT

METHOD

Finely chop the vegetables. To be truthful, I chop the carrot, celery and leek in the food processor. Heresy, I know, but there you are, I'm a lazy cook. But I always chop the onion by hand. Onions do not take kindly to processing. Heat the olive oil in a saucepan and, when hazy with heat, add the vegetables, stirring to coat them in oil. Cook over a medium heat for 5-7 minutes, stirring occasionally, until they are well wilted and the onion transparent. Rinse the lentils under cold water and add them to the vegetables, stirring them around. Add the stock, bring to the boil and simmer until the lentils are tender but have not disintegrated. This could take anywhere between 15-25 minutes, depending on your lentils. You just have to try them from time to time. Cool slightly and add the flavourings of your choice.

I serve these by putting a tablespoon or two of the lentils into a ramekin and plonking the poached egg on top. I then eat it with a teaspoon. But there's no need to be so refined. On the plate with the egg on top is just fine. I am not going to tell you how to poach an egg.

MICHAEL CAINES

SLOW ROASTED SADDLE OF VENISON, RED CABBAGE AND CHESTNUT PURÉE
Serves 4

INGREDIENTS

800g   Venison saddle
Ground juniper berries
Salt & pepper
Vegetable oil
Unsalted butter

Red cabbage

100g   Onions, diced
1 garlic clove, crushed
70g   Butter
250   Red wine
70ml   Red wine vinegar
50ml   Port
Juice of ½ lemon
Juice of ½ orange
80g   Demerara sugar
80g   Redcurrant jelly
1kg   Red cabbage, finely sliced
Spice muslin bag: ½ cinnamon stick,
1 dried orange peel, 1 clove, 4
juniper berries, 4 black peppercorns,
1 star anise, 3 sprigs of thyme,
1 bay leaf
70g   Smoked belly pork trim
Salt & pepper

Chestnut purée

20g   Onions, sliced
1 garlic clove
Salt
20g   Unsalted butter
100ml   Chicken stock
Bouquet garni
200ml   Water
250g   Frozen chestnuts
10   White peppercorns,
              in a plastic money bag

Garnish

2   Figs cut into quarters
12   Pan-roast wild mushrooms

METHOD

Red cabbage

Preheat the oven to 180°C/350°F/ gas mark 4. Place the onions and garlic in a pan with the butter and cook until soft and transparent. In a separate pan, mix the red wine, red wine vinegar, port, lemon and orange juice, demerara sugar and redcurrant jelly. Warm together and then place in an ovenproof dish, along with the red cabbage. Add the spice bag, smoked belly pork and season with salt and pepper. Place in the oven and cook for 1 ½ to 2 hours. When cooked, remove from the oven, check the seasoning and leave to cool.

Chestnut purée

To make the chestnut purée, place the onions, garlic and salt in a pan with the butter. Cook until soft and transparent then add the chicken stock, bouquet garni, water, chestnuts and bag of peppercorns. Bring to the boil then reduce to a simmer and cook for about 10-15 minutes. When cooked, remove from the heat and leave to cool before straining the liquid into a bowl, leaving the mixture in the colander. Remove the bouquet garni and bag of peppercorns then place the mixture in a blender or food processor and blend until a fine purée. Use some of the braising stock to get it to the correct consistency.

Venison

Preheat the oven to 200°C/400°F/ gas mark 6. Season the meat with a little of the ground juniper berries, salt and pepper. Then heat a little oil with some butter in a thick bottomed pan, add the venison and cook in the foaming butter, turning from time to time to ensure it is cooked evenly. For medium rare, simply take a kitchen skewer and insert it into the middle of the venison and count to 7. Remove and place the skewer below your lip to feel if it is warm to the touch. If it is, remove the venison and rest for 20 minutes.

TO SERVE

Reheat the chestnut purée and red cabbage. Warm the figs and wild mushrooms, place the venison into the preheated oven for 5 minutes. Place a small amount of chestnut purée on the plate in a line from left to right, then a large spoonful of red cabbage into the middle of the plate. Remove the venison from the oven and slice it into medallions. Place even amounts on top of the red cabbage, garnish around with figs and wild mushrooms and serve.

SALAD LYONNAISE
Serves 4

INGREDIENTS

400g	Dandelion leaves or frisée salad
180g	Smoked streaky bacon
4 tbsp	Olive oil
	White wine vinegar
20	Thin slices of small baguette bread
2	Garlic cloves, cut
4	Free-range eggs
2 tbsp	Red wine vinegar
	Salt & pepper

METHOD

Pick, wash and dry the salad leaves. Cut the bacon into strips or batons, place them in a non-stick pan with a drop of olive oil and cook slowly over a medium heat. Put a saucepan of water on to boil with a generous splash of white wine vinegar. Bake the baguette slices in a warm oven until dry and crisp, then rub with the garlic.

Bring the pan of water to a simmer, crack the eggs and carefully drop them into water to poach. The eggs should take about 4 minutes for the whites to be cooked, yet the yolk should still be very runny. Pour the golden-brown bacon and fat onto the salad with the bread, vinegar and remaining olive oil. Season lightly with salt but generously with pepper, toss and place the drained, hot eggs on top.

MICHEL ROUX JR

The classic salade Lyonnaise should be made with dandelion leaves, but they can be a little bitter for some people. If you are lucky enough to have a garden with untreated areas in it, you can pick your own leaves. Alternatively, use frisée salad, also called curly endive.

NATHAN OUTLAW

YOUNG SEA SPINACH SOUP WITH CRISPY CORNISH DUCK EGG

Serves 4

INGREDIENTS

Soup

Oil
1	Small onion, peeled and sliced
2	Garlic cloves, germ removed and sliced
1	Large potato, peeled and thinly sliced
1kg	Young sea spinach, picked and washed
1 litre	Chicken stock

Salt

Eggs

4	Duck eggs boiled in water for 5 minutes

Flour for dusting
1	Egg

Milk
White breadcrumbs
Salt & pepper
Oil for deep frying

METHOD

Heat a saucepan and add some oil. Place the onion and the garlic in the pan and cook for 1 minute with no colour. Add the sliced potato and cover with chicken stock. Simmer until the potato is cooked and transfer to a blender. Place a frying pan on the heat and add a little oil. Put the spinach in the frying pan and sweat and wilt. Add the spinach to the soup base in the blender and blend for 3 minutes or until smooth.

Taste and add salt accordingly. Chill the soup over ice to retain the green colour. Place in the fridge until required.

Eggs

Season the flour, peel the duck eggs and flour them. Mix the egg and the milk together and roll the duck eggs in the mixture, then coat with the breadcrumbs. Place on a tray until required.

TO SERVE

Heat a deep fat fryer. Heat the soup and adjust the consistency if required with chicken stock. Fry the eggs for 30 seconds or until crisp. Lay out four warmed bowls. Trim off the bottom of the eggs, sprinkle with a little salt and stand in the bowl. Pour in the soup and serve.

FREE-RANGE SCRAMBLED EGGS, HASH TOMATO
Serves 2

INGREDIENTS

Scrambled eggs

4	Large free-range eggs
20g	Butter
Salt & pepper	
Few drops double cream	

Hash tomato

2	Ripe plum tomatoes
10g	Butter
2 dashes of Worcestershire sauce	
Dash of Tabasco	
Salt & pepper	
Fresh parsley, to serve	

NEIL WIGGLESWORTH

METHOD

Scrambled eggs

Crack the eggs into a bowl, do not whisk. Mix with a fork until the egg yolks are broken into the whites while still retaining a streaky white and yellow look.

In a medium pan add the butter and egg mix, season with salt and pepper. Put on a medium heat and stir slowly with a wooden spoon for 2-3 minutes, add the cream once cooked.

Hash tomato

Roughly chop the tomatoes.

In a hot non-stick frying pan add the butter and tomatoes. Cook until the tomatoes have broken down and started to caramelise. Add the Worcestershire sauce and a dash of tabasco. Season with salt and pepper.

TO SERVE

Place a good spoonful of scrambled egg onto the plate, hash tomato on top and finish with fresh parsley.

NICK NAIRN

Serves 4

INGREDIENTS

1	1.3-1.8 kg free-range organic chicken
1	Lemon
4-5	Garlic cloves

Handful of flat leaf parsley
4-5 tbsp Olive oil
Freshly ground sea salt and freshly ground pepper

8	Large floury potatoes
8	Medium parsnips

Vegetable oil

1	Glass of white wine
½	Chicken stock cube

Steamed broccoli to serve

METHOD

Preheat the oven to 200°C/400°F/ Gas 6. Untruss the chicken and let it come to a cool room temperature before cooking. Cut the lemon into eight wedges and lightly crush the whole garlic cloves so that they just crack open. Feel inside the cavity between the legs and pull out any large pieces of fat still clinging to the insides. Stuff the cavity with the lemon wedges, garlic cloves and a huge handful of flat leaf parsley, stalks and all. Rub the outside of the bird all over with olive oil and season with salt and pepper. Slash down through the skin between the legs so that they go floppy; this lets the heat of the oven into the legs. Sit the bird in a roasting tin and pour in the remaining olive oil. Roast on the middle shelf of the oven for 20 minutes.

Meanwhile, peel the potatoes and par-boil in a large pan of boiling salted water for 8 minutes. Peel the parsnips, trim and cut into halves or quarters lengthways depending on size and set aside. Drain the potatoes well, then use a fork to roughen the outside of each potato – this will make the crunchy crust. Pour a thin layer of vegetable oil into another roasting tin on top of the stove and heat until smoking hot. Carefully add the potatoes, turning them in the oil to coat, and making sure the oil has heated up again.

Open the oven door, remove the chicken and baste it with the juices in the tin. Add the parsnips, turning them in the pan juices. Return the chicken to the oven and put the potatoes on the highest shelf above the chicken. Roast for another 40 minutes, basting everything occasionally and turning the potatoes at least once during cooking.

When everything is looking good and golden brown, test the chicken to see if it is cooked by sticking a skewer in the thickest part of the leg. If the juices run clear, remove the chicken from the tin and place on a warm plate covered loosely with a piece of foil, and leave to rest for 10 minutes. Tip the excess fat out of the pan, return to the oven and let the parsnips crisp up for 10 minutes. Remove the parsnips and potatoes from the oven. Turn the oven off. Lift the potatoes out of the tin with a slotted spoon into a warm serving dish and do likewise with the parsnips; keep them warm in the oven with the door propped open.

Now make the gravy. Set the chicken roasting tin on the heat, add the wine, stock cube and 150ml water. Bring to the boil and boil furiously for 2-3 minutes, scraping up all the sticky bits from the bottom of the tin. Taste and season very well. Tip any juices that have flowed out of the chicken into the gravy, then strain into a warm jug or gravy boat. Allow to settle, then spoon off the fat from the top. Serve immediately with some steamed broccoli (or as pictured with carrots and coarsely chopped onions, roasted).

PORT OF LANCASTER SMOKED SALMON ON TOASTED CRUMPETS

Serves 1

INGREDIENTS

2	Crumpets
25g	Butter
2 large tsp	Cream cheese
6	Small slices of Port of Lancaster smoked salmon
20	Nonpareil capers
¼	Finely shredded red onion
1 dstspn	Chopped chives
8	Turns of the black pepper mill

METHOD

Toast the crumpets well on both sides, then butter them. Place a teaspoon of cream cheese on top of each crumpet. Add the slices of smoked salmon and garnish with the capers, onions, chopped chives and a few turns of the black pepper mill.

NIGEL HAWORTH

POACHED RED FRUITS WITH CHILLED ORGANIC CREAM (RØD-GRØD-MED-FLØDE)

Serves 4

INGREDIENTS

Handful of chopped rhubarb
2 large tbsp   Sugar
Half a vanilla pod
1   Punnet strawberries, halved
1   Punnet raspberries
Handful of redcurrants
Sugar
Lemon juice
200ml   Chilled organic cream

METHOD

Simmer, over a medium heat, the chopped rhubarb together with two large tablespoons of sugar and a halved vanilla pod for about ten minutes. Add to the pan the strawberries, raspberries and redcurrants and poach for a further minute.

Add sugar and lemon juice to taste – the amount of sugar required will depend upon the season and the sweetness of the fruits.

Chill the fruit stew and serve together with chilled organic cream.

PAUL CUNNINGHAM

ONE HOUR HERB ROASTED CHICKEN WITH BUTTERED PEAS, LETTUCE AND BAY LEAF

Serves 4

INGREDIENTS

Good sprig of tarragon, finely chopped
Good sprig chervil, finely chopped
Good sprig rosemary, finely chopped
25g   Soft cream cheese
25g   Butter
Finely grated zest of half lemon
Sea salt & black pepper
1 x 1½-2kg   Chicken
Olive oil
1   Carrot

Buttered peas with lettuce and bay leaf

1 tsp   White wine vinegar
2 tsp   White wine
1   Shallot, peeled and finely chopped
1   Bay leaf
½ tsp   English mustard
⅛   of an iceberg lettuce finely shredded
2 tsp   Double cream
100g   Hard unsalted butter, diced
Salt & freshly ground white pepper
250g   Cooked peas

PAUL HEATHCOTE

METHOD

Place a roasting tray or cast iron pan in an oven preheated to 180°C/350°F/gas mark 4.

First mix the herbs with the cream cheese, butter and zest, season well with salt and pepper and reserve to one side.

To prepare the chicken remove the parson's nose and trim up any excess fat. Loosen the skin from the breast by gently working your fingers over the meat and under the skin to make a pocket repeat on the other side. Stuff the herb mix evenly under both breasts.

With a sharp knife, score the legs with two or three incisions, this will make the legs crispy and allow them to cook quicker. Tie up the legs of the chicken.

Rub olive oil over the chicken and season with salt and pepper. Take out the hot tray or pan and place the chicken on its side with the thigh of the chicken pressed firmly down. Use the carrot to prevent the chicken breast falling onto the tray and to balance the chicken.

Cook for 25 minutes before turning over and repeating for around another 20 minutes.

Sit the chicken upright for a further 15 minutes before removing. Check that it is cooked by inserting a small knife into the wing knuckle of the bird to test for blood.

Allow to rest at room temperature for 10 minutes or so.

Buttered Peas with Lettuce and Bay Leaf

Place the vinegar, wine, shallot and bay leaf in a small pan and boil until only a teaspoon of the liquid remains, then add the mustard. Add the lettuce and cream and bring back to the boil for 15 seconds or so. Add the diced butter, little by little, and whisk in until a sauce is formed. Season to taste, reheat the peas and add to the sauce.

TO SERVE

Carve into 4 portions and serve with the peas.

CHICKEN BREAST EN PAPILLOTE WITH CHERRY TOMATOES AND ROSEMARY

Serves 4 as a main course

PETER GORDON

Cooking en papillote is a brilliant way to keep poultry (and fish) moist while cooking, and unless you add oil to it, it can be a very low-fat way of cooking. Also, if you wanted to serve a steamed meal to 8 people you'd need to have a huge steamer – cooking en papillote allows you to do this, but bake it on several trays in the oven instead.

INGREDIENTS

Non-stick (but definitely not waxed) baking parchment
4   Chicken breasts (I like to keep the skin on)
Handful of flat parsley leaves, off the stem
1   Large finger of fresh ginger, peeled and thinly sliced
2 tbsp   Olive oil
2 tsp   Fresh rosemary leaves
2 tsp   Fresh thyme leaves
6   Garlic cloves, peeled and thinly sliced
32   Cherry tomatoes
Salt & pepper

METHOD

Preheat the oven to 180°C.

Cut 4 pieces of parchment to approximately 30-40cm square, then fold each one in half to produce a centre seam and re-open. Lightly season the chicken breasts, sprinkle with the parsley and ginger and place one on each sheet of parchment, up tight against the centre fold.

In a wide pan over moderate heat sauté the rosemary, thyme and garlic in the olive oil until the garlic begins to turn golden. Add the tomatoes and cook until around a quarter of them have popped, shaking the pan from time to time. Spoon 8 tomatoes on top of each chicken breast and drizzle with the pan juices.

Now the origami bit begins. Place the chicken on the parchment in front of you with the centre seam going away from you. Fold the left side of the parchment over the breast and bring it level to the right-hand side. Take the furthest end of the paper in your right hand, and put your forefinger next to the top of the breast (furthest from you). Fold the parchment to the right at a 90° angle. Now it's just a matter of twisting the right hand edge of the paper towards the breast, moving around it as you do so, in order to seal it. Don't make it too tight though as you need to allow some space for the cooking steam to expand. Once the bag is twisted into a package it's a good idea to tuck the final fold under itself to keep it sealed, or secure with a paper clip!

If this all seems too difficult, use a small oven bag or foil (which is easier to seal).

Place the packages on a baking tray and cook for 18-20 minutes. Take from the oven and leave to rest for 5 minutes before serving, snipping the package open with scissors at the table.

Serve with new potatoes and a green salad.

POT ROASTED PHEASANT WITH ROOT VEGETABLES AND SHERRY

Serves 4

INGREDIENTS

5g	Sugar
500ml	Warm water
55g	Yeast
1kg	Strong flour
25g	Salt
75ml	Olive oil
50g	Duck fat
2	Pheasants, trussed with bacon
Salt & pepper	
1	Carrot, peeled and cut into 8
1	Parsnip, peeled and cut into 8
¼	Celeriac, peeled and cut into 8
½	Swede, peeled and cut into 8
1	Medium turnip, peeled and cut into 8
4	Chestnuts, peeled
8	Button onions, peeled
1	Bay leaf
100ml	Medium dry sherry
200ml	Brown chicken stock

PHIL HOWARD

METHOD

Dissolve the sugar in the warm water, add the yeast and leave to sit for 20 minutes. Place the flour in the bowl of a food mixer, add the salt, olive oil and water/yeast mix and, using the dough hook, knead to a smooth elastic dough – this will take 3-4 minutes. If doing this by hand you will to have knead the dough for a good 5 minutes.

Turn the dough into a large bowl and move to a warm place to prove. When it has doubled in volume, after about 30 minutes, knock it back, turn it onto a floured surface and briefly knead again. Return to the bowl and set aside in the fridge.

Place a large ovenproof dish over a medium heat and leave for 2 minutes. Add the duck fat, season the pheasants and lightly brown in the pot. Remove the pheasants, move to a medium heat, add all the vegetables and sauté until golden. Add the bay leaf, the sherry and the chicken stock, place the pheasants back into the pot and remove from the heat. Wipe the rim of the pot down with a damp cloth.

Roll the dough out on a lightly floured work surface into a long 'sausage' so that it can wrap around the entire pot. Press gently around the rim and, while supporting the dough, place the lid on top. Ensure this is a tight, sealed fit. Dust the excess dough around the edges with flour and place the pot in a warm place for ½ hour for the dough to prove. Now bake in the oven at 220°C/425°F/gas mark 7 for 10 minutes.

Remove from the oven and leave to cool for half an hour. Break the lid open, remove the birds and take the breasts and legs off the bone. Keep warm. Gently reduce the liquid by half. Carefully spoon some of the vegetables and some sauce onto each plate and finish with a breast and leg of pheasant. Serve a piece of the bread crust on the side.

363

OX CHEEK BRAISED IN RED WINE (JOUE DE BOEUF EN DAUBE)

Serves 4

INGREDIENTS

700g	Ox cheek, cut into 12 large pieces
100g	Seasoned flour
50ml	Vegetable oil
150g	Carrots roughly diced
150g	Onions roughly diced
1.1 litre	Good red wine
4	Garlic cloves, chopped
1	Bouquet garni
120g	Button onions peeled
30g	Butter
½ teaspoon sugar	
Salt & pepper	

PIERRE KOFFMANN

METHOD

Preheat oven to 200°C/400°F/gas mark 6.

Roll the pieces of meet lightly in the seasoned flour. Heat the oil in a large heavy heatproof casserole until very hot, then brown the meat quickly and evenly. Add the diced carrots and onions, cover and sweat gently for 10 minutes.

Remove all the fat from the pan. Deglaze the casserole with the red wine and bring to the boil. Add the garlic and bouquet garni and season. Replace the lid and cook in the oven for about two and half hours until the meat is very tender, stir regularly during the cooking, adding a little water if there is too much evaporation.

Meanwhile put the button onions into a pan large enough to hold them all in a single layer. Pour over enough water to cover, add the butter, salt and sugar, cover with a piece of greasproof paper and press down. Bring to the boil and simmer over a low heat, tossing the onions very gently from time to time until they are brown and shiny. Keep warm until ready to serve.

Remove from the oven. Lift out the meat with a slotted spoon, and place in a serving dish, pass the sauce through a sieve add to onions and pour over the meat.

TO SERVE

Serve with mash potato and carrots.

TARTE TATIN
Serves 4

INGREDIENTS

The tart

200g	Bought puff pastry, thawed if frozen
8	Large Cox's apples, peeled, halved and cored with a melon baller
10g	Unsalted butter, melted
1 tbsp	Caster sugar

For the caramel

50ml	Water
100g	Caster sugar
25g	Unsalted butter

METHOD

Preparing the pastry

On a lightly floured surface, roll out the puff pastry to 2mm thick and prick it all over with a fork. Transfer to a baking tray, cover with cling film and refrigerate for 20-30 minutes to firm it up and prevent shrinkage while cooking. Cut out a 20cm circle, using a plate or cake tin as a template, prick with a fork and chill again.

Making the caramel

Put the water in a small, heavy-based saucepan and scatter the sugar over it in an even layer. Let the sugar absorb the water for a few minutes, then place the pan on a medium heat and leave, without stirring, until the sugar has dissolved and formed a syrup. Simmer until it turns to a golden brown caramel. Stir in the butter and immediately pour the caramel into an 18cm round baking tin, 4-5cm deep.

RAYMOND BLANC

This amazing, sensuous dessert was invented at the turn of the 20th century by two elderly spinsters, the Tatin sisters – the world owes them a great deal! All the elements of pleasure are here: the dark caramel, the sweet and acidic taste of the apple, the crisp pastry. Serve with the very best crème fraîche (full fat, please) or a scoop of vanilla ice cream. Should you wish, you can cook the tart one day in advance, keep it in the tin and reheat it at 150°C/300°C/ gas mark 2 for 20 minutes. However, the best way to eat it is an hour or so after cooking, when it is still warm.

Filling the tin with the apples

Preheat the oven to 190°C/375°F/ gas mark 5. Arrange 12 apple halves upright around the edge of the tin to complete a full circle. In the middle sit half an apple, flat-side up, then top with another half apple. Cut the remaining apple into slices and wedge them into the empty spaces. You need to pack tight as many apple pieces as you can into the tin, so that you leave as little space as possible; this will give the perfect density and the perfect slice. Brush the melted butter over the apples and sprinkle the caster sugar over the top.

Baking the tart

Place the tin in the oven and bake for 35 minutes, until the apples are partly cooked. Remove from the oven, place the puff pastry circle on top of the hot apples and tuck the edge of the pastry inside the tin. Cook for a further 30 minutes until the pastry is golden brown. Place the tarte tatin next to an open window, if possible, and leave for 1-2 hours, until barely warm.

Unmoulding the tart

Slide the blade of a sharp knife full circle inside the tin to release the tarte tatin. Place a large dinner plate over the tart and, holding both tin and plate together, turn it upside down, shaking it gently sideways to release the tart on to the plate.

RICHARD
CORRIGAN

SALT CHILLI SQUID AND LIME AIOLI
Serves 4

INGREDIENTS

Lime aioli

Juice of 5 limes
5   Egg yolks
5   Garlic cloves
500ml   Olive oil
Salt & pepper

Salt chilli squid

5   Birds eye chillies
250g   Rice flour
25g   Salt
400g   Medium squid rings
3tbsp   Warm water
Chopped coriander or finely chopped
green chillies to serve

METHOD

Using a blender blitz the lime juice,
egg yolks and garlic cloves together.
Drizzle the olive oil into the mix and
season with salt and pepper.

Blitz together the birds eye chillies,
rice flour and salt to make a coating –
this will keep in an airtight container
for up to one week.

Put the squid rings in a bowl
and add the warm water. Coat with
the flour. Deep fry at 180°C until
crispy. Drain and serve with chopped
coriander or finely chopped
green chillies.

PRAWN CLUB SANDWICH
Serves 4

INGREDIENTS

425g   Cooked prawns, roughly chopped
1   Plum tomato, peeled, seeded and chopped
6 tbsp   Mayonnaise
Handful of freshly chopped basil leaves
8   Hard boiled quails' eggs, shelled and chopped
4   Thin slices of pancetta
Salt & pepper
12   Thin slices fresh white crusty bread
Butter for spreading
Dressed mixed salad leaves, to garnish

METHOD

In a large bowl, mix together the prawns, tomato, half the mayonnaise and the basil leaves, season to taste.

In another bowl, mix together the quails' eggs, pancetta and remaining mayonnaise, and season. Toast the bread until golden then butter it.

Spread a portion of the prawn mixture on one slice of the toast, top with a second slice of toast and spoon a portion of pancetta mix on top.

Sandwich with a third slice of toast on top and cut in half, place on plates, garnish with salad leaves and serve.

ROBBIE MILLAR

SMOKED EEL SALAD WITH BACON AND GARLIC BEURRE BLANC

Serves 8

INGREDIENTS

500g	Mixed leaves, ideally some lettuce, a little curly endive and some rocket
600g	Smoked eel
125g	Streaky bacon
50g	Butter

Beurre blanc

1	Shallot
4	Garlic cloves
Pinch of sea salt	
Pinch of milled white pepper	
½ glass	Dry white wine
1 tbsp	Double cream
150g	Unsalted butter

Vinaigrette

½ tsp	Sea salt
½ tsp	Cracked black pepper
½ tsp	Dijon mustard
2 tsp	White wine vinegar
2 tbsp	Olive oil
4	Rashers of crispy bacon, to garnish

METHOD

Wash and dry the salad leaves. Cut the smoked eel into 20cm long slices and lay out on a tray and keep chilled. Cut the streaky bacon into very small dice. Put it in a small saucepan, cover with cold water and bring to the boil before draining and refreshing in cold water. Fry the blanched streaky bacon in 50g of butter, turning regularly until perfectly crisp on all sides, then drain well and reserve.

Chop the garlic and shallots quite finely and put in a small saucepan together with the salt, pepper and white wine. Stew on a very gentle heat for ten minutes, reducing the liquid to a syrupy tablespoonful. Add the cream, bring quickly to the boil before adding the butter, cut into small cubes, whisking very well as you do so. The butter will liaise with the reduction into a smooth, pale sauce. Strain the result through a fine sieve into a warm (not hot) bowl.

Vinaigrette

Make the vinaigrette by mixing the salt, pepper, mustard and vinegar very well before whisking in the oil.

TO SERVE

To assemble the salad, dress the leaves lightly with the vinaigrette and arrange in the middle of the plates. Drape three slices of eel per person over the salad and sprinkle with the bacon. Place the salads under a hot grill for thirty seconds or until the leaves are just starting to wilt. Remove immediately from the grill and anoint with a tablespoon or two of the beurre blanc over the salads, garnish with the crispy bacon and serve immediately.

SALT AND PEPPER OYSTERS
Serves 4

INGREDIENTS

Rapeseed oil for deep frying
24   Rock oysters (Cumbrae)
        opened
1   Red chilli, sliced
1   Shallot, sliced

Tempura batter

70g   Cornflour
30g   Plain flour
Pinch   Szechuan pepper
Pinch   Maldon sea salt
Sparkling water, iced

To serve

Maldon sea salt
4   Limes, cut into wedges
Bunch of coriander

METHOD

To make the batter, mix the flours, salt and pepper together. Add a little iced sparkling water and all the juices from the oysters.

Clean out the oyster shells; assemble on the plate on a bed of sea salt.

Heat up the rapeseed oil to 180°C in a small deep fat fryer.

Dip the oysters and the chillies into the batter along with the shallot. Fry until golden brown, shake off any excess oil and lay on a cloth to dry.

Pop the oysters back into the shells and garnish with the shallots, chillies and lime wedges. Just to be really cheffy sprinkle with a few sprigs of coriander to finish off.

ROY BRETT

HOME

S A T
B A I N S

CHORIZO EGGS
Serves 1

INGREDIENTS

50g   Chorizo, chopped into cubes
2   Organic eggs
Salt and pepper
Fresh herbs (optional)

METHOD

Pan fry the chorizo in a dry pan, when caramelised add the egg and cook to your liking, season with salt and pepper and serve with a thick slice of toasted Hovis or other brown bread. Sprinkle with herbs if desired.

WHOLE ROASTED BANANA
Serves 1

INGREDIENTS

1	Ripe banana skin on
25g	Unsalted butter
30 tbsp	Caster sugar
1 tbsp	Vanilla ice cream

METHOD

Cook the banana in a warm oven at 190°C/375°F/gas mark 5 for 5 minutes then turn the banana over and cook for a further 5 minutes. The skin should be black.

Allow the banana to cool for 20 minutes.

Remove the top third of the banana skin using sharp knife.

Warm a frying pan suitable for oven use and big enough to fit the banana. Add the butter and when it is foaming, add the banana flesh side down. Add the sugar and turn the heat up to full. When the sugar and butter start to caramelise turn the banana over and spoon the liquid caramel over the top.

Put the pan into the oven at 210°C/ 415°F/gas mark 6.5 for 3 minutes. Remove the banana from the pan and leave to cool for 5 minutes before eating.

TO SERVE

Serve with vanilla ice cream.

SHANE OSBORN

TREACLE TART WITH CLOTTED CREAM AND FRESH RASPBERRIES

Serves 8-10

S H A U N   R A N K I N

This dish is fit for so many occasions from a sumptuous dinner with friends to a family Sunday lunch, even with a good cup of tea. It's so diverse you can dress it up or leave it simple, but no matter how you serve it, it will always bring back childhood memories.

INGREDIENTS

Pastry

518g	Plain flour
202g	Icing sugar
67g	Ground almonds
250g	Butter, diced
2	Free-range eggs, lightly beaten

Egg wash (2 eggs mixed with 1 tbsp milk)

Treacle tart filling

165g	Brown breadcrumbs
92g	Butter
130g	Eggs
70g	Double cream
9.5g	Salt
720g	Golden syrup

Fresh raspberries
Lemon juice
Icing sugar
Cracked black pepper
Clotted cream, to serve

METHOD

Pastry

In a large bowl add the flour, sugar, almonds and diced butter together; using your finger tips, mix together until it reaches the crumb stage (like a crumble should look like) then add the eggs and mix well, cover and rest in the fridge for 30 minutes. Roll out to approx 2mm thick and line a 22.5cm tart ring, letting it hang over the sides. Bake blind on 180°C/350°F/gas mark 4 for approximately 20 minutes until cooked through and lightly golden. Using a pastry brush egg wash the tart well and put back in the oven for a further 3 minutes, remove and set aside until needed.

Treacle tart filling

Remove the crusts from the bread and blitz in a food processor to make bread crumbs.

Cook the butter in a pan until it starts to foam (it will start to turn brown at that stage), remove from the heat and sieve, leaving the sediment behind.

Mix the eggs, cream and salt in a bowl. Heat the golden syrup gently until hot and pour in the butter, mix well until it goes cloudy (that's when you know the butter is mixed properly) then add the cream mix. Next, add the breadcrumbs, mixing in well, pour the mixture into the cooked tart base and cook for 25 minutes at 160°C/325°F/gas mark 3 and then turn down to 140°C/275°F/gas mark 1 for 20 minutes. When cooked, leave to cool on a wire rack for around 2 hours until cold – the top should be chewy, the middle soft and moist with the pastry being crunchy.

Raspberries

Place the raspberries into a bowl, add the lemon juice and icing sugar, mix well and finish with the cracked black pepper. Set aside until needed.

TO SERVE

Cut the tart into portions and place on the plate. Scatter the dressed raspberries over and around, then serve straightaway with the clotted cream.

Notes and tips for the cook
It's so important that you add the treacle and the butter while they are both still hot and mix well before adding any other ingredients as this will stop the mix separating.

For a perfect presentation when cutting the tart use a wet, warm knife.

Also, always make extra, you will certainly need it!

PEPPER STEAK
Serves 4

INGREDIENTS

4	170g fillet steaks
3 tbsp	Black peppercorns
3 tbsp	White peppercorns
2 tbsp	Coriander seeds
1½ tsp	Fine sea salt
2 tbsp	Vegetable oil
2 tbsp	Soft butter
75ml	Cognac
200ml	Brown chicken stock
180ml	Double cream
3 tbsp	Soft green peppercorns in brine

Chips and green salad, to serve

METHOD

Coarsely grind the black and white peppercorns together with the coriander seeds (using a spice grinder or a pestle and mortar). Transfer the crushed peppercorns to a sieve, shake to release and discard any pepper dust.

Roll the steaks in the crushed pepper, pressing firmly to embed them into the meat – set aside and keep at room temperature.

Heat a large, heavy, cast-iron frying pan over a high heat. Add the vegetable oil, season the steaks with salt and place carefully into the frying pan (it is vital that the pan is very hot at this stage as the addition of the cold steaks will cool the pan, resulting in the meat stewing rather than frying if not hot enough). Cook for 2 minutes over a high heat and then add the butter. Continue cooking until blood rises to the surface.

TERRY LAYBOURNE

Turn the meat over at this point. Cook for another 2 minutes for rare, 4 minutes for medium rare or continue until blood rises again to the surface, which indicates that your steak is medium. Remove from the pan when you are happy that the cooking is to your liking and transfer to a plate which has a smaller, upturned plate on top (this is to help collect any juices which may be released whilst resting the meat and while the sauce is being made).

Leave to rest in a warm place, above the stove or on the open door of a low oven.

Discard any excess fat from the frying pan and swill out with Cognac.

Return to the heat and boil until reduced to 1 teaspoon before adding the chicken stock. Boil until reduced by three-quarters and then pour in the cream. Simmer gently until reduced to a coating consistency. Strain through a fine sieve into another small saucepan and stir in the soft green peppercorns. Check the sauce for seasoning and set aside to keep warm. Transfer the steaks to warm serving plates, tip any collected juice into the sauce and spoon the sauce over the meat.

TO SERVE

Serve with thin, crispy chips and a green salad dressed in olive oil, best quality red wine vinegar and a little Dijon mustard.

RISOTTO DI PEPERONI
Serves 4

INGREDIENTS

2	Red peppers
1	Red onion
3	Sticks celery
Olive oil	
300g	Risotto rice
Half a glass of white wine	
2 litres	Chicken stock
2	Yellow peppers
4	Ripe plum tomatoes (skinned, deseeded and finely chopped)
150g	Parmesan
Handful of fresh basil (ripped)	
75g	Unsalted butter
Salt & pepper	

METHOD

Char grill the red peppers until black, place in a bowl and cover with cling film. Peel off the black skin. Wash off seeds, chop finely and set aside.

In a large saucepan soften the onion and celery in a little olive oil, add the rice, cook for 5 minutes, add the white wine then the stock and stir continuously until the rice has absorbed all the stock. When the rice is almost ready add the chopped peeled peppers, tomatoes, parmesan, basil and butter and stir vigorously to obtain a lovely creamy consistency. Season with salt and pepper. Serve.

COCK-A-LEEKIE
Serves 4-6

INGREDIENTS

1	Whole free-range chicken
1	Leek
1	Onion
2	Carrots
1	Sprig of thyme
5	White peppercorns
1	Bay leaf
Salt	

Garnish

200g	Basmati rice
50g	Chopped prunes
20g	Chopped parsley
1	Chopped leek

METHOD

In a large pan cover the chicken with cold water and bring to the boil. Add the vegetables and herbs and cook slowly for 2-3 hours until the chicken is cooked.

Remove the chicken and vegetables from the stock and season to taste.

Meanwhile, cook the basmati rice and chopped leeks in boiling salted water. Chop the prunes and parsley, keeping aside for garnish. Break away the chicken from the bone.

TO SERVE

In a bowl place the cooked rice, chicken, prunes and chopped parsley. Cover in stock and serve.

TOM KITCHIN

DEVILLED KIDNEYS
Serves 4

INGREDIENTS

3 tbsp   Plain flour
2 tsp   Cayenne pepper
2 tsp   Colman's English mustard
              powder
Sea salt and freshly ground black
pepper
Knob of butter
10   Lamb or calf kidneys,
              slit in half and cored
Splash of chicken stock
Splash of tabasco
Worcestershire sauce, to taste
2   Slices thick brown toast
Squeeze of lemon juice
Handful of flat leaf parsley, chopped

METHOD

Mx together the flour, cayenne
pepper, mustard powder, salt and
pepper. Then heat a pan until
hot and drop in the butter. Toss
the kidneys in the flour mixture
and shake to remove any excess.
Cook for 2 minutes on each side,
adding the stock, tabasco and
Worcestershire sauce. Then remove
the kidneys from the pan and place
on the toast. Squeeze over lemon
juice and sprinkle with parsley.

The Artistry of Champagne

www.champagne-roederer.com

BRUT PREMIER*

LOUIS ROEDERER

CHAMPAGNE

BRUT   REIMS

12 % VOL.   ℮ 750 ml

WINE MAN

NORTHCOTE'S RESIDENT WINE MATCHER CRAIG BANCROFT TELLS ROSIE BIRKETT ABOUT HIS YEARS OF CHOOSING WINES FOR THE FESTIVAL.

Over the ten years of its term to date, Obsession has been lauded for its sophisticated and innovative cuisine. But one very crucial factor of the event's success is the wine, which, over the years, has become Craig Bancroft's labour of love. For the first year, Craig enlisted the expert help of wine critic Charles Metcalfe, with whom he liaised to choose the appropriate wines for each dish of the festival. But the following year Craig, who considers himself a wine enthusiast rather than an expert, felt he wanted to take on the wine element.

"It started in 2002 with me choosing a flight of wine to go with each chef's menu," he says. "It was very daunting because you have to understand the chef's food in order to pick an accompanying wine, and in terms of actually getting the menus off the chefs, this is usually quite a last minute thing. I'd normally get them just ten days prior to event, so I set myself a difficult task. Sometimes I'd ask Nigel to mock up a dish to help me with the flavours. "

Once Craig has the often-elusive menu from a particular chef in his hands, his next stage is to look at it carefully and think about which flavours would work with which wines. He also talks to that particular chef's sommelier for some guidance, and to get a better steer on the wine. "Every dish is matched by a different wine, to give the diner a better experience," says Craig, who has rarely repeated the same wine twice in any one festival.

Creating a wine list to sate the often exacting standards of each particular chef is a challenge in itself, as Craig found out in 2007, when choosing wines for Raymond Blanc. "I was invited to attended The Champagne Academy of 2005 with his sommelier, Xavier Rousset (now of Texture Restaurant London), then after I'd chosen them I called him and he said they looked good. But when Raymond showed up he wanted to taste them all, and was just about to try and change them when I slipped into conversation that they had partly been chosen by his sommelier."

"Some chefs are precious, and there are some who won't have non-French wines on menu, but most have been good fun. Paul Cunningham made us have a very expensive bottle of wine from a Danish vineyard that I couldn't match with anything, and that no one drank."

So where does Craig's enthusiasm for matching wine with food come from? He puts it down to his love of food and his gourmet upbringing. "My parents were real gourmands," he says. "From a very young age we ate at one, two and three Michelin-starred restaurants all over the world. When you're brought up like that good food and wine becomes a way of life, as it has for me and my children now. It's quite embarrassing when we're in public because even my kids can say where they think a wine is from and occasionally be spot on," he chuckles.

Craig sees his passion for food as an advantage when choosing wines for the festival, and something that gives him the edge over most sommeliers. "My first love is food, which is good because it means that I look at wine in a different way to most sommeliers. The choices I make are more to do with my food than my wine knowledge," he says. "What I'm looking for is what is going to go best with a certain dish – so I'm searching for flavours that match ingredients. Of course sommeliers are incredibly good at what they do, but many don't tend to eat that much and normally concentrate on the wine rather than the food. For a food and wine matching, you need to be equally enthusiastic."

Within the week of the festival, Craig tries to create intrigue, excitement and surprise. But he goes even further than that to give the diner some variety. "Usually in my flight I try to use a different country in each course unless I am working with the origin of the chef or his restaurant as was the case of Dieter Koschina in 2006 where the wine were in the main Portuguese." Though Northcote dabbled with wine sponsorship for some of the festivals, Craig put a stop to this because he found it too restrictive. "We could have got a lot of financial underpinning for the nights, but I'm not a wine prostitute," he says.

"Sometimes with the sponsored nights I couldn't find the wines with the flavour I needed, and I realised that it wasn't helping us give the client the best delivery, so I stopped it."

In terms of wines that have particularly stood out during the festivals, Craig remembers a Pinot Noir he matched with Phil Howard's roasted foie gras with raisin purée pain d'epice and a sweet and sour glaze in 2007. "It was a particularly memorable wine," he says. "A Pinot Noir Beerenauslese – Willi Opitz 2005, which was a seamless match for the foie gras. They were just made to go with each other. The wine's acidity came through to cut the foie gras perfectly, but its sweetness also worked incredibly well with the raisins."

Portuguese wines strike a real chord with Craig, and over the years he's really come to love Portuguese red wine in particular. "Using Portuguese wines has been interesting for our chefs because it's still not something represented that well in restaurants. Over the years we've had some crackers, like the Cartuxa de Evora Reserva, Fundação Eugénio de Almeida, 1999 which went particularly well with Dieter Koschina's saddle of venison and port sauce. Because Dieter's restaurant Vila Joya is in the Algarve in Portugal, I used the opportunity to have all Portuguese wines, except for with the dessert.

"Portuguese wines tend to be robust and full bodied, so they go fantastically well with Nigel's food in particular as he has a real depth of flavour in his cooking – so I can match them quite easily to his food. In 2009 we did a fantastic roast loin of braised shoulder of Herdwick mutton with smoked mash and yellow beets and we served a Portuguese Vinha Pan Beiras Luis Pato 2003 with that."

Choosing wines year in, year out is a challenge, but one Craig enthuses about nonetheless. Does he ever get palette fatigue from all those tastings? He insists not. "There's a lot of tasting but I tend to use my brain as much as my palate. Like if there's a port wine in the sauce then porty style wine will go. It's not rocket science but it's about picking up on nuances of flavour and knowing what works together. After years of eating all over the world, which I've been lucky enough to do with Nigel, you learn what works."

Craig and Nigel would like to thank all those who have given them help and guidance with their wine choices over the years, especially our team of sommeliers who have worked alongside us over the 10 years. Special thanks goes to Julian Kaye from the Wright Wine Company, Guy Cliffe and all the team at Louis Roederer, Charles Metcalfe, Nick Adams MW, Miles Corish and all our wine friends.

Encruzado, Dao, Quinta dos Roques, 2008	2010	Tom Kitchin
Blanc de Blancs, Clos Mireille, Côtes de Provence-Domaines Ott, 2006	2010	Tom Kitchin
Albariño, La Val, Rias Baixas, 2008	2010	Tom Kitchin
Cheval Des Andes, Mendoza, Cheval Blanc and Terrazas de Los Andes, 2005	2010	Tom Kitchin
Vin de Constance, Klein Constantia, Constantia, 2004	2010	Tom Kitchin
Vinho Frisante Gaseficado, "Bomfinal" Vinhos Messias	2010	Matthew Fort & Tom Parker Bowles
Gavi di Tassarolo, "Piedmont", La Zerba, 2008	2010	Matthew Fort & Tom Parker Bowles
Sauvignon Blanc, Marlborough, Isabel, 2008	2010	Matthew Fort & Tom Parker Bowles
Hunter Semillon, VAT 1, Hunter Valley, Tyrrell's, 2002	2010	Matthew Fort & Tom Parker Bowles
Chianti Classico, Tuscany, Fattoria Ormanni, 2005	2010	Matthew Fort & Tom Parker Bowles
Muscat, Campbells, Victoria, Rutherglen NV	2010	Matthew Fort & Tom Parker Bowles
Frangelico Liqueur, Barbero	2010	Matthew Fort & Tom Parker Bowles
Pinot Gris, Le Fromenteau, Alsace, Josmeyer, 2006	2010	Theo Randell
Vouvray, Le Mont Sec, Domaine Huet, 2007	2010	Theo Randell
Dolcetto di Dogliani, San Luigi, Piedmont, Pecchenino, 2008	2010	Theo Randell
Reserva, Alión, Ribera del Duero, Bodegas y Viñedos, 2005	2010	Theo Randell
Moscato d'Asti, Piedmont, Pio Cesare, 2008	2010	Theo Randell
Grüner Veltliner, Kamptal, Fred Loimer, 2008	2010	Ken Hom
Saké, Daiginjo, Akashi-Tai Brewery, Akashi	2010	Ken Hom
Riesling Saering, Grand Cru, Alsace, Schlumberger, 2007	2010	Ken Hom
Robert Arnoux, Bourgogne 'Pinot Fin', 2007	2010	Ken Hom
Goldackerl, Beerenauslese, Willi Opitz, 2007	2010	Ken Hom
Vinhas Velhas Branco, Bairrada, Luis Pato, 2008	2010	Angela Hartnett & Lisa Allen
Roero Arneis, Piedmont, Giacosa, 2008	2010	Angela Hartnett & Lisa Allen
Amontillado (c18th Solera) Bodegas Tradicion	2010	Angela Hartnett & Lisa Allen
Leione, Dominio Dostares, Castile y Leon, 2005	2010	Angela Hartnett & Lisa Allen
Riesling Late Harvest, Niagara-on-the-Lake, Château des Charmes	2010	Angela Hartnett & Lisa Allen
Ramos Pinto LBV, 2004	2010	Angela Hartnett ; Lisa Allen
Sauvignon Blanc, Single Vineyard, Marlborough, Fairhall Downs, 2007	2010	Nathan Outlaw
Redoma, Douro, Dirk Niepoort, 2008	2010	Nathan Outlaw
Gran Reserva, Blanco "Capellania", Marqués de Murrieta, 2004	2010	Nathan Outlaw
Zinfandel, Geyserville, Santa Cruz, California, Ridge Vineyards, 2006	2010	Nathan Outlaw
Vino Dolce, Vulcaia Après, Veneto, Inama, 2004	2010	Nathan Outlaw
Sancerre Rosé, Pascal Jolivet, 2008	2010	Phil Howard
Sauvignon Blanc, Te Koko, Marlborough, Cloudy Bay, 2006	2010	Phil Howard
Sito Moresco, Langhe, Piedmont, Gaja, 2006	2010	Phil Howard
Réserve de La Comtesse, Pauillac, Bordeaux, 2001	2010	Phil Howard
Quinta da Ervamoira, 10 Year Old Tawny, Ramos Pinto	2010	Phil Howard
Château Bastor-Lamontagne 2005	2010	Phil Howard
Louis Roederer, Blanc de Blancs , Reims 2003	2010	Jacob Boerma
Chablis, l'er Cru 'Beauroy', Domaine Hamelin, 2007	2010	Jacob Boerma
Condrieu, Les Chaillets, Yves Cuilleron, 2008	2010	Jacob Boerma
Chardonnay Reserve, Franschhoek, Chamonix, 2008	2010	Jacob Boerma
Châteauneuf-du-Pape, Les Vieilles Vignes Domaine de Villeneuve, 2005	2010	Jacob Boerma
Tokaji Aszú, 5 Puttonyos, Oremus, 2000	2010	Jacob Boerma
Pinot Gris, Marlborough, Fairhall Downs, 2006	2010	Andrew Fairlie
Chardonnay, Hermanus, Walker Bay, Hamilton Russell, 2007	2010	Andrew Fairlie
Crozes Hermitage, Domaine Mule Blanche, Paul Jaboulet Aîné, 2007	2010	Andrew Fairlie
Garrafeira, Casa de Saima, Bairrada, Graça Miranda, 2001	2010	Andrew Fairlie
Jurançon Moëlleux, Sélection des Terrasses, A Capcéu, Domaine Larreyda, 2006	2010	Andrew Fairlie
Rose of Virginia, Rosé, Barossa Valley, Charles Melton, 2008	2010	Nigel Haworth
Sancerre Blanc, Harmonie, Vincent Pinard, 2006	2010	Nigel Haworth
Vinhos Barbeito, Single Harvest Madiera, 1997	2010	Nigel Haworth
Vosne Romane, Burgundy, Vosne Romanée René Engel, 2002	2010	Nigel Haworth
Red Muscadel, Nuy Winery, Worcester, 2007	2010	Nigel Haworth
Châteauneuf-du-Pape Blanc, La Bernardine, M. Chapoutier	2009	Daniel Clifford
Rully l'er Cru "Les Clous", Olivier Leflaive, 2006	2009	Daniel Clifford
Sito Moresco, Langhe, Piedmont, Gaja, 2006	2009	Daniel Clifford
Jurançon Moëlleux, Sélection des Terrasses, A Capcéu, Domaine Larredya, 2006	2009	Daniel Clifford
Mönchhof Erdener Treppchen, Riesling Kabinett, 2002	2009	Shaun Rankin
Chablis l'er Cru, Fourchaume, Domaine Séguinot-Bordet, 2007	2009	Shaun Rankin
Fugue de Nenin, Pomerol, 2002	2009	Shaun Rankin
Shiraz, T & C Soderstrom, Barossa Valley, Viking, 1999	2009	Shaun Rankin
Sauvignon, Late Harvest Maule Valley, Concha y Toro, 2004	2009	Shaun Rankin
Verdejo, Conclass, Sitios de Bodega, 2007	2009	Glyn Purnell
Pouilly-Fuissé, Métertière, Thierry Drouin, 2006	2009	Glyn Purnell
Riesling, Les Princes Abbés, Organic, Domaines Schlumberger, 2005	2009	Glyn Purnell
Cabernet Sauvignon, Don Melchor, Puento Alto Vineyard, Concha y Toro, 1998	2009	Glyn Purnell
Muscat de Beaumes de Venise, Le Chant des Griolles, Paul Jaboulet Aîné, 2006	2009	Glyn Purnell
Don Nuño, Dry Oloroso, Emilio Lustau	2009	Phil Howard & Brett Graham
Chardonnay, Hermanus, Walker Bay, Hamilton Russell, 2007	2009	Phil Howard & Brett Graham
Pinot Noir, Beernauslese, Willi Opitz, Illmitz, 2005	2009	Phil Howard & Brett Graham
Château Leydet-Valentin, St Emilion, Grand Cru Classé, 2004	2009	Phil Howard & Brett Graham
Inama, Vulcaia Aprés Vino Dolce, Veneto Bianco, Verona, 2006	2009	Phil Howard & Brett Graham
Marsanne, Vin de Pays des Collines Rhodaniennes, Domaine Yves Cuilleron, 2007	2009	Atul Kochar
Rose of Virginia, Rosé, Barossa Valley, Charles Melton, 2008	2009	Atul Kochar
Chenin Blanc, Piekenierskloof, Tierhoek, 2004	2009	Atul Kochar
Pinot Noir, Central Otago, Amisfield, 2006	2009	Atul Kochar
Tokaji Aszú, 5 Puttonyos, Oremus, 2000	2009	Atul Kochar
Pinot Gris, Marlborough, Fairhall Downs, 2006	2009	Jason Atherton
Gran Reserva, Blanco "Capellania", Marqués de Murrieta, 2003	2009	Jason Atherton
Zinfandel, Sonoma County, Seghesio, 2006	2009	Jason Atherton
Côteaux du Layon, Chaume, Domaine des Forges, 2006	2009	Jason Atherton
Quinta da Ervamoira, 10 Year Old Tawny, Ramos Pinto	2009	Jason Atherton

Wine	Year	Name
Mâcon Village, Quintaine, Domaine de la Bongran,, J. Thévenet, 2001	2009	Nigel Haworth & Paul Heathcoate
Hildegard, Bien Nacido, Santa Barbara, Au Bon Climat, 2004	2009	Nigel Haworth & Paul Heathcoate
Don Nuño, Dry Oloroso, Emilio Lustau	2009	Nigel Haworth & Paul Heathcoate
Vinha Pan, Beiras, Luis Pato, 2003	2009	Nigel Haworth & Paul Heathcoate
Recioto della Valpolicella, Corte Sant Alda, 2002	2009	Nigel Haworth & Paul Heathcoate
Château Partarrieu, Sauternes, 2005	2009	Nigel Haworth & Paul Heathcoate
Soave Classico, Inama Azienda Agricola, 2006	2008	Anthony Flinn
Blanc de Blanc, Clos Mireille, Cotes de Provence-Domaines Ott, 2004	2008	Anthony Flinn
Terra do Zambujeiro, Alentejo, Quinta do Zambujeiro, 2002	2008	Anthony Flinn
Botrytis Riesling, Mellifera, Stellenbosch Jordan, 2006	2008	Anthony Flinn
Erdener Treppchen Riesling Kabinett, Dr Loosen, 2005	2008	Mark Edwards
Pinot Grigio, Ramato, Venezia Giulia, Azienda, Specogna, 2006	2008	Mark Edwards
Chinon, Cuvée de la Cure, Charles Joguet, 2005	2008	Mark Edwards
Nuits-Saint-Georges, Vieilles Vignes, Domaine Patrice Rion, 2003	2008	Mark Edwards
Chambers Rutherglen Muscadelle, Rutherglen	2008	Mark Edwards
Meursault, "Les Grandes Charrons", Domaine Michel Bouzereau, 2003	2008	Pierre Koffmann
Chablis, Suzanne Reynard, Domaine J Durup, 2006	2008	Pierre Koffmann
Châteauneuf-du-Pape Les Vieilles Vignes Domaine de Villeneuve, 1998	2008	Pierre Koffmann
Chateau Romassan, Bandol, Domaines Ott, 2002	2008	Pierre Koffmann
Côteaux, du Layon Saint-Aubin de Luigné Domaine des Forges, 2003	2008	Pierre Koffmann
Châteauneuf-du-Pape, La Bernardine M. Chapoutier, 2005	2008	Angela Hartnett
Verdicchio di Matelica, La Monacesca, 2005	2008	Angela Hartnett
Sancerre Rouge, Pascal Jolivet, 2005	2008	Angela Hartnett
Moscato d'Asti, Pio Cesare, 2006	2008	Angela Hartnett
Sauvignon Blanc, Late Harvest, Semi-Dulce, Bornos, 2004	2008	Angela Hartnett
Albarino, Lagar de Cervera, Rias Baixas, 2005	2008	Phil Howard
Pinot Gris, Marlborough, Mudhouse, 2005	2008	Phil Howard
Rully, l'er Cru "Les Clous", Olivier Leflaive, 2006	2008	Phil Howard
Gloria Reynolds, Alentejo Julian Cuellar Reynolds, 2002	2008	Phil Howard
Essensia, Orange Muscat, Andrew Quady, 2006	2008	Phil Howard
Sylvaner, Vieilles Vignes Organic-Domaine Ostertag, 2006	2008	Shane Osborn
Gavi di Tassarolo "Terrarosa", La Zerba, 2006	2008	Shane Osborn
Condrieu, Invitare, M. Chapoutier, 2006	2008	Shane Osborn
Zinfandel, Sonoma County, Seghesio, 2004	2008	Shane Osborn
Pedro Ximénez, San Emillio Lustau	2008	Shane Osborn
Gewürztraminer, les Folastries, Josmeyer, 2005	2008	Nigel Haworth
Marismeno Fino, Sanchez Romate	2008	Nigel Haworth
Puligny Montrachet, Domaine Louis Carillon, 2005	2008	Nigel Haworth
Pinot Noir, San Antonio, Leyda Valley, Amayna, 2005	2008	Nigel Haworth
Château Lafaurie-Peyraguey l'er Cru Classe, Sauternes, 1995	2008	Nigel Haworth
Alvarinho Soalheiro, Vinho Verde, Minho, António Esteves Ferreira, 2005	2007	Andrew Pern
Gewürztraminer, Domaine Albert Mann, 2005	2007	Andrew Pern
Pera Manca Tinto, Fundação Eugénio de Almeida, 1998	2007	Andrew Pern
Essensia, Orange Muscat, Andrew Quady, 2005	2007	Andrew Pern
Mercurey 'Meix Foulot', Paul de Launay, 2005	2007	Raymond Blanc
Château Bouscaut Blanc, Pessac Léognan, Grand Cru Classé, 2003	2007	Raymond Blanc
Menetou–Salon, Clos des Blanchais, Domaine Henry Pellé, 2005	2007	Raymond Blanc
Gigondas, Domaine les Palliéres, H. Brunier, 2001	2007	Raymond Blanc
Goldackerl, Beerenauslese, Willi Opitz, 2005	2007	Raymond Blanc
Condrieu, Invitare, M. Chapoutier, 2005	2007	Michel Roux Jr
Auxey-Duresses Blanc, Domaine du Comte Armand, 2002	2007	Michel Roux Jr
Chassagne-Montrachet, Domaine Louis Carillon, 2003	2007	Michel Roux Jr
Rasteau, Vin Doux Naturel, Domaine des Escaravailles, 2003	2007	Michel Roux Jr
Grüner Veltliner, Kamptal, Fred Loirmer, 2005	2007	Paul Cunningham
Meursault, Domaine Henri Boillot, 2001	2007	Paul Cunningham
Vino Dolce, Veneto Bianco, Inama, 2001	2007	Paul Cunningham
Pinot Noir, Geelong and Yarra Valley, Shadowfax, 2003	2007	Paul Cunningham
Chateau Ålsgårde, 2005, Denmark	2007	Paul Cunningham
Banyuls, Vin Doux Naturels, M. Chapoutier, 2004	2007	Paul Cunningham
Verdicchio de Matelica Riserva, Mirum, La Monacesca, 2005	2007	Michael Caines
Gewürztraminer, les Folastries, Josmeyer, 2005	2007	Michael Caines
Sauvignon Blanc, San Antonio-Leyda Valley, Amayna, 2005	2007	Michael Caines
Le Cigare Volant, Bonny Doon Winery, 2002	2007	Michael Caines
Domaine des Forges, Coteaux de Layon, Saint-Aubin de Luigné, 2004	2007	Michael Caines
Cotes de Provence-Domains Ott, 2004	2007	Phil Howard
Pouilly-Fumé, Cuvée d'Eve Vieilles Vignes, Jean Claude Dagueneau, 2003	2007	Phil Howard
Pinot Noir Beerenauslese-Willi Opitz, 2005	2007	Phil Howard
Chianti Classico Riserva, Berardo, Castello di Bossi, 2001	2007	Phil Howard
Boal, Colheita Cask 81A, Vinhos Barbeito, Maderia	2007	Phil Howard
Gewürztraminer, les Folastries, Josmeyer, 2005	2007	Nigel Haworth
Pinot Grigio, Ramato, Venezia Giulia, Azienda Specogna, 2005	2007	Nigel Haworth
Mâcon-Village, Quintaine, Domaine de la Bongran, J. Thévenet, 2001	2007	Nigel Haworth
Nuits St Georges Clos de Forêts St Georges Domaine de L'Arlot, 2001	2007	Nigel Haworth
Thwaites Lancaster Bomber	2007	Nigel Haworth
Late Harvest Orange Muscat and Flora, Brown Brothers, 2005	2007	Nigel Haworth
Pinot Gris, Marlborough, South Island- Kim Crawford, 2005	2006	Claude Bosi
Auxey-Duresses Blanc, Domaine Compte Armand, 2002	2006	Claude Bosi
Chardonnay "Wild Boy", Santa Barbara, California-Au Bon Climat, 2003	2006	Claude Bosi
Château Partarrieu, Sauternes, 2001	2006	Claude Bosi
Châteauneuf-du-Pape, Cuvée Etienne Gonnet, Domaine Font de Michelle, 1996	2006	Claude Bosi
Plantagenet off the Rack, Chenin Blanc-Great Southern, 2003	2006	Claude Bosi
Gewürztraminer, les Folastries, Josmeyer, 2002	2006	David Thompson
Viognier, Rapel Valley Special Reserve, Anakena, 2004	2006	David Thompson
Juliénas, Domaine Gérard Descombes, 2003	2006	David Thompson

Wine	Year	Name
Pinot Grigio, Ramato, Venezia Giulia, Azienda Specogna, 2003	2006	David Thompson
Mâcon-Clessé-Quintaine, Sélection de Grains Cendrés, Guillemot-Michel, 1992	2006	David Thompson
Sauvignon Blanc, Late Harvest, Semi-Dulce Bornos, 2002	2006	David Thompson
Pinot Gris Grand Cru Brand, Cave de Turckheim, 2001	2006	Fergus Henderson
"R" Rosé Côtes de Provence, Domaine de Rimauresq, 2004	2006	Fergus Henderson
Rimauresq Blanc Côtes de Provence, Domaine de Rimauresq, 2004	2006	Fergus Henderson
Beaune l'er Cru Epenottes, Vallet Frères, 2001	2006	Fergus Henderson
Vin de Paille Hermitage Gambert de Loche, Cave de Tain, 1999	2006	Fergus Henderson
Albariño, Lagar de Cerveza, Rias Baixas, 2004	2006	Andoni Luis Aduriz
Blanc de Blancs, Clos Mireille, Cotes de Provenance-Domaines Ott, 2001	2006	Andoni Luis Aduriz
Jurançon, Vendanges Tardives, "Symphonie de Novembre", Domaine Cauhapé, 2002	2006	Andoni Luis Aduriz
San Vincente, Tempranillo-San Vincente, Rioja, 1994	2006	Andoni Luis Aduriz
Rasteau, Vin Doux Naturel, Domaine de Trapadis, 2001	2006	Andoni Luis Aduriz
Riesling, Eden Valley, Rockford, 2001	2006	Mark Hix
Cartuxa Branco de Évora, Reserva, Alentejo, Fundação Eugénio de Almeida, 2001	2006	Mark Hix
Napoleon, Oloroso Abocado, Vinicola Hidalgo	2006	Mark Hix
Pinot Noir, San Antonio, Leyda Valley, Amayna, 2003	2006	Mark Hix
Late Harvest, Three Choirs Vineyard, 2002	2006	Mark Hix
Montagny l'er Cru, Château de la Saule, Alain Roy, 2004	2006	Bruce Poole
Pinot Noir, Marlborough South Island, Isabel, 2002	2006	Bruce Poole
Riesling, Les Princes Abbés, Organic-Domaine Schlumberger, 2001	2006	Bruce Poole
Cartuxa de Évora Reserva, Fundação Eugénio de Almeida, 1999	2006	Bruce Poole
Maury Vins Doux Naturels, Domaine Pouderoux, 2003	2006	Bruce Poole
Pinot Grigio, Ramato, Venezia Giulia, Azienda Specogna, 2005	2006	Phil Howard & Nigel Haworth
Sauvignon Blanc, San Antonio-Leyda Valley, Amayna, 2003	2006	Phil Howard & Nigel Haworth
Riesling Mount Barker, Plantagent,1998	2006	Phil Howard & Nigel Haworth
Gevrey Chambertin, Les Sevrees, Vieilles Vignes, Domaine Michel Magnien, 2000	2006	Phil Howard & Nigel Haworth
De Bortoli, Noble One Botrytis Semillon, Riverina 2000	2006	Phil Howard & Nigel Haworth
Grand Millésime, Champagne Gosset, 1996	2005	Eric Chavot
Dry Furmint, "Mandolas", Tokaji-Oremus, 2002	2005	Eric Chavot
Menetou-Salon, Clos des Blanchais, Domaine Henry Pellé, 2002	2005	Eric Chavot
Chambolle Musigny, Frédéric Mugnier, 1998	2005	Eric Chavot
Muscat de Rivesaltes, Domaine Piétri Géraud, 2003	2005	Eric Chavot
Quincy, Domaine des Ballandors, 2003	2005	Sat Bains
Viognier, Podere di Montalupan, Ascheri, 1997	2005	Sat Bains
Château de Fonsalette, Jacques Reynaud, 1993	2005	Sat Bains
Boal, Colheita Cask 81A, Vinhos Barbeito, Madeira	2005	Sat Bains
Château Partarrieu, Sauternes, 2001	2005	Sat Bains
Jurançon, Vendanges Tardives, "Symphonie de Novembre", Domaine Cauhapé, 2002	2005	Sat Bains
Bairrada Reserva, Casa de Saima, 1996	2005	Dieter Koschina
Quinta do Bom-Retiro, 20 Year Old Tawny, Ramos Pinto	2005	Dieter Koschina
Alvarinho Soalheiro,Vinho Verde, António Esteves Ferreira, 2001	2005	Dieter Koschina
Cartuxa de Évora Reserva, Fundação Eugénio de Almeida, 1999	2005	Dieter Koschina
Opitz One, Vin de Paille, Willi Opitz, 2000	2005	Dieter Koschina
Mud House Sauvignon Blanc, Marlborough, 2004	2005	Roy Brett
Gran Reserva Rioja Blanco, Marqués de Murrieta, 1998	2005	Roy Brett
Mercurey Blanc, Clos Rochette, Domaine Faiveley, 2001	2005	Roy Brett
Sancerre Rouge, Pascal Jolivet, 2003	2005	Roy Brett
Quinta da Ervamoira, 10 Year Old Tawny, Ramos Pinto	2005	Roy Brett
Pinot Grigio, Ramato, Venezia Giulia, Azienda Specogna, 2002	2005	Phil Howard
Pera Manca Branco, Alentejo-Fundação Eugénio de Almeida, 2001	2005	Phil Howard
Montagny, l'er Cru, Château de la Saule, Alain Roy, 2003	2005	Phil Howard
Pinot Noir, Yarra Ranges and Geelong, Shadowfax, 2002	2005	Phil Howard
Essensia, Orange Muscat, Andrew Quady, 2003	2005	Phil Howard
La Bernadine M. Chapoutier, Châteauneuf-du-Pape Blanc, 2003	2005	Richard Corrigan
Tokay Pinot-Gris, Le Fromentau, Josmeyer, 2002	2005	Richard Corrigan
Château Marsac-Séquineau, Cru Bourgeois-Margaux, 1996	2005	Richard Corrigan
Côteaux du Layon, Saint-Aubin de Luigné, Domaine des Forges, 2003	2005	Richard Corrigan
Maury Domaine Pouderoux, 2001	2005	Richard Corrigan
Gewürztraminer, les Folastries, Josmeyer, 2002	2005	Nigel Haworth
Malvasia, Colheita Cask 3, Vinhos Barbeito, 1993	2005	Nigel Haworth
Rasteau, Cuvée Prestige, André Roméro, 2000	2005	Nigel Haworth
Sauvignon, Late Harvest, Semi-Dulce, Rueda 2001	2005	Nigel Haworth
Elysium, Black Muscat Quady, 2003	2005	Nigel Haworth
Tokay Pinot-Gris, Le Fromentau, Josmeyer, 2002	2004	Peter Gordon
Chardonnay, Barossa Vines, Grant Burge, 2001	2004	Peter Gordon
Cartuxa Branco de Évora, ReservaFundação Eugénio de Almeida, 2000	2004	Peter Gordon
Zinfandel, Sonoma Country-Pedroncelli, 1999	2004	Peter Gordon
Recioto di Soave-Anselmi, I Capitelli, 1995	2004	Peter Gordon
Pinot Grigio, Venezia Giulia-Vinnaioli Jermann, 2000	2004	John Campbell
Viognier, Eden Valley-Heggies, 2002	2004	John Campbell
Sancerre Rouge, Pascal Jolivet, 2002	2004	John Campbell
Pinot Noir, Geelong and Yarra Valley-Shadowfax, 2001	2004	John Campbell
Essensia, Orange Muscat-Andrew Quady, 2000	2004	John Campbell
Esporão Reserva, Alentejo-Herdade do Esporão, 2001	2004	Rowley Leigh
Montagny l'er Cru, Château de Saule-Alain Roy, 2002	2004	Rowley Leigh
Château Haut Pezat-St Emilion Grand Cru, 2000	2004	Rowley Leigh
Champagne Vilmart and Cie, Grand Cellier d'Or, Rilly-La-Montagne, 1997	2004	Rowley Leigh
Vin Santo Villa di Vetrice, 1985	2004	Rowley Leigh
Marqués de Murrieta, "Capellaina", Blanco Gran Reserva-Marques de Murrieta, 1997	2004	Darina Allen
Chardonnay "Wild Boy", Santa Barbara, California-Au Bon Climat, 2000	2004	Darina Allen
Esporão Reserva, Alentejo-Herdade de Esporão, 2000	2004	Darina Allen
Vinhos Barbeito, Boal, Colheita Cask 81a, 1995	2004	Darina Allen
Late Harvest Muscat-Brown Brothers, 2002	2004	Darina Allen

Wine	Year	Name
Pinot Gris, Boyzone Vineyard, Marlborough, Kim Crawford, 2003	2004	Phil Howard
Palo Cortado Regenta, Sánchez	2004	Phil Howard
Menetou-Salon, Clos des Blanchais, Domaine Henry Pellé, 2002	2004	Phil Howard
Cartuxa de Évora Reserva-Fundação Eugénio de Almeida,1997	2004	Phil Howard
Banyuls, Vin Doux Naturel, M. Chapoutier, 1997	2004	Phil Howard
Taittinger Brut Réserve NV	2004	Giorgio Locatelli
Taburno Greco, Cantine Del Taburno, 2002	2004	Giorgio Locatelli
Vernaccia di San Gimignano, 2002	2004	Giorgio Locatelli
Barbera d'Alba "Ornati" Parussa, 2001	2004	Giorgio Locatelli
Barolo, E. Pira, 1999	2004	Giorgio Locatelli
Targa Riserva 1840, Marsala Superiore Riserva, Florio	2004	Giorgio Locatelli
Muscat "Collection" Series Kuentz Bas, 2000	2004	Nigel Haworth
Sauvignon Blanc Fairhall Downs, 2002	2004	Nigel Haworth
Cabernet Merlot, Lark Hill, Canberra District, 1999	2004	Nigel Haworth
Palladius, Eben Sadie, 2002	2004	Nigel Haworth
Pedro Ximénez, San Emilio Lustau	2004	Nigel Haworth
Menetou-Salon, Clos des Blanchais-Domaine Henry Pellé, 2000	2003	The Galvin Brothers
Dry Oloroso, Don Nuño-Emilio Lustau	2003	The Galvin Brothers
Pinot Grigio, Isonzo-Giovanni Puiatti, 2001	2003	The Galvin Brothers
Château de Ferrand, Grand Cru Saint Emilion, 1994	2003	The Galvin Brothers
Clos Labère, 2ème Vin de Château Rieussec -Sauternes Bordeaux, 1990	2003	The Galvin Brothers
La Gitana, Manzanilla-Vinicola Hidalgo	2003	Christian Olsson
Gewürztraminer, Grand Cru Hengst-Josmeyer, 1996	2003	Christian Olsson
Muscadet de Sevre et Maine, Sur lie, Château de Chasseloir-Chéreau-Carré, 1994	2003	Christian Olsson
Sauvignon Blanc, Adelaide Hills-Shaw and Shaw, 2001	2003	Christian Olsson
Valduero Reserva-E Valduero, Ribera del Duero, 1997	2003	Christian Olsson
Elysium Black Muscat-Andrew Quady California, 2000	2003	Christian Olsson
Muscadet de Sèvre et Maine, Sur Lie Château de Chasseloir Vinifié en Futs de Chêne Neufs Château-Carré, 1994	2003	Phil Howard
Gewürztraminer, les Folastries, Josmeyer, 2000	2003	Phil Howard
Montagny l'er Cru Château de la Saule-Alain Roy, 2000	2003	Phil Howard
Cartuxa de Évora Reserva-Fundação Eugénio de Almeida, 1997	2003	Phil Howard
Mâcon Clessé Selection de Grains Sendrés Quintaine-Guillemot-Michel, 1992	2003	Phil Howard
Bourgogne Blanc-Vallet Frères, 2000	2003	Heston Blumenthal
Vouvray, Cuvée des Fondraux-Champalou, 1997	2003	Heston Blumenthal
Esporão Reserva, Alentejo-Herdade de Esporão, 1999	2003	Heston Blumenthal
Sauvignon Blanc, Late Harvest, Semi-Dulce, Bornos, 2000	2003	Heston Blumenthal
Recioto di Soave, Capitelli-Anselmi, 2000	2003	Heston Blumenthal
Fino Marismeno, Reservas Especiales-Sánchez Romate	2003	Neil Wigglesworth
Viognier-Chardonnay, Bien Nacido Cuvée-Qupé, 2000	2003	Neil Wigglesworth
Tokay Pinot-Gris, Le Fromentau, Josmeyer, 1999	2003	Neil Wigglesworth
Late Picked Muscat-Brown Brothers	2003	Neil Wigglesworth
Zinfandel, Les Vieilles Vignes, Napa Valley-Fife Vineyards, 1998	2003	Neil Wigglesworth
Essensia, Orange Muscat, Andrew Quady, 1999	2003	Neil Wigglesworth
Cava, Rosado, Brut-Juvé y Camps	2003	Nigel Howarth & Charles Metcalfe
Esporão Reserva, Alentejo-Herdade do Esporão, 2000	2003	Nigel Howarth & Charles Metcalfe
Dry Oloroso, Don Nuño-Emilio Lustau	2003	Nigel Howarth & Charles Metcalfe
Reserva-Marques de Murrieta, 1997	2003	Nigel Howarth & Charles Metcalfe
Sauvignon Blanc, Late Harvest, Semi-Dulce, Bornos, 2000	2003	Nigel Howarth & Charles Metcalfe
Viognier-Chardonnay, Bien Nacido Cuvée, California Qupé, 1998	2002	Germain Schwab
Dry Oloroso, Don Nuño, Emilio Lustau	2002	Germain Schwab
Albariño, Martin Codax, 2000	2002	Germain Schwab
Reserva, Monte Real, Bodegas Riojanas, Rioja, 1996	2002	Germain Schwab
Essensia, Orange Muscat, Andrew Quady, 1999	2002	Germain Schwab
Dry Oloroso, Don Nuño, Emilio Lustau	2002	Phil Howard
Esporão Reserva, Alentejo-Herdade de Esporão, 2000	2002	Phil Howard
Rubicon, Stellenbosch, Meerlust, 1997	2002	Phil Howard
Montagny l'er Cru, Chateau de la Saule, Alain Roy, 1999	2002	Phil Howard
Ratafia de Champagne, Vilmart et Cie, Rilly-La-Montagne	2002	Phil Howard
Tokay Pinot-Gris, Le Fromentau, Josmeyer, 1997	2002	Robbie Millar
Juliénas, Domaine Gérard Descombes, 1999	2002	Robbie Millar
Pouilly-Fumé Cuvee d'Eve, Vieilles Vignes, Jean Claude Dagueneau, 1999	2002	Robbie Millar
Rioja Gran Reserva, Bodegas Sierra Cantabria, 1994	2002	Robbie Millar
Muscat de Frontignan, Midi, Château de la Peyrade	2002	Robbie Millar
Chardonnay, Eden Valley, Heggies, 1998	2002	Brian Turner
Gewürztraminer, Domaine Albert Mann, 1998/99	2002	Brian Turner
Bergerac Rosé, Château Tour des Gendres, 2000	2002	Brian Turner
Côteaux du Layon, Saint-Aubin de Luigné, Domaine des Forges, 1996	2002	Brian Turner
Saumur Cardinal, Noir de Noirs, Gratien & Meyer	2002	Brian Turner
Chablis l'er Cru, Montmain, Denis Race, 2000	2002	Daniel Couet
Gewürztraminer, Domaine Albert Mann, 1999	2002	Daniel Couet
Sauvignon Blanc, Ponder Estate, Marlborough, 2001	2002	Daniel Couet
Pedroncelli Zinfandel, Sonoma County, 1999	2002	Daniel Couet
Noble Riesling, Brown Brothers, Victoria, 1996	2002	Daniel Couet
Champagne Boizel Brut Réserve N/V	2002	Nigel Howarth & Charles Metcalfe
Chassagne Montrachet l'er Cru 'Clos St Jean', Domaine Ramonet, 1997	2002	Nigel Howarth & Charles Metcalfe
Chablis l'er Cru 'Beauroy' Domaine, L. Tribut, 1999	2002	Nigel Howarth & Charles Metcalfe
Nuits St George l'er Cru 'Les Pruliers', Domaine D Durban, 1996	2002	Nigel Howarth & Charles Metcalfe
Tokaji Furmint Vendage Tardine, 2000	2002	Nigel Howarth & Charles Metcalfe

YES CHEF! MAGAZINE

AN OBSESSION WITH QUALITY

YES CHEF! Magazine was born out of the need for a professional magazine which celebrated the skill, creativity and sheer hard work that goes into working in a restaurant kitchen. What are the secrets of the masters? How did they get where they are today? What really goes on behind the kitchen door? The original idea came from Gary Rhodes, who remarked to publisher Peter Marshall that, when he was working his way up as a young chef, there was a magazine called Chef which appeared as a quarterly supplement to one of the catering trade magazines. It was full of recipes, stories about the great chefs and tips and tricks of the trade and he read it from cover to cover and filed every copy. Then, one day, it stopped coming. The publishers had decided to drop it, for reasons of their own, and Gary bemoaned the fact that there was nothing similar for ambitious young chefs currently available.

Inspired by this conversation Peter Marshall, an experienced magazine publisher, conceived the idea of YES CHEF! Magazine. It started out aimed at young professionals, maybe chefs de partie, sous-chefs or even commis who were ambitious and determined to get ahead in the industry. Features have included profiles of the great chefs of yesteryear and today, successes in the food guides, seasonal and prime ingredients, the latest kitchen gadgets and, of course, recipes demonstrating the individual skills of the people who make the running in modern professional cookery.

Interestingly, the magazine has evolved since then and, probably as a result of the much higher profile of chefs – another Obsession of the 21st century – many readers from outside the profession have come to it simply out of a fascination with food, restaurants, the people behind them and what's happening in new ideas, equipment and techniques. Add to this the tendency for many people to take an interest in healthy eating, sustainable farming, animal welfare and 'food-miles' and the way modern chefs approach local and seasonal produce becomes even more relevant. YES CHEF! Magazine is still, first and foremost, aimed at professionals in the industry, but welcomes enthusiastic 'foodies' who, themselves, have an obsession with quality, purity and the sheer joy of eating wonderful food. The editorial board includes Heston Blumenthal (The Fat Duck), Michel Roux Jr (Le Gavroche), Andrew Fairlie (Gleneagles) and Brian Turner (all contributors to this book), who oversee the content and make sure that it's always fresh, up-to-date and relevant.

As the flagship publication for Peter Marshall's publishing company YES CHEF! Magazine has become an Obsession that has led him into the publication of cookbooks for some of the finest chefs of today. The magazine is published quarterly, and there are more details at **www.yeschefmagazine.com**.

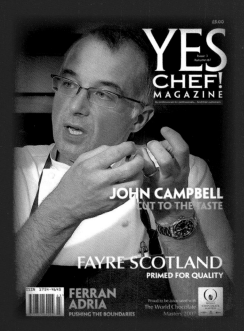

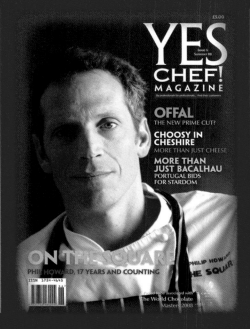

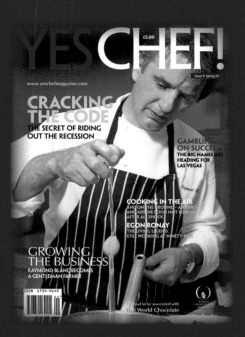

HOSPITALITY ACTION

For over 170 years Hospitality Action, the Hospitality Industry Benevolent Organisation, has been at the forefront of the industry providing specialised support to all who work, or have worked within hospitality in the UK and who, through no fault of their own, find themselves in crisis.

Hospitality Action offers vital assistance to those who need it most. The organisation supports people suffering from serious illnesses and helps those experiencing poverty, domestic violence and bereavement. Over 80 per cent of the help given to beneficiaries is due to severe financial hardship or life-changing illness while 74 per cent of those supported are under the age of 60.

The hospitality industry can be a demanding place to work with many employees exposed to drink and drugs. The Ark Foundation, part of Hospitality Action, helps tackle the problems of the excessive effects of these substances via educational seminars. These seminars are carried out by experienced industry professionals who have fallen victim to substance abuse. Since 2001 The Ark has spoken to 40,000 catering students offering advice on how to avoid peer pressure and cope with their heavy workplace demands.

Hospitality Action also issues grants to help with the cost of basic essential items such as food, clothing and central heating and supports those who have worked within the industry, but are now retired. This Family Members Scheme is a great way for beneficiaries to make new friends and catch up at regular lunches. They also receive a newsletter with interesting features and relevant news stories as well as being visited in their own homes by a friendly volunteer. The Volunteer Visitors provide someone to talk to in confidence as well as friendship for this often forgotten about group of individuals.

Hospitality Action hosts numerous exciting fundraising events throughout the year in the UK to raise much needed funds. The organisation is very fortunate to have support from a whole host of fabulous chefs, including Nigel Haworth with the Obsession festival and this cookbook.

For more information and ways to get involved and support the charity please visit the website at: www.hospitalityaction.org.uk

Registered Charity No. 1101083

OBSESSION RECIPES / CHEFS' RESTAURANTS INDEX

OBSESSION RECIPES / CHEFS' RESTAURANTS INDEX

JACOB JAN BOERMA
Restaurant De Leest
Netherlands
00 31 578 571 382
www.restaurantdeleest.nl
Lightly Grilled Turbot with Pumpkin,
Two Preparations of Scallops, Winter
Truffle, Purslane and Jus of Truffle
and Olive Oil
page 46

JASON ATHERTON
The Maze
London
020 7107 0000
www.gordonramsay.com
Sweetcorn Vanilla Panna Cotta
page 82

JEFF GALVIN
Galvin La Chapelle
London
020 7299 0400
www.galvinrestaurants.com
Smoked Quail Consommé,
Pithiver of Quail page
page 252

JOHN CAMPBELL
Coworth Park
Ascot
01344 8388
76 6000
www.coworthpark.com
"Mandarin" Parfait, E'spuma, Granita
page 222

KEN HOM
Maison Chin
Bangkok
+66 (0) 2266 0505
www.maisonchin.com
www.kenhom.com
Spicy Hot and Sour Soup
page 28

LISA ALLEN
Northcote
Lancashire
01254 240555
www.northcote.com
Valrhona Chocolate Cylinder,
Smoked Nuts, Salted Organic
Sheep's Milk Ice Cream
page 34

MARK EDWARDS
Nobu
London
020 7290 9222
www.noburestaurants.com
Blackcod with Sweet Miso
page 98

MARK HIX
Hix Oyster and Chop House
London
020 7017 1930
www.hixoysterandchophouse.co.uk
Baked Razor Clams with Chorizo and
Wild Garlic
page 172

MATTHEW FORT &
TOM PARKER BOWLES
Petto D'Anatra con Orzotto E Zucca
(Duck Breast with Barley Risotto
and Pumpkin)
page 20

MICHAEL CAINES
Gidleigh Park
Devon
01647 432367
www.gidleigh.com
Pan Fried Scallops with Celerica
Purée and Truffle Vinaigrette
page 140

MICHEL ROUX JR
Le Gavroche
London
020 7408 0881
www.le-gavroche.co.uk
Bitter Chocolate and Pear Tart,
White Chocolate Ice Cream
page 132

NATHAN OUTLAW
Restaurant Nathan Outlaw
Cornwall
www.themarinahotel.co.uk
www.nathan-outlaw.co.uk
Wreckfish, Mussels and Saffron with
Red Pepper and Black Olives
page 38

NEIL WIGGLESWORTH
Formerly of Twin Farms
USA
Heather-Fed Bowland Lamb,
Morecambe Bay Shrimp, Dry-Cured
Ham and Herb Polenta
page 270

NICK NAIRN
Nick Nairn Cook School
Scotland
01877 389900
www.nicknairncookschool.com
Warm Salad of Wood Pigeon,
Stornoway Black Pudding, Fifeshire
Bacon and Cumberland Sauce
Topped with Crispy Parsnips
page 318

NIGEL HAWORTH
Northcote
Lancashire
01254 240555
www.northcote.com
"Hindle Wakes" Goosnargh Chicken
Broth Flavoured with Dried Plums,
Brown Rice, Streaky Bacon and Basil
page 274

Apple Crumble Soufflé, Lancashire
Cheese Ice Creame
page 300

Confit Shoulder of Lamb Studded
with Rosemary and Garlic, Poached
Plum Tomatoes, French Beans,
Purée Potatoes
page 310

Local Game Baked in Butter Puff
Pastry, Celeriac Purée
page 118

Tiny Melting Valrhona
Chocolate Desserts
page 88

Venison Carpaccio, Mushroom Pâté,
Pickled Damsons, Hazelnuts
page 54

Reg Johnson's Seared Cornfed
Duckling, Spicy Red Cabbage, Mead
page 212

Seared Dexter Beef, Wild Herb and
Salsify Salad, Lime Caramel, Roast
Marrowbone
page 182

Treacle Salmon, Scallops, Ginger
page 244

Warm Loin of Herdwick Mutton,
Jerusalem Artichokes,
Honey and Mint Dressing
page 150

PAUL CUNNINGHAM
The Paul
Copenhagen
00 45 3375 0775
www.thepaul.dk
Local Rabbit Grilled with
Langoustines from Læsø
page 136

PAUL HEATHCOTE
Heathcotes
Preston
01772 200 232
www.heathcotes.co.uk
Heathcote's Bread and Butter
Pudding, Apricot Compote,
Clotted Cream
page 86

OBSESSiON

COOKING AT HOME INDEX

THE MALL BLACKBURN

VILLEROY & BOCH

EBLEX

BMI HEALTHCARE

THE WRIGHT WINE COMPANY LTD

H G STEPHENSON LTD

MAUREEN COOKSON LTD

SHARROCKS FRESH PRODUCE LTD

BARCLAYS COMMERCIAL BANK

BLACKBURN ROVERS FOOTBALL CLUB

BOOTHS SUPERMARKETS

ASHE PARK FINE WATERS

THWAITES BREWERY

NEALES WASTE MANAGEMENT LTD

THE BEARDWOOD HOSPITAL

BOWKER BMW

NORTH WEST FINE FOODS

BAKER BOOTHMAN & EDY LTD

RICKETT MITCHELL AND PARTNERS LTD

WELLGATE FISHERIES

RILEYHOLMES LTD

EPS LTD

SYNEXUS CLINICAL RESEARCH LTD

J R TAYLOR ST ANNES

LANCASHIRE AND BLACKPOOL TOURIST BOARD

FARMHOUSE FARE LTD

ASHLEIGH SIGNS LTD

ST JOHN'S COLLEGE CATERING & CONFERENCE CENTRE

THE LIVESEY GROUP

TOTAL FOOD SERVICE SOLUTIONS LTD

RIBBLE VALLEY JOINERY AND BUILDING

HALLIWELLS COMMERCIAL LAW FIRM

M N H PLATINUM LTD

CARDBOARD BOX COMPANY LTD

H GREAVES & SON (MEAT PRODUCTS) LTD

TASTE LANCASHIRE

DUNBIA

C N G FOOD SERVICE EQUIPMENT LTD

WAVERLEYTBS

BEGBIES TRAYNOR GROUP

BELL TRAILER RENTAL LTD

RICHARD WELLOCKS & SON

TASTE TRADITION LTD

ZEUS GROUP

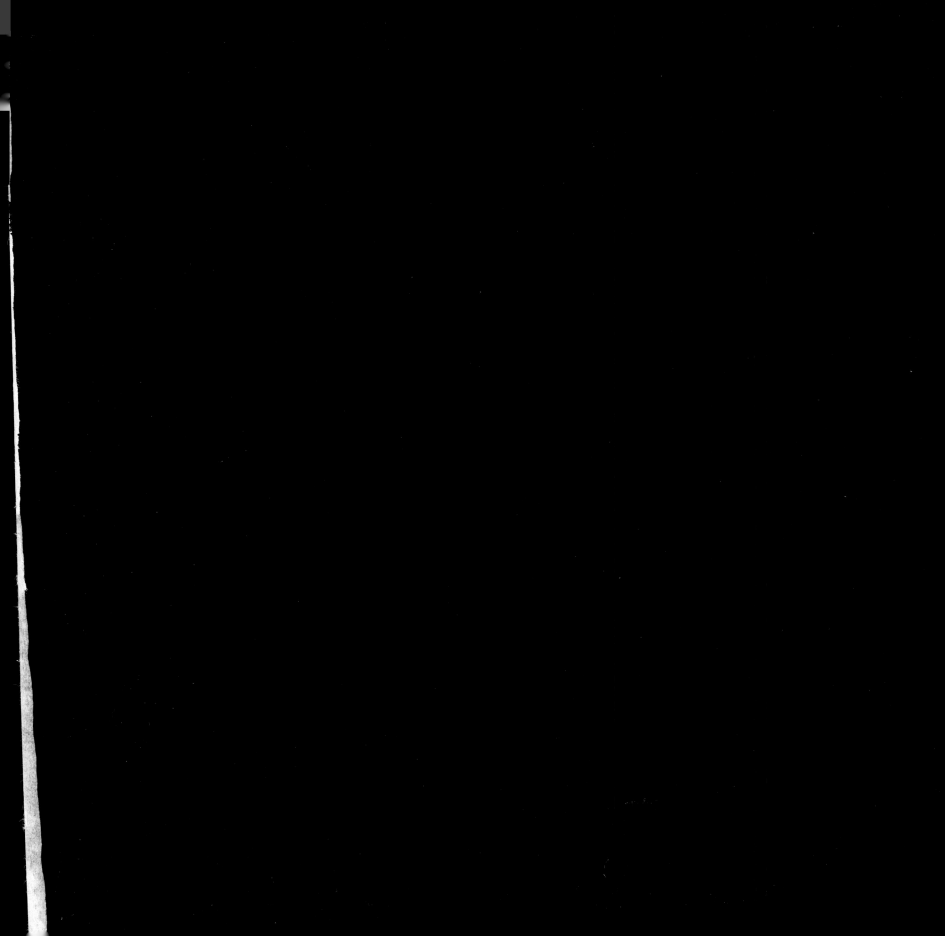